Doing Semiotics

Doing Semiotics

*A Research Guide for Marketers
at the Edge of Culture*

LAURA R. OSWALD

OXFORD
UNIVERSITY PRESS

OXFORD
UNIVERSITY PRESS

Great Clarendon Street, Oxford, OX2 6DP,
United Kingdom

Oxford University Press is a department of the University of Oxford.
It furthers the University's objective of excellence in research, scholarship,
and education by publishing worldwide. Oxford is a registered trade mark of
Oxford University Press in the UK and in certain other countries

First Edition published in 2020

Impression: 1

Published in the United States of America by Oxford University Press
198 Madison Avenue, New York, NY 10016, United States of America

British Library Cataloguing in Publication Data
Data available

Library of Congress Control Number: 2019956694

ISBN 978–0–19–882202–8 (hbk.)
ISBN 978–0–19–886211–6 (pbk.)

Printed and bound by
CPI Group (UK) Ltd, Croydon, CR0 4YY

For Christian Metz

Acknowledgments

For several years, various colleagues of mine have asked for a practical guide that would introduce the principles and methods I presented in *Marketing Semiotics* and *Creating Value* to marketing students. However, it was a request I received from a young professor in Calcutta that made me realize that a research guide to semiotics could serve the needs of teachers, students, and practitioners on a larger scale. I designed the learning tools and methods in *Doing Semiotics* with them in mind.

I am grateful to Marcel Danesi, Rachel Lawes, Christian Pinson, and Laura Santamaria for contributing the reading sections in various chapters. I invited their contributions to expand the discourse on marketing semiotics and provide food for thought and class discussion.

I have been privileged to work with Ellen Newborn and Lynn Childress on the production of this book. Their expertise and support over the years have been invaluable for ensuring the clarity and accessibility of the texts to readers. I am also grateful for the on-going support of staff and services at the Northwestern University libraries for providing valuable information and a quiet setting for completing the manuscript. The author is grateful to Elsevier Publications for enabling me to incorporate Pinson's 1998 essay, "Marketing Semiotics," into the reading for Chapter 4. The author is also grateful for the use of verbatim comments from informants for the reading in Chapter 5, and for tacit permission to publish advertising images where the permission holder could not be reached directly.

I am particularly grateful to Søren Askegaard, Russell Belk, Daniel Chandler and Robert Kozinets, for reviewing and providing feedback on the manuscript. I look forward to continuing our conversation on semiotics.

Laura R. Oswald
Chicago, Illinois
September 2019

Contents

List of Figures

Whilst every effort has been made to secure permissions to reproduce the illustrations, we may have failed in a few cases to trace or reach the copyright holders. If contacted, the publisher will be pleased to rectify any omissions at the earliest opportunity.

List of Tables

Introduction

Structural semiotics is a hybrid of communication science and anthropology that accounts for the deep cultural codes that structure communication and sociality, endow things with value, move us through constructed space, and moderate our encounters with change. *Doing Semiotics: A Research Guide for Marketers at the Edge of Culture*, shows readers how to leverage these codes to solve business problems, foster innovation, moderate cultural difference, and create meaningful experiences for consumers. The case examples also illustrate the malleability of codes in the construction of meaning and culture in daily practice. In addition to the basic principles and methods of applied semiotics, the book introduces the reader to branding basics, strategic decision-making, and brand equity management.

Doing Semiotics is a primer for forward-thinking researchers, students, and marketers who wish to teach, learn and apply some basic semiotic concepts to marketing areas ranging from advertising research to consumer behavior. The book can stand on its own as a research guide or can be used in the classroom to supplement my previous, more theory-oriented books, *Marketing Semiotics* (2012) and *Creating Value* (2015) with practical exercises, examples, extended team projects, and evaluation criteria. The course work guides students through the application of learnings to all phases of semiotics-based projects for integrated marketing communications, brand positioning, design strategy, new product development, and public policy management. In addition to grids and tables for sorting data and mapping cultural dimensions of a market, the book includes useful interview protocols for conducting semiotics-based focus groups, in-depth interviews, and ethnographic studies. Each chapter also includes an expert case study or essay from the perspectives of Marcel Danesi, Rachel Lawes, Christian Pinson, Laura Santamaria. I contributed the reading for the last chapter.

The Interpretive Tradition in Consumer Research

Publication of *Marketing Semiotics* and *Creating Value* sparked a resurgence of interest in semiotics for marketing, a research stream that has origins in the interpretive tradition in market research beginning in the 1980s (e.g., Belk 1988; Belk, Wallendorf, and Sherry 1989; McCracken 1990; Thompson and Haytko 1997). In brief, interpretive researchers make sense of consumers' symbolic encounters with the market, from their relationship to goods to their response to advertising. Inspired by the seminal work of Mary Douglas and Baron Isherwood in *The World of Goods: Toward and Anthropology of Consumption* (1996 [1979]), the interpretive tradition in consumer research responded to the general reorientation of marketing itself from a focus on product benefits and functions to the symbolic functions that consumers assign to goods and rituals such as shopping or serving a meal.

According to the theory of symbolic consumption, goods are more than the passive objects that consumers use to meet practical needs for food, clothing, and housing; they are signs endowed with meanings that deliver to consumers intangible benefits, from status and belonging to self-actualization and relationship. Thus the "anthropology of consumption" is essentially a semiology[1] that accounts for the normative dimensions of meaning production that form culture.

Over the years the interpretive tradition has evolved into a multidisciplinary stream of literature on symbolic consumption known as Consumer Culture Theory, a term coined by Eric Arnould and Craig Thompson (2005) in the article, "Consumer Culture Theory (CCT): Twenty Years of Research." Though a lengthy discussion of the rich CCT literature is beyond the scope of this introduction, this movement represents a shift in interpretive research from a focus on individual consumers, consumer psychology, and the meaning of advertising for the single reader, to the normative aspects of consumer behavior that define culture. For a more detailed review of the literature, please see *Marketing Semiotics* (Oswald 2012) and *Creating Value* (Oswald 2015).

The Early Literature on Semiotics and Marketing

Although semiotics-based research evolved in tandem with emerging trends in consumer research in the 1980s, the early literature on marketing and semiotics does not generally address the semiotic dimensions of consumer behavior, but focuses on either the structure of meaning in advertising and popular culture (e.g., Williamson 1998 [1978]; Stern 1988, 1996a & b; Sherry 1991; Sherry and Camargo 1987; Mick 1986; McQuarrie and Mick 1992; Mick and Buhl 1992; Scott 1994a; Schroeder 2002; Brunel and Nelson 2000; Beasley and Danesi 2002) or consumers' response to advertising meaning (e.g., McCracken 1986; Mick 1986; Holbrook and Hirschman and 1993; Scott 1994b; Arnold and Fischer 1994; Darley and Smith 1995, Ritson and Elliott 1999).

Proceedings from the 1986 North American conference (Umiker-Sebeok 1987) and the 1989 Copenhagen Colloquium (Larsen et al. 1991) on semiotics and

---

[1] The term "semiology", in contrast to "semiotics", defines the general epistemological dimension of the discipline, i.e. a world view centered on meaning production rather than, for instance, metaphysics.

marketing reflect three principle characteristics of the early research that shaped the direction of semiotics-based marketing research for several decades.

- An orientation to North American traditions in pragmatic philosophy (Peirce 1988 [1955]), linguistics (Morris 1971 [1946]), and literary theory (Richards 1929);
- A focus on the form of meaning in the closed system of the advertising text; and
- A philosophical orientation of consumer response to the phenomenology of perception, which anchors meaning and being in the closed framework of a transcendental subject impervious to the effects of culture, ideology, and sign play.

A Social Science Perspective

Though marketing semiotics research emerged in line with the interpretative tradition in consumer research, the early semiotics-based literature sidelines the prolific European scholarship on the implication of semiotics and the social sciences, beginning in the nineteenth century with the seminal influences of Ferdinand de Saussure (2011 [1916]) and Émile Durkheim (1995 [1912]). Developments in theoretical semiotics reflect how linguistics and the social sciences were intertwined throughout the twentieth century, as evidenced in the work of the Moscow Linguistic Circle in the 1910s and '20s (i.e. Jakobson 1990; Volisinov 1986 [1929]), the Bakhtin Circle in the 1920s and 30s (i.e. Bakhtin 1981–1993 [1934–1935]), the Prague Linguistic Circle in the 1930s (Toman 1995), and developments in post-structural semiotics in post-war Paris (i.e. Bourdieu [1976] 1984). It was this stream of research that led to the application of semiotics to anthropology by Claude Lévi-Strauss (1974 [1963]), who claimed that culture is a form of language. Even as North American anthropologists, such as Clifford Geertz (1973a & b), Marshall Sahlins (1976), and Michael Herzfeld (1983) acknowledged Levi-Strauss' influence on their innovative developments in semiotic anthropology, there remained an entrenched assumption in the marketing literature that semiotics applies mainly to textual analysis and advertising research.

It goes without saying that meaning production is contingent upon the inter-dependency of cognitive functions and the cultural codes and conventions structuring the interpretation of discourse in society. However, *Doing Semiotics* focuses on the embedded complexity of signs and meaning in consumer culture rather than theories of cognition. In contrast to theories of information processing, behaviorism or experimental psychology, based upon hypothesis testing in controlled environments (i.e. Hall 1980; Skinner 1938; Peirce (1988 [1955]), structural semiotics is oriented to the sociality of meaning production and the play between codes and performance in the practice of meaning production (Saussure 2011 [1916]).

For example, based in European traditions in structuralism, *Doing Semiotics* does not draw from the semiotics of American philosopher Charles Sanders Peirce. Though marketers reference Peirce to understand the effects of the formal structure of signs on consumer perceptions (i.e., Grayson & Martinec 2004 and Belk & Sobh 2019), Peirce's semiotic does not directly consider relationships between meaning and reference to the context of active discourse and therefore eludes questions of the effects of irony, cultural difference, and change on the meaning production and consumer identity. Framed within a theory of logic, Peirce's semiotic side steps the essentially collective nature of meaning production, focusing instead on the ways human subjects infer meanings based upon the formal properties of signs. In contrast, *Doing Semiotics* focuses on ways that advances in post-structuralism expand the reach of semiotics beyond the sign or the individual text and considers the play between code and performance in active discourse (i.e. Oswald 1999). When applied to marketing communication, experience-centered design, and consumer ethnography, the semiotic analysis both identifies the codes structuring the normative aspects of culture and also accounts for the ways consumers manipulate these codes to negotiate cultural difference, competitive distinctions, identity construction, and ambiguity.

Semiotics in the Brand Management Arena

The meanings that consumers attach to goods, services and brands deliver valuable benefits that satisfy emotional and social needs, benefits which exceed the use-value of goods (see Levy 1959, 1981; Ries and Trout 2000 [1981]; Aaker 1991; Oswald 2012, chapter 1). The most basic marketing functions, from pricing and product placement to packaging design and distribution strategy, contribute to the perception of the value, distinction, and cultural relevance of the brand for consumers.

Moreover, this principle applies not only to commercial goods per se but also to political personalities, cultural practices, and even public policy initiatives, such as marketing medical care to underserved populations. Furthermore, from the most obvious cases of iconic brands to the least obvious, such as an individual's personal style, branding creates value by defining and setting apart the branded product, process, or individual from the crowd, enhancing their favorability and creating the terms for a long-term relationship (Oswald 2015).

The Semiotic Solution

Though experts agree that brand semiotics has measurable impact on the organization's bottom line (Interbrand Group 2018), the brand management literature lacks a guidebook for managing these meanings in order to grow brand equity. My recent books on marketing semiotics address this need because they explain the principles at work in meaning production, present methods for leveraging these meanings in marketing strategy, and illustrate principles and methods through examples and case studies drawn from actual consulting projects.

In *Marketing Semiotics: Signs, Strategies, and Brand Value* (Oswald 2012), I explain how semiotics-based research can be used to guide strategy at all stages of the planning process to build, strengthen, and clarify brand meanings. Semiotics can be applied systematically to the full spectrum of brand management processes, including consumer research, market segmentation, brand positioning, creative strategy, and the design of products, packaging, service sites, and digital retailing.

In *Creating Value: The Theory and Practice of Marketing Semiotics* (Oswald 2015), I expand the discussion beyond the basics of structural semiotics to engage readers in theoretical advances in post-structural semiotics, particularly in areas such as semiotic ethnography, multicultural consumer behavior, the digitalization of consumer experience, and the movement of consumer attention in the multi-media hypertext. *Creating Value* also reviews contemporary thinking on topics ranging from behavioral economics, cultural branding, and brand rhetoric to digital media management and service site design.

The decision to write the present book, *Doing Semiotics: A Guide for Marketers at the Edge of Culture*, was prompted by a growing demand for a guide to the basic concepts and methods of marketing semiotics research. The book is designed to support professors, students, and industry experts in the application of semiotics to marketing. Although the guide can stand alone as an introduction to marketing semiotics research methods, readers will benefit from using the workbook in conjunction with my previous marketing books. I refer the reader to *Marketing Semiotics* and *Creating Value* from time to time throughout the book to find a more detailed treatment of semiotic theories, principles, examples, case studies, and academic references.

A Practical Approach

In my research, teaching, and commercial practice I attempt to illustrate the multi-disciplinary scope of semiotic studies for marketing. In *Doing Semiotics*, I focus on a few basic concepts related to signs, discourse, and semiotic perform-ance and show how to apply them across the marketing research spectrum to make sense of the market, grow brand value, and moderate cultural difference. *Doing Semiotics* initiates readers in the practice of strategic semiotic research methods and principles for industry as well as not-for-profit organizations.

The workbook format helps students internalize concepts by means of active learning tasks and illustrations (Bonwell and Eison 1991). It provides classroom tools for teaching semiotics-based research, including simple exercises, problem-solving tasks, and team projects. The extended projects measure students' grasp of learnings by inviting them to apply chapter concepts to typical business problems in branding, creativity, and product innovation.

The book breaks down the research process into a series of action steps, from stating project objectives to performing a semiotic analysis of data. It includes instructions for decoding cultural dimensions of data, interview protocols, and grids for analyzing the strategic dimensions of findings. It includes instructions for teasing out the cultural codes structuring meaning production across multiple areas of marketing research, including advertising and branding, design development, and primary research with consumers.

To broaden the book's perspective on semiotics, I enlisted four other scholars and scholar-practitioners to write short articles and case studies for a reading included in each chapter. They include Marcel Danesi on brand names; Rachel Lawes on the human factor in semiotic research; Laura Santamaria on semiotics and user experience design, and Christian Pinson on twenty years of marketing semiotics research. I contributed the final reading on a semiotic ethnography in the inner city and its implications for public policy.

It is hoped that this book will stimulate ongoing discussion and debate among scholars and practitioners on important questions related to the role of semiotics in value creation, cross-cultural consumer behavior, and interdisciplinary thinking on meaning in the marketplace.

Post-structural Semiotics

My approach to marketing semiotics is steeped in the continental literature on post-structural semiotics, originating with two formative years I spent in Paris studying cinema semiotics under Christian Metz at the École des hautes études en sciences sociales and took Barthe's seminar on literary hedonics at New York University in Paris. Though the early structuralists emphasized parallels between language and rhetoric and the structure of visual and literary discourses (for instance, Barthes [1964] 2000 and Metz 1991 [1971]), post-structural semiotics considers the ways semiotic performance deconstructs the formal structure of texts through sign play, subject-address, and reference to the cultural context (Metz 1981 [1975] and Derrida 1983 [1972]).

The Semiotic Square

For example, Jean-Marie Floch (2001 [1990]) introduced Greimas's (1984 [1966]) theory of structural semantics to market research in order to move his clients' brands to the competitive edge of culture. Floch exposed the complex semantic dimensions of brands, product categories, and service experiences by deconstructing the dominant codes that define a category into a set of intersecting binaries on the Semiotic Square. For example, rather than simplify the competitive dimensions of the personal care category in terms of a dominant binary such as beauty/science, the Semiotic Square reveals opportunities for a new cultural positioning in the grey areas between beauty and science and opens up a potential space for brand innovation and competitive distinction, where beauty is scientific and science creates beauty.

Furthermore, a comprehensive perspective on structural semantics asks us to take the process even further by exposing the open-ended dynamic that the semiotic square puts into play. Greimas explains that in active meaning production, multiple cultural categories, such as gender, power, and ethnicity overlap and play off of each other. These overlaps create tensions between the cultural categories that constantly shift and reframe the semantic context of discourse, suspending indefinitely the possibility of a synthesis of binary oppositions in a coherent cultural space or meaning. I illustrate this principle in Chapter 5. Findings from a study of inner-city communities showed that public policy initiatives often come into conflict with the minority culture of the people they are meant to help. By analyzing these tensions on the semiotic square, I placed in question the social ideal of cultural assimilation or "acculturation" with a resistant cultural space that thrives on a kind of play between "us" and "them".

The Subject in Question

In my early research on postmodernism in the arts, I encountered the limitations of structuralism to account for the messy slips and slides of meaning and narrative identity in contemporary literature, theater, and film.

Under the influence of works by Umberto Eco (1979), Émile Benveniste (1967, 1971), Christian Metz (1981 [1977]), and Jacques Derrida (1983 [1972]), I moved attention from the structural analysis of texts to the organization of meaning, subjectivity, and reference in discourse. From this research I developed a theory of semiotic performance (Oswald 1987, 1989) that accounts for the unruly give and take between formal codes and the manipulation of codes in semiotic practice, whether in the arts or the marketplace.

After writing and teaching in the humanities for many years, I discovered that the theory of semiotic performance applied directly to the ways consumers play with cultural identities in day-to-day life. While teaching at Northwestern University, I found my way to a seminar on "Deconstruction and Consumer Behavior" at the Kellogg School of Management, directed by John Sherry, a marketing anthropologist. Sherry's interdisciplinary perspective on consumers, culture, and postmodern philosophy exposes the humanistic dimensions of markets and marketing and the rich potential of applied semiotics for the field of consumer research.

The seminar project provided an opportunity to test my theory of semiotic performance in the consumer setting. I published the research from that seminar (1999) in an article on symbolic consumption in the multicultural household. The study proved that consumers, like actors in a play or characters in a postmodern novel, move between multiple identities in everyday life and communicate these shifts in identity through language as well as their symbolic use of goods. The study also proved that my theory of semiotic performance had broad applications to global consumer culture and fostered a rich research stream on issues related to consumer identity and acculturation and their implications for marketing in multi-cultural and emerging markets.

The study also prompted a rethinking of long-standing marketing principles such as demographic segmentation and consumer targeting. By showing that ethnic consumers are always and already divided in their allegiances between home and host cultures in their day to day lives, the theory of semiotic performance deconstructed the traditional interpretation of ethnicity and cultural identity in terms of strict binary distinctions between the cultural mainstream and its margins, between "us" and "them." The findings from this study can also be extended into a general theory of consumer identity construction, since we all "change outfits" as we move from one cultural space to another in our daily lives, from work to play, home to office, and from gym to cocktail party.

My semiotic encounter with consumers and markets opened a career path that continues to reveal the limitless potential of semiotics to expose the interface between meaning production and value creation, mitigate tensions between cultures in contact, and generally make sense of our world.

The Marketing Semiotics Paradigm

In summary, the approach to marketing semiotics outlined in *Doing Semiotics* extends and simplifies the approach presented in *Marketing Semiotics* and *Creating Value*. It embraces various applications of semiotics to market research, including communication theory, cultural brand management, design strategy, and consumer behavior. Like the previous books, *Doing Semiotics* reinforces the fundamental principle that meaning production creates value for brands, consumers, and the market generally. The present approach extends the earlier focus of research on semiotics and marketing in the following ways:

- It expands the object of semiotic analysis from the text to the cultural codes and norms that structure the meaning and value of goods in a given market;

- It broadens the scope of marketing semiotics research beyond advertising to consumer behavior, design, architecture, brand management, and social organization;
- It orients the theory of semiotics to European developments in linguistics and the social sciences;
- It also pushes the limits of structural semiotics by orienting meaning production to the theory of semiotic performance, a theory that takes into account the slips and slides of meaning and cultural difference in active meaning production or semiosis.

Chapter Summaries

The chapters are designed to include a brief discussion of semiotic principles and concepts, examples from actual projects, team exercises, and a final project. Each chapter also includes a reading by outside experts on issues in semiotics for marketing and consumer research.

Chapter 1 introduces readers to the semiotic dimensions of brands and the methods used by semioticians to leverage competitive difference in a given market. In order to understand the basic analytical tools of semiotics, I limit analysis to advertising campaigns rather than design or consumer research.

Marcel Danesi contributed the Reading on brand names for this chapter. Danesi reviews the critical role played by brand names to identify brands, differentiate them from competitors, and evoke the brand's intangible benefits. As Danesi puts it, "A lipstick product without a name...will not sell in today's world." The author provides an overview of historical trends in brand naming. Using examples from advertising, he then describes the various semiotic strategies and name types used by marketers in the naming process, including manufacturer, fictitious character, suggestive, iconic, and symbolic names and descriptors.

Chapter 2 takes a closer look at the strategic dimensions of brands and the methods used to identify, clarify, and develop brand positioning in a competitive environment. The chapter guides the reader through a strategic positioning project for new product development, including a semiotic analysis of competitive advertising, a brand mapping exercise that exposes new cultural spaces in the category, and development of a positioning statement for the new brand.

Rachel Lawes contributed the Reading for this chapter on the human dimension of semiotics-based research. Lawes proposes that though data analytics have advantages over human-driven research as relates to the speed with which it can sort through large amounts of data, it cannot replace the subtlety and complexity of the live semiotician's analytical process. By embedding the structure of meaning in the context of the communication event, the semiotician can solve an array of semantic puzzles missed by the machine by examining relationships between meaning and reference in marketing discourse. Lawes classifies these semantic puzzles into types and lists action steps taken by the researcher to make sense of the data.

Chapter 3 walks the reader through basic semiotic principles and methods for developing design strategy and planning for service sites and packaging. The chapter includes exercises that raise awareness of the semiotic dimensions of the lived environment and the architectural and design elements that shape the consumer's experiences of public space. Students also learn to compare and contrast the consumer impact of design at two distinct service categories: fast food venues and owner-operated restaurants.

Laura Santamaria contributed the Reading for this chapter on design strategy and innovation. Santamaria presents a theory review and case analysis to illustrate the application of a semiotics-driven methodology called *Con[text]* to guide design innovation. A form of user-experience design research, *Con[text]* grounds design strategy in emerging trends and consumer needs in a given market and translates them into a set of design elements. She illustrates her process through a step-by-step analysis of a case study for Crop Drop, a locally sourced produce business located in the United Kingdom.

Chapter 4 illustrates how semiotics can be applied to standard qualitative research methods to gain deeper insights, encourage respondent creativity, and improve the consistency and validity of findings for the client. The chapter includes sample research guides for conducting focus groups and in-depth interviews. It engages the reader in team exercises and a final project that tests their skills in study design, interviewing, and the semiotic analysis of data. It also includes tips for managing clients, the recruitment process, and interview moderation.

Christian Pinson contributed the Reading for this chapter. Pinson reflects on advances in semiotics since the first wave of applied semiotics research dating back to the late 1980s. Pinson reviews developments in structural semiotics leading from the formalism of early writers to Greimas' semiotic square. The semiotic square is an advanced tool of structural analysis that provides a more nuanced analysis of cultural binaries by mapping the subtler relationships that fall between the strict opposition of terms such as good/evil. They include relationships of implication and contrariness and enable the researcher to find common ground and even new cultural space in a data set where the binary analysis only found division and incompatibility.

Chapter 5 reviews the advantages of ethnographic research for gaining more nuanced findings about consumers and their environments. Chapter exercises and projects put into play the skills and semiotic principles learned in the four previous chapters related to project design, data collection, the binary analysis, brand mapping, and decision making. They also extend the learnings in Chapter 4 on the design and execution of primary research to consumer ethnography. The chapter focuses on comparing and contrasting the cultural factors that shape consumer perceptions, experiences, and brand preferences in settings that include service sites, dwellings, and community space. The final team project engages students in fieldwork related to an ethnic household. By means of observations and semi-structured interviews at home, at the store, and in social gatherings, students learn to identify cultural factors at work in consumer choices and behaviors and identify managerial implications of findings for marketing and new product development.

I contributed the Reading for Chapter 5 on the methods used to conduct an exploratory ethnography of community gardening in the inner city of Chicago. The research uncovered a cultural divide between the local community and the Garfield Park Conservatory, a horticultural institution on Chicago's West Side, which interfered with the Conservatory's efforts to serve local residents with new programming. Research findings led to solutions for mitigating this divide through community outreach and cultural exchange. The study has important implications for public policy, cultural production in the inner city, and urban agriculture.

Concluding Remarks

Doing Semiotics is designed to support the aims of *Marketing Semiotics* and *Creating Value* to achieve three broader goals: (1) promote broader interest in semiotic studies generally, (2) expand the scholarship on marketing semiotics, and (3) inspire changes to the brand management and consumer behavior curricula at business schools. Though the chapter summaries reflect the broad scope of applied semiotics for consumer research, design, brand strategy and organizational culture, they do not tell the whole story of *Doing Semiotics*. The advantages of this work over my earlier books consist specifically in the learning resources it provides. The book places the reader squarely on center stage in this adventure by teaching them to view the world semiotically, work through the research process, and immerse themselves in the multidimensional world of meanings in the marketplace.

1

Brand Equity and Semiotics

"Consumers shop for meanings, not stuff." Laura Oswald, *Marketing Semiotics*

Marketers generally agree that consumers make brand choices based upon intangible benefits such as status, belonging, or sex appeal, rather than product attributes alone, such as ingredients or technologies. Intangible benefits are delivered to consumers through communications or brand semiotics, which include the brand's cultural positioning, service and packaging design, media content, and innovation strategy. The semiotic dimensions of brands are not just the icing on the cake, or a "value added" to the brand's functional benefits; they form the foundation and sine qua non of brand equity. The brand equity equation banks on the strength of branding to build and differentiate the brand in an increasingly cluttered market, prompting consumers to choose one brand over the other.

Chapter 1 focuses on meaning production in advertising because the relatively simple semiotic structure of print ads lends itself to a basic introduction to a semiotic analysis. I discuss the more complex, performative systems of digital hypertexts in *Marketing Semiotics* (2012, chapter 7). The remaining chapters apply semiotics to brand strategy, design, and consumer semiotics. As with all of the chapters, Chapter 1 introduces the reader to the basic methods of marketing semiotics research by means of group exercises, discussion, and concept development and conclu

Brand Equity and Semiotics

The chapter is rooted in four basic principles of marketing semiotics.

- The semiotic value of brands exceeds their use value.
- Marketing semiotics research leverages brand meanings to grow brand value.
- The brand's semiotic value is observable and measurable.
- The object of semiotics is not the individual text but a data set of texts defined by project objectives, including advertising, cultural artifacts, and consumer interviews.

Laura R. Oswald, *Brand Equity and Semiotics* In: *Doing Semiotics: A Research Guide for Marketers at the Edge of Culture.*
Edited by: Laura R. Oswald, Oxford University Press (2020). © Laura R. Oswald. © Marcel Danesi, Reading 1.
DOI: 10.1093/oso/9780198822028.003.0001

Semiotic Value

This chapter presents the basic tools used by semioticians to grow value for their clients by clarifying and strengthening the brand's meaning across the marketing mix. Though business schools generally characterize intangible brand attributes as non-essential "added value" to the quantifiable factors such as sales or brand awareness, in both of my previous books (2012 and 2015) I prove that brand semiotics has a direct impact on the firm's financial performance by clarifying the brand's value proposition, growing customer loyalty, and developing innovative brand experiences. Over the years consultancies such as the Interbrand Group actually rank brands on the basis of the market value of the brand's semiotic associations. In their annual ranking of the top global brands, Interbrand recently valued Apple at over $200 billion (2018) based upon the strength of semiotic assets such as clarity, commitment, relevance, differentiation, breadth, consistency, and engagement (Interbrand Group 2018).

Branding across the Marketing Mix

By adapting a user-friendly positioning from the beginning, Apple built a constellation of relatable and aspirational attributes such as creativity, innovation, intelligence, and design leadership. Apple's user friendly identity positioned them in diametrical opposition to IBM whose positioning to big business and distant, high-tech image intimidated ordinary consumers in the early days of consumer technology. Over time, IBM dropped out of the personal computing market and Apple emerged as the category leader by expanding personal computing beyond computers to include lifestyle devices, beginning with the iPod, which integrated technology into every facet of consumption. All of these activities contribute to brand semiotics and enabled Apple to topple Coke's long-standing reign as the number one most valued global brand (Elliott 2013).

Although a cursory look at the brand's historical advertising can provide a snapshot of the brand's positioning, the brand system includes not only advertising messaging but also the meanings consumers associate with the most basic marketing functions, such as pricing or product innovation (Figure 1.1). The high price of luxury brands is part and parcel of the perception of luxury. Brands like Chanel would deplete their luxury status if they held regular sales or offered discounts. Likewise, technological innovation is integral to the perception of cultural leadership and modernity. When Apple launches the latest iPhone or Nike innovates in sports footwear design, these technologies do not gain traction in the marketplace on their own; they also draw from their association with the iconic, cool, culture-bending ethos that these brands represent. In dialectical fashion, these functional innovations contribute in turn to the brand ethos.

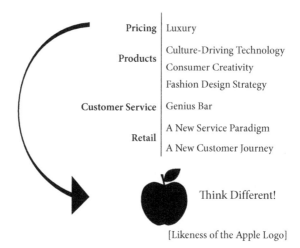

Think Different!

[Likeness of the Apple Logo]

Figure 1.1. Apple—branding across the marketing mix. © 2018 Marketing Semiotics

Apple's investments in advanced technologies sustain a core segment of brand loyalists that will wait in line for hours for a device that ensures their place at the cutting edge of digital culture.

"Think Different"

For example, Apple's "Think Different" positioning has traction with its youthful target market because it suggests independence, risk-taking, and fun. Apple consistently communicates this positioning in all marketing functions. First of all, the brand name itself is whimsical and irreverent in an industry that relies upon science and difficult technologies. That's "different." Apple redefined the meaning and purpose of computer technology by developing consumer lifestyle technologies that transcend computers and work and enrich consumers' daily lives through entertainment, digital mobility, and personal creativity. Apple recently broke from the pack when they positioned the brand as luxury, hiring the former Burberry CEO to lead their customer experience operations. Apple's luxury positioning is reflected in their pricing strategy, design philosophy, their cutting-edge retail architecture, and even the gift-wrapped packaging on the products. They "think different."

The Brand Value Pyramid

Semiotic value exceeds the functional value of goods. The symbolic equities consumers associate with brands evolve over time and build upon formal marketing

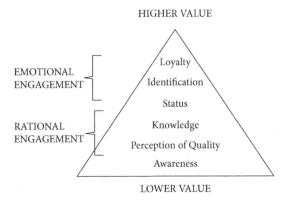

Figure 1.2. The Brand Value Pyramid. © 2018 Marketing Semiotics

programs such as media campaigns, merchandising, and public relations, as well as informal events, such as their shopping and service experiences and word of mouth on social media and in real time (see Oswald 2012, 2015). Consumers also form brand perceptions based upon the brand's reputation for product quality and reliability, cutting-edge technology, cultural relevance, and category leadership.

The Brand Value Pyramid (Figure 1.2) shows how the perception of value grows from one campaign to the next, one new product to the next by growing the degree of consumer engagement with the brand, from awareness to loyalty. Loyal consumers will assert their brand engagement through repeat purchases, not only strengthening the brand's promise of future growth but also sparing the company the costs associated with acquiring new customers.

Awareness

Researchers measure awareness by the number of consumers who recognize the brand name, its presence in the media, and the number of times it is mentioned on the social media. Awareness does not necessarily correlate with brand preference or purchase or even the perception of quality.

Perception of Quality

The perception of quality reflects the brand's reputation for things like customer service and product reliability and performance. Consumers develop perceptions of a brand's quality through word of mouth, consumer reports, the company reputation, or their actual use of the product. In a study of the luxury market in China (Oswald 2011), consumers told me that their perceptions of quality were influenced by the frequency with which they saw the brand in promotional advertising. They said that companies that spent lots of money on advertising must have high quality.

Knowledge

Knowledge reflects the breadth and depth of consumers' associations with the brand name and logo and adds value to the brand whether or not the consumer actually buys the product. Brand value grows value in direct proportion to the scope of brand semiotics across multiple cultural categories. The broader the scope of brand meanings, the more likely consumers will connect with one of these meanings and internalize the brand as their own. This explains why Coke identifies the brand with polar bears, Santa Claus, family, global music culture, and many things in between.

Engagement

Consumer engagement relates to the degree of emotion consumers invest in the brand persona, ethos, or mission. Even for non-users, iconic brands often become catalysts for social engagement in brand communities (Muniz and O'Guinn 2001) where consumers coalesce around the brand's values and mythology. Even if engagement does not equate with purchase, the passion that consumers feel for brands like Harley Davidson or Tesla increases brand value because it generates free publicity and elevates the brand story to the level of myth and legend in the broader culture. For this reason the luxury automotive brand Tesla runs a promotional program that invites drivers from all walks of life to test drive their vehicles. Likewise Nike launched a politically divisive campaign featuring NFL football player Colin Kaepernick, who was fired for kneeling during the national anthem to protest against the racial injustice he witnessed in American society. Although the campaign came with risks—the market value dropped and some consumers burned their Nike's or called for a boycott—Nike banked on the "buzz" factor of the campaign to stir dialogue and debate and place Nike squarely in the bull's eye of the current media cycle.

Loyalty

Repeat purchase behavior is the surest indicator of brand strength and long-term value, since it indicates both the long-term sustainability of the brand and also reduces the marketing costs associated with acquiring new customers.

Summary

Apple has achieved Best Global Brand status for many years running by growing strength at every level of the Brand Value Pyramid. Apple enjoys ubiquitous awareness in the everyday lives of consumers whether they use the brand or not. As the harbinger of culture at the cutting edge, Apple enjoys broad presence on social media and connects users on-line in brand communities that encourage brand personalization and expand brand knowledge. Furthermore, among users, Apple has grown and retained customers' loyalty by becoming synonymous with a culture of innovation, market leadership, authenticity, superior quality, and responsible customer service. In Chapter 2, I extend the discussion of Apple with a focus on the brand's strategic positioning in relation to competitors in the personal technology market.

The Basics of Applied Semiotics

Whether working with corporate clients or business students, managing the conversation about brands is fundamental to a successful branding project or lesson plan. For most clients I've worked with, even those with MBAs from prestigious business schools, the implications of brand meaning for brand value are not obvious, because marketing education still emphasizes operational factors in their approach to brand equity. To ensure that all students agree on the semiotic function of brands, I walk the reader through some experience-based exercises for identifying the brand persona, differentiating it from competitors, and mapping it on a strategic grid.

Underlying Principles

The semiotic analysis operates on the basis of several underlying assumptions, including the idea that consumers engage in symbolic consumption when they project meanings into goods. They are able to use goods symbolically due to a fundamental cognitive capacity to form symbols, whether choosing one brand over the other or co-creating brand meaning on the social media.

Symbolic Consumption

Brands target specific consumer groups by identifying a fit between the brand's cultural positioning and consumers' unmet needs. When marketers speak of "unmet needs," they are not referring specifically to product attributes per se, such as functions, technologies, or flavor, but to emotional needs for things like relationship, identity, or self-affirmation that consumers seek in brands. This practice is known as symbolic consumption.

For example, consumers seeking a fun ride at a low price would choose the Ford Focus, whereas they would choose the Mustang to satisfy their needs for adventure, social appeal, and excitement. In other words, the Focus and the Mustang represent distinct cultural positions in the marketplace. The strategic semiotic analysis finds that fit.

The Symbolic Function

The power of brands to influence consumer behavior is rooted in the human capacity to gratify emotional needs through symbols. This cognitive function is the condition of possibility for the practice of symbolic consumption.

The symbolic function originates in early childhood development at the stage of language acquisition. Freud (1955 [1909]). observed that young children use symbols to mitigate the inevitable separation from their symbiotic relationship to the mother. The reader might recall that they themselves found comfort in a favorite toy or "security blanket" in early childhood for this purpose. Psychological projection continues into adulthood and enables symbolic behaviors ranging from language use to indulging our fantasies through shopping.

The Role of Marketing

Though things like price and product quality influence the perceived value of specific product categories, such as luxury goods or organic foods (see Askegaard Kristensen & Ulver 2017), branding increases the symbolic appeal and market value of un-branded products. Even the appeal of obvious eye-catchers such as desserts or jewelry increases in relation to the reputation, we associate with the brand. Strong brands not only clarify the product's quality but symbolize the intangible benefits sought by consumers, such as status or an aspirational lifestyle.

Marketing communication plays a key role in brand building by consistently linking the brand name and logo with a set of unmistakable meanings, values, and beliefs over a prolonged period of time. Furthermore, long-standing brands such as Coca-Cola have sustained their equity for over one hundred years by adapting the message to the precise context of consumers at a given time, from heart-tugging images of GIs returning home from World War II to the heart-lifting sounds of music that invite consumers from across the globe to dance to the same beat.

I begin the book with the semiotic analysis of brand communication because it provides a snapshot of the broad cultural dimensions of a market and the distinct cultural positionings of brands that are competing for market share within the category. The tools and principles used in this chapter hold true for the semiotic study of more complex semiotic systems, including but not limited to packaging and service space design and consumer behavior.

Exercise 1.1 Name that brand!

Brand semiotics consists of the signs, symbols, and rhetorical strategy employed by marketing communications to deliver the brand's emotional message. In Exercise 1.1, students learn firsthand some basic tools for using and analyzing brand semiotics.

Exercise 1.1 consists of a collage-building activity that teaches students to tease out brand meaning from its functional attributes. Each team presents their collage to the larger group and asks them to "Name that brand!" by means of associations with the mood, color scheme, or design presented in the collage. Exercise 1.1 tests students' ability to identify the brand's intangible equities, find words and pictures that communicate these equities, and communicate the brand message without the aid of the brand name or logo. This kind of work drives home the very visceral and emotional nature of the brand experience and provides insight into the creative process.

Exercise Overview

The collage exercise is a fun group activity designed to prompt students to think creatively and learn to foreground brand symbolism, including mood, target customers, and perception of quality. Working in teams, students create a mood board or collage using pictures cut out of magazines for a given brand. When the technology in the room permits, teams can also collaborate on-line and choose pictures from the Internet and project the collage on a screen. The mood board should communicate the brand's essence to the rest of the class without using the logo or brand name.

Instructions

Below are listed the steps involved in completing the exercise.

Form Teams
Divide the group into teams of three to four students. Teams assign leaders who will lead discussion and present the collage to the group. *For the game to succeed,*

each team chooses a well-known brand but conceals their brand choice from the other teams.

Preparation
Distribute to each group one medium-sized (28″ × 22″), colored poster board, dry markers, glue sticks, and half a dozen old magazines with lots of pictures. Teams may wish to select a specific color poster board that seems to fit with their brand.

Timing
The collage exercise should take about one hour, including time to give instructions, form groups, and distribute materials to the group, collage production, and class presentations and discussion. It is at the discretion of each instructor to tailor the exercise to the time frame of the class or workshop.

The Brand Mood Board

The mood board is a common creative ideation tool that advertising agencies use to develop language and visuals that communicate their creative concepts. The exercise trains the mind to focus on the brand associations evoked by semiotic elements such as colors, shapes, themes, and cultural references in visual media, rather than the brand's functional benefits. The instructor encourages the group to free associate on the brand's emotional meanings that they recall from advertising and to expand upon the brand's purely functional aspect.

Once each team has chosen their brand, they brainstorm to identify a few words or concepts that they associate with the brand name, such as "creative," "high tech," and "user-friendly." These concepts should guide the group's selection of words and images from the magazines to be used in the collage. Since the group must guess their brand based upon the collage of images and words, every element of the collage must communicate the main brand attributes. For instance, students may represent Coca-Cola by means of things such as the red color, fizz, or polar bears, because these are highly recognizable symbols for the brand (Figure 1.3). They may free associate on these symbols to account for the breadth and depth of the brand's semiotic reach, which correlates to the brand's value.

Class Participation—Name That Brand!

The exercise takes on the aspect of a quiz show when each team presents their mood board to the whole group and asks them to guess the brand—Name That Brand! Since teams could not use Coke imagery, language, or logo to produce the mood board, the class must guess the brand based solely on the familiarity

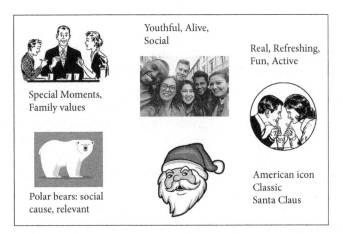

Figure 1.3. A basic mood board for Coke. © 2018 Marketing Semiotics

and strength of the brand's intangible associations, as well as the team's ability to communicate those associations in the collage. The winning team is selected on the basis of the shortest amount of time it takes for the class to "name that brand."

Brand Rhetoric

As teams worked through the exercise, they identified intangible brand attributes by making cognitive connections between seemingly unrelated ideas and cultural categories, as between a sweet carbonated drink and Santa Claus. In other words, they learned the role of metaphorical thinking in the production of brand meaning. Rhetoric adds emotional and psychic force to a statement to underscore the speaker's state of mind or their desire to drive home their point of view to the listener. The next section is devoted to brand rhetoric because of its importance in value creation, including brand building, creative development, and brand engagement.

Some Basic Principles of Rhetoric

Rhetorical expressions begin as cognitive operations in the mind that enable us to compare dissimilar things in order to clarify or add emphasis to a statement. It is manifested in visual and verbal communication in the association or substitution of a literal term, such as anger, with a figurative term, such as a nuclear explosion. We use these kinds of metaphors all the time to communicate the emotional force of a thought, as for example, "My boss went nuclear when he heard the news."

Metaphor

Brands are essentially metaphorical in nature, inasmuch as they form the world of meanings that consumers associate with a product or service. The brand world is built on a strategic positioning that management develops up stream in the new product development process. Smart managers realize that the strategic positioning extends beyond functional attributes or price, because competitors can easily copy these, diminishing the brand's distinction in the marketplace. Brand rhetoric is responsible for creating the intangible assets we associate with brands that distinguish them from competitors and satisfy unmet consumer needs for things like status, identity or relationship.

Metaphor abounds in advertising. The associations represented on the mood board (Figure 1.3) actually personify Coke in terms such as "youthful, alive, and social,"—giving the brand attributes traditionally associated with humans. When consumers are exposed to the same messaging repeatedly over time, they eventually begin to think about these appealing attributes when they see a Coke logo or ad.

Rhetoric is sometimes called the art of persuasion because the emotional appeals of brand communication elicit strong consumer response, draw attention to the brand, and engage consumers in a relationship. For example, early adopters take pride in being first to try a new technology and will stand in line for hours to buy the latest iPhone or Nike sneaker. It is not the technology alone that prompts this kind of behavior, but management's decision to position Apple and Nike at the cutting edge of consumer culture.

Classical Rhetoric

Aristotle (1984 [347–322 BC]) defines rhetoric as a form of verbal art that speakers use to persuade an audience to their point of view (Stanford 2013). Aristotle distrusted rhetorical discourse because it deviated from the logical meaning of words. He nonetheless supplied us with a rigorous categorization of figures of speech or tropes based on their formal structure. For example, *metaphor* and *simile* both compare two terms on the basis of their similarity. However *metaphor* substitutes one word for another, absent term, as in "My boss went ballistic." The comparison of a man with a nuclear explosion is implied but not stated in the sentence. In contrast, *simile* aligns both terms of the comparison in the statement by means of comparative adverbs, as in the sentence, "My boss's anger was like a nuclear explosion."

Although the average reader may associate rhetoric with metaphor, in fact metonymy, the association of things on the basis of logical or spatial contiguity, is a forceful rhetorical form itself, because it demands that consumers participate in meaning production by filling in some missing information (see Genette 1972 and Lakoff 1992). In the figure, "smoke billowed on the horizon," the smoke signals danger but leaves us in suspense about the source or intensity of the fire.

Aristotle differentiates between metonymy and other contiguity tropes such as synecdoche. *Metonymy* per se represents a term by one of its constituent attributes, such as the use of "suits" to represent lawyers. Synecdoche, in contrast, represents something by one of its parts, as in "smoke" for "fire."

Metaphor and Metonymy

The logic of metonymy also bridges differences between the two terms of metaphor in the context of discourse (Genette 1972). Take, for example, the simile [love = red rose] in the figure, "My love is like a red, red rose that's newly sprung in June" (Robert Burns). The metaphor builds upon two metonymies. First, the term [love] is a metonymy for the poet's mistress, based upon a logical connection between the poet's affection and the object of his affection, the "bonnie lass" he mentions in stanza two. A second metonymy linking "rose" to "newly sprung in June" expands the meanings we associate with a red rose, such as fragrant, beautiful, and passionate, to include the freshness, youth, and warmth of a June day. Metonymy also invites the reader to create their own image of the woman based upon their own experiences of red roses blossoming in June (Figure 1.4).

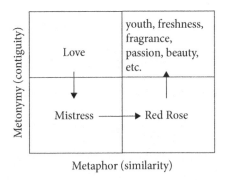

Figure 1.4. The play of metaphor and metonymy. © 2018 Marketing Semiotics

Thus, the simple comparison, "my love is like a red, red rose," is in fact a fairly complex system of rhetorical associations that are motivated by both similarity and contiguity and engage the reader in the poet's world.

Rhetoric in Semiotic Perspective

Semiotics brings a modern perspective to the study of rhetoric because it moves the focus from figures of speech or *tropes* to the broader cognitive operations that facilitate rhetorical associations, regardless of the medium of expression. While classical rhetoric, going back to Aristotle, focuses on hair-splitting classifications of tropes based on their formal attributes, semiotics is more concerned with the way we discover or create new connections between disconnected ideas in order to say what we mean. Rhetorical thinking is at the heart of creativity and innovation because it challenges logical thought, forming new pathways between formerly disjointed concepts.

Visual Rhetoric

The same principle applies to visual rhetoric. For example, while Coke, a carbonated soft drink, and Santa Claus are not really similar, they are spatially connected in historical advertising showing Santa drinking Coke. Metonymy also extends the metaphor into Christmas as a whole by connecting Santa to happy families drinking Coke at Christmas celebrations (Figure 1.5).

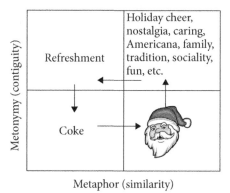

Figure 1.5. Coke's Santa connection. © 2018 Marketing Semiotics

Coke's identification with Santa creates value by expanding the brand's reach into the hearts and minds of consumers around themes consumers throughout the world associate with this secular symbol for the Christmas season. Santa evokes holiday cheer, nostalgia, sociality, and fun even in non-Christian countries such as China. Santa belongs to an elaborate repertoire of brand symbols and associations that reinforce Coke's positioning as the refreshing break, a playful mood, and a celebration.

To make sense of visual rhetoric, print advertising must anchor the figure in a tagline that explains what it means. The examples below illustrate how a British company, Woodbury Dream Cosmetics, experimented with visual metaphor in the 1950s. The first example, "Tropical Dream," illustrates the pitfalls of relying too much on visuals to make metaphors. In order to suggest the dream state promised by Dream cosmetics, advertisers superimposed a woman's glowing face in the sky hovering over a scene with her in a romantic encounter on the beach. The metaphor is too literal to be pleasing or even trustworthy, because the large face hovering over the horizon is too implausible (Figure 1.6).

Tropic Dream (1950)   Dreams for Sale! (1957)

Figure 1.6. Woodbury Dream Cosmetics

The comparison of dreams and cosmetics in the 1957 ad, "Dreams for Sale," is more plausible because advertisers anchor the visual metaphor in a tagline that substitutes the term [cosmetics] with [dream]. The bottom of the page features a product display, including lipstick, creams, and powders. The top represents a woman in expensive dress, artful make-up, and glittering jewelry. The aura created by backlight, soft focus, billowing chiffon, and sparkling earrings suggest a dreamy, imaginary space. The woman's soft gaze upwards toward an undefined object reinforces the aerial mood of the image. The graphic placement of the tagline, "Dreams for Sale," at the center of the ad structures a relationship of cause-to-effect between the real products below and the dream-like benefits above. This logical connection weaves the cosmetics/dream metaphor into the logic of the brand discourse.

The metaphors in early print ads rely on words to make sense. However, just as the cinema evolved away from its dependency on words in the 1960s to its current emphasis on visual expression and direct experience, advertising followed suit, aided by advancements in digital technology. In the SUV ad in Figure 1.7, the visual metaphor speaks for itself and language anchors it in the brand message. Rather than substitute one term for another in verbal metaphor, the advanced digital imaging used to create this image allowed the artist to literally integrate the chassis and body of the SUV with the body of a rhinoceros. We get it—the vehicle operates like a rhinoceros. But what exactly does that mean?

Figure 1.7. "It's more than technology. It's instinct." Advert for Mitsubishi Motors. Developed at Africa São Paolo. Photography by Platinum Studio (2018)

On its own, the visual metaphor opens up a Pandora's Box of associations, including the untamed continent of Africa, wild animals, toughness, weight, larger than life, horned, and so on. The original tagline referring to the SUV brand's reputation for advanced safety technology does not create the metaphor so much as it narrows and clarifies the precise meaning of the image and ties it to the brand message. The khaki background color references safari outfitter gear and reinforces the SUV brand/rhinoceros connection by placing the SUV in Africa, navigating rough terrain in the manner of a rhinoceros.

Video and cinema have the advantage over photography in this regard because moving pictures build meaning by mixing word and image in a single representation and juxtaposing multiple meanings in a chain of shots in montage. A good example of visual metaphor can be found in the silent film, *City Lights* (1931), in which Chaplin succeeded in creating a visual comparison between a rose and his romantic interest by juxtaposing an image of the girl with a close-up shot of a rose.

Advertising rhetoric grows brand value by broadening the range of meanings and experiences—the semantic scope—of brands in the marketplace. By drawing associations between the functional attributes of products and the brand's proprietary symbols, meanings, and mood states, brand rhetoric increases brand awareness and knowledge, engages consumers in a brand relationship, and builds customer loyalty.

In Chapter 2, I illustrate how the rhetorical style of a given ad forms an element of the brand's broader semiotic system.

The Basics of Strategic Semiotic Research

Semiotic research enables clients to manage brand meanings across the brand life cycle in order to grow brand value. We begin by expanding the range of analysis beyond the single text to the relationships between texts in the brand system. The research begins with the collection, classification, and semiotic analysis of a large group of ads representing the brand legacy and competitive environment. The methodologies are drawn from discourse theory, which accounts for the intersection of codes and meaning in a set of texts.

The Brand System

The structural analysis of a single campaign forms a building block of the brand system. The analysis of advertisements for Dream Cosmetics and an SUV brand illustrates in very simple terms how the formal elements in print advertising structure advertising meaning and form semiotic associations with the brand. They include the visual elements (color scheme, shapes, visual perspective, etc.) and their organization within the frame (left/right, top/bottom, etc.), the rhetorical style (metaphor or metonymy), and the story or message.

Although a building block of the brand system, the textual analysis of a single campaign may not reflect the brand's historical legacy, core message, or strategic positioning, leaving consumers feeling confused or betrayed. This principle has important implications for creative strategy as well, since successful campaigns must align with the brand strategy or fail in consumer testing.

Clients routinely commission semiotics research to explain why a costly new campaign failed with consumers, though they spent big budgets on cutting-edge creativity and famous celebrities. In every instance, the new campaign conflicted with the brand's historical identity, blurred the brand's distinction from competitors, or was out of touch with contemporary culture. The three examples that follow illustrate how introducing semiotics upstream in the creative strategy process could have prevented costly problems by aligning creative strategy with the brand legacy, competitive environment, and consumer culture.

Creative Strategy

In my experience, advertisers use the term "creative strategy" to describe the process of developing signs, symbols, and language to draw attention to the brand name, entertain consumers, or fulfill the creative ambitions of the artistic director. They need to anchor creative strategy in the brand's cultural positioning or historical legacy. Creative directors usually reach out to Marketing Semiotics to move along the production process by matching creative concepts to esthetic elements such as colors, forms, words, and rhetorical style. In this way, advertisers both misunderstand the full benefits of strategic semiotic research and overlook the basic marketing functions of advertising to (1) sustain the brand legacy and (2) differentiate the brand from other brands in the marketplace.

Creative directors, being groomed in the production of beautiful ads, may create campaigns that are award-quality for creativity but fail in the marketplace because they are (1) off-message and fail to represent the brand's long-standing image; (2) they mix messages and communicate two or more brand positionings; or (3) they fail to align the communication with the culture of consumers, lagging behind current trends or even offending consumers. In every case, advertisers banked on the creativity of a campaign to carry the show rather than align the new campaign with the brand's strategic context.

Example 1—The USA Oil Company

Take, for example, an advertising research case for a brand of motor oil we will call USA Oil. The advertising agency was revising advertising for the long-standing brand because they were retiring the actor who had represented Charlie the friendly service station attendant in advertising for almost twenty years. The agency created five prototypes of 30- to 60-second TV spots (yes, they were that long back then) and hired me to select the best one to be used in the new campaign. The client said their favorite prototype was a rather surreal, fast-paced montage of an empty gas station at night, ending with a shot of the moon. The ad was esthetically appealing, but would it support the brand legacy?

To gauge which ad aligned best with the brand legacy we obtained from the client findings from their recent consumer study. The results confirmed that consumers associated the brand with the downhome friendly personality that Charlie embodied. The very modern campaign was clearly off-message and could weaken the brand's competitive strength. The winning campaign succeeded in translating the brand's down-to-earth legacy into a crisp creative style that would satisfy both new and loyal customers.

Example 2—Is It Mass, Luxury, or Gourmet?

In another case, the client came to me because their pet artistic project, an innovative digital imaging ad for a premium brand of instant coffee, failed in testing (see Oswald 2015, chapter 2). Once again the client thought I could find the solution through a structural analysis of the single ad. And once again I needed more context, so I built a foundation for the analysis by decoding what coffee means across the category. After analyzing communication strategies for multiple brands across the coffee spectrum, regardless of price or format, I discovered that each category communicated value by means of very distinct visual and verbal appeals or codes.

A thorough category analysis identified multiple codes at play in each category. For instance, mass brands such as Folgers emphasize the sociality of coffee for groups. In contrast, premium brands emphasize the individual experience. Thus, we conclude that the cultural binary [social/self] structures a strategic distinction between mass and premium brands. Within the premium category itself, gourmet brands such as Intelligentsia focus on the connoisseur's appreciation of fine coffee; luxury brands such as Starbucks emphasize consumer pleasure with added milk and flavorings. Thus, we conclude that the cultural binary [connoisseurship/pleasure] structures a strategic distinction within the premium coffee category between gourmet and luxury brands.

Given these insights, we returned to the print ad under review. The campaign failed in testing because it represented all three cultural codes in the same image, blurring the brand's value proposition: is it mass, gourmet, or luxury? These kinds of mistakes confuse the brand in consumers' minds, foster distrust, and deplete brand value.

Example 3—A Kardashian Moment

The last example concerns Pepsi's "Live for Now Moments" campaign (2017), a mini-film in which drinking Pepsi is a catalyst for stepping out of your comfort zone and joining in the political conversation. The ad features top model Kendall Kardashian at a photo shoot watching a peace and love demonstration pass by on the street. One by one various characters leave their comfort zones at work or play and join the march, Pepsi in hand. Kendall has her "now" moment, casts off her model's wig and joins the march. She presses to the head of the march where some police officers are lined up and hands one of the officers a Pepsi as a kind of peace offering. Pepsi emerges the hero in this conflict by settling all disputes with a smile.

The ad had all the earmarks of a successful campaign—a top model and reality star, popular music, and a peace and love demonstration. However it provoked a swift and widespread denunciation on the social media because it dismissed the burning issues of our time with a smile and a Pepsi (Watercutter 2017). Management failed to gauge the public mood on issues such as sexual harassment, police brutality, and racial equality. By inserting a global brand into the conversation, Pepsi added fuel to the fire because corporate culture is often a target in these debates. These kinds of mistakes speak to a brand that is out of touch with consumer culture.

In all three cases, we identified a strategic problem by embedding the textual analysis in the broader brand system, the set of codes that drive the brand positioning from one campaign to another over the years. From this standpoint we then developed a new creative strategy that was both esthetically appealing and also consistent with consumer culture and the brand's historical legacy.

The Brand Roadmap

In the previous section, we reviewed the role of visual rhetoric to transfer intangible benefits to the functional attributes of brands, as in the comparison of an SUV with a rhinoceros. We also focused our understanding of rhetoric on the mental operations that enable us to make associations between two contiguous terms in metonymy and associations between two similar terms in metaphor. While rhetorical figures link the brand name to the brand's intangible benefits, they do not account for the iteration of these meanings in various forms from one campaign to another over time. In the next section, I discuss the role of the similarity and contiguity functions of discourse.

Brand discourse defines the underlying code system that defines the brand culture and differentiates it from competitors (Oswald 2012, ch. 4). However, strong brands are both consistent and relevant. Marketers continually restore and refresh the brand by calibrating the message to changes in consumer culture, including fashion, design, and consumer behavior. Taking a cursory look at historical ads for Coca-Cola over a 100-year period, we notice that vintage ads from 1900 communicate refreshment in rather formal, conservative images of women in Victorian dress enjoying Coke from a small glass. Fast-forward to 2017 and the ads show two young women in bathing suits drinking Coke from the bottle on the roof of an apartment building. WWII advertising may include soldiers returning from war, 1950s ads show an emerging youth culture complete with bobby socks and saddle shoes, and recent ads emphasize cultural diversity and global consumer culture. However Coke's signature emphasis on the refreshment break, sociality, and family values defines a kind of brand code that dictates brand messaging over the years and remains the same over the years.

Semiotic codes motivate the tension between constancy and change by supplying an underlying blueprint for guiding the creative process. In language, code systems such as grammar and syntax are the shared norms that enable speakers to communicate with each other. Codes are not the same as content, however. They define the norms or abstract rules that ensure some level of understanding and communication among speakers. However, it is the dialectic between code and performance that enables speakers to create any number original statements by means of substitution. The malleable nature of codes enables us to generate a limitless number of messages, create metaphors, or recreate brands on the social media.

For instance, grammar and syntax structure the positioning statement, "Coke is refreshing." From the standpoint of grammar, I can substitute an infinite number of terms in place of subject, verb, and direct object in the sentence, for example, Cola/is/refreshing, Coke/is/funny, or wine/tastes/refreshing. However, insofar as advertising represents the brand's cultural positioning, advertisers are constrained in their substitutions by the semantic framework (i.e., the brand codes that structure the brand identity and world). Rather than limit creativity, these codes enable marketers to grow market share over the years by expanding, rather than changing, the semantic framework. By doing consumer research, management routinely finds original ways to communicate the idea of "refreshing."

The tensions between codes and creativity draw from what Jakobson (1990, 115–33) calls the "double axis of discourse," including the linear, "syntagmatic" axis, the axis of alignment, and the vertical, "paradigmatic axis," the axis of substitution. The play between selection and substitution in active communication resembles the relationship of theme to variation in music or poetry, which is constrained by the formal and semantic codes structuring the work as a whole, but also leaves room for creativity and innovation. The alignment of elements in any given ad defines the "syntagmatic" axis of discourse, and the substitution of one element for another across multiple historical campaigns defines the vertical, paradigmatic dimension of Coke's brand system (Figure 1.8).

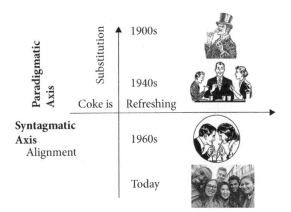

Figure 1.8. Code and performance: The double axis of discourse. © 2018 Marketing Semiotics

The Two-Dimensional Structure of Discourse

By mapping the syntagmatic and paradigmatic dimensions of the brand discourse on a double-axis grid, the semiotician clarifies how far afield the creative team can expand new brand associations without digressing from the brand's basic positioning (Figure 1.8).

Similarity/Contiguity Functions

It is no coincidence that these two axes correspond to the metonymical and metaphorical dimensions of rhetoric, inasmuch as they both draw from the mental operations forming associations by contiguity and similarity. The connection does not stop there. Indeed, brand rhetoric is responsible for expanding the brand's semantic field, motivating brand metaphors such as "Coke is Santa Claus." A metonymy of cause and effect between refreshment, Santa, and Christmas cheer motivates the association.

Brand Extensions

The double-axis structure of brand discourse contributes to the brand's long-term value and growth. With a clear understanding of the underlying cultural codes that structure the brand meaning, management can also extend the product portfolio without disturbing the integrity of the brand name. The ability to find parallels among multiple iterations of the brand message also enables marketers to develop product extensions that perpetuate the brand positioning from the core brand to other products in a category. This principle explains how a company such as Coca-Cola can leverage its intangible equities in Refreshment beyond the primary product category, i.e., the Coke beverage, to include "all Ready to Drink (RDT) beverages," such as non-Coke sodas, tea, juice, and bottled water (Figure 1.9).

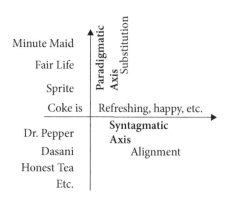

Figure 1.9. Coke's brand extension system. © 2018 Marketing Semiotics

Exercise 1.2 The Brand Audit

Exercise 1.2 walks the reader through the steps involved in an audit of the brand's historical legacy by finding recurring themes across a set of historical campaigns. The Brand Audit is particularly useful upstream in the creative process because it produces a blueprint for aligning creative strategy with the brand's historical positioning.

The Brand Audit is an entry-level exercise for the budding semiotician. It introduces the readers to strategic semiotic thinking in relation to advertising research, preparing them for later chapters, which focus on more complex semiotic systems such as consumer ethnography and architectural design. For example, by combing through a set of the brand's historical advertising in search of recurring patterns of meaning, the reader grasps firsthand the concept of semiotic codes, the underlying mechanisms responsible for building the brand system.

In Chapter 2, I perform a brief Brand Audit of the Nike sportswear brand that illustrates in more detail what the exercise entails. Teams should include between three and four students.

Study Design

Working in teams, students select an iconic brand with a strong track record in the specific product category. They sort through multiple historical advertising campaigns in order to define the brand's consistent underlying message and positioning.

Objectives

The purpose of this study is to identify a set of semiotic codes responsible for communicating a consistent strategic positioning for [Brand X] in historical advertising. Research will also make note of evolutions in the creative style and cultural reference of advertising as the brand responds to cultural change, category trends, and new markets.

Scope and Data Set

Researchers will collect samples of the brand's major advertising campaigns reaching back five to ten years, either in print or other media. The data set would be more limited if the audit were part of a three-day workshop, but more extensive if taught within the context of a full semester course, where students can work in teams outside of class. To simplify the exercise, the data should include short texts (i.e., print ads, 30-second TV spots, the home page on a website, etc.) rather than full-fledged marketing media campaigns.

Timing

This exercise could take two to three hours of class time depending on the instructor. If students have more time to develop the exercise in more detail, it could take two to three days of data collection, analysis, and write-up.

Instructions

The Brand Audit prepares teams to conduct a more complete audit of the iconic brand of their choice. Please choose a category other than sportswear, since we will continue our discussion of that category in Chapter 2. The steps for completing the team assignment are outlined below and include exercise grids for organizing the campaigns in the data set and tracking the recurring elements over multiple campaigns.

Data Collection and Organization

Data collection includes selecting the brand for analysis, collecting campaigns for the data set, and organizing the campaigns numerically on a grid. For purposes of this exercise, please choose a brand with sufficient legacy and clarity to enable you to complete the exercise.

To simplify the exercise, I recommend focusing on a single medium, such as a single image in print or digital advertising, since television spots, websites, and social media include many more variables for analysis. The Internet search is the easiest path to collecting a set of recent and historical campaigns through Google searches, company websites, and YouTube.

Data Organization

To keep track of the data, create a table similar the Data Set Table 1.1 located in the Appendix. The data set for Exercise 1.2 should include at least five campaigns in a data set drawn from five to ten years of historical advertising. If you choose a medium other than print, please note the medium in the heading.

On your Data Set Table, organize the campaigns numerically by year, beginning with the most recent campaign and working back. Include on this grid only the number, title, and a general organization and theme of each ad. If you cannot find the agency's title for the campaign, come up with your own title for use in your discussions.

The Semiotic Analysis

At this stage, teams analyze each campaign in greater detail by identifying semiotic elements in each ad and tracing the recurrence of signs and meanings across the historical spectrum.

- First, create and complete a Paradigmatic Analysis Table modeled after Table 1.2 located in the Appendix. This table lists the campaign number and year, and three semiotic dimensions. As students review their data, they may wish to include additional semiotic dimensions to the analysis as their brand demands. Keep in mind, however, that simplicity is key for this instructional exercise.

The Brand System

- Next, create and fill in a Brand System grid modeled after Table 1.3, located in the Appendix. This table illustrates the consistent association of specific signs with the brand's key meanings in the data set.
- After filling in both tables, record how you tracked recurring semiotic elements across the data set, a positioning statement, and an analysis of the syntagmatic and paradigmatic dimensions of the brand system.

The Positioning Statement

In one sentence define the brand positioning and support your statement with a brief summary of key details from the data that reinforce this positioning over the years. Alternatively, you may state the overall historical positioning and also point out instances where certain campaigns went astray of the brand's historical positioning.

Key Learnings from Exercises 1.1 and 1.2

Exercise 1.1

Exercise 1.1 created awareness of the semiotic dimensions of brands and walked students through the basic steps involved in a simple brand analysis.

- Working in teams, students learned to distinguish product benefits from the brand's symbolic attributes.
- They learned to identify brands on the basis of these attributes.
- Teams uses free associations in word and image in order to stimulate creativity within the group.
- Teams also learned how consumers engage with brands by identifying with the brand's intangible benefits and projecting their own experiences into the brand persona.
- They also engaged in rhetorical thinking, the mental operations that are responsible for creating and communicating the brand's intangible emotional benefits, such as fun or trust.

Exercise 1.2

Exercise 1.2 introduced students to the strategic dimension of brand semiotics by situating the analysis of a single campaign in context with the brand's historical legacy.

- Students learned to assess a large sampling of historical ads and track the recurrence of cultural codes that structure the brand's positioning (i.e., is it fun or serious? social or personal? formal or casual?). In addition to tracking these codes, the assessment also tracks the recurrence of visual and rhetorical codes employed consistently across the data to reinforce the brand's look and appeal. To the extent that these codes recur over time, they support the brand's strategic force in the marketplace year upon year.
- The exercise walked students through the Brand Audit of historical communications, the first stage in a full-scale brand positioning or creative strategy project.
- Teams learned the basics of data collection and created tools for summarizing findings on tables and grids.
- Teams learned how to identify the paradigmatic dimension of a set of ads by tracking recurring themes and visuals over time and multiple campaigns.
- Teams learned to develop a positioning statement based on an analysis of the recurring signs and meanings in the brand system.

Chapter Summary

The discussions and team exercises walked students through the practice of three basic principles of semiotics-based research for marketing. First, strategic semiotic research situates the textual analysis within a broader analysis of recurring, paradigmatic codes across a large sampling of historical advertising. Second, successful advertising campaigns both attract audience attention and also align the creative process with the brand strategy and consumer culture. Third, by initiating a semiotic audit of the brand's historical advertising upstream in the creative process, management can avoid costly mistakes and anchor campaign development in the codes that sustain the brand positioning over time.

Appendix

Table 1.1 The data set in historical perspective

Brand A – (Medium)			
No.	Year	Title	Summary description
1			
2			
3			
4			
5			
6			
etc.			

Table 1.2 A paradigmatic analysis of semiotic elements

Brand A			
No. & year	Language	Visuals	Rhetoric
1.			
2			
3			
4			
5			
6			
etc.			

Table 1.3 The brand system

Years	Signs	Meanings
	Language	
	Visuals	Brand (X) is ... (main positioning)
	Rhetoric	
	etc.	
	Language	
	Visuals	Brand (X) is (secondary positioning)
	Rhetoric	
	etc.	

Reading 1
Semiotic Techniques behind Brand Naming

Marcel Danesi
University of Toronto, Canada

Introduction

The brand names of everyday products and services are as recognizable as the names of celebrities. Names such as *Coca-Cola, Apple, Kleenex, Calvin Klein, Chanel, McDonald's, Ivory Soap, Scotch Tape,* and the like have become veritably and literally household names. This would not have occurred if they were simply called soft drinks, hamburgers, running shoes, computers, and so on. Naming brands is pivotal to creating an identity or image for products, since this assigns a "semiotic code" to them. The brand name has become so important to the marketing world that it is now fiercely protected by law. Anyone who trademarks a brand name acquires the legal right to prevent others from using a similar one (see Martin 2017 for the histories of famous brand names). *Brand naming* is definable as a semiotic strategy designed to communicate qualities associated with products through the name.

Names breathe life into things. Across cultures, a neonate is not considered a person until they are given a name. The act of naming is the first rite of passage into the world. A similar kind of "life breath" is injected into products after they are named. For marketers and manufacturers, the coinage of an appropriate brand name is thus the first crucial step in transforming a product into a brand. At a practical level, naming a product has, of course, an identifier function, allowing consumers to identify what particular product they may wish to purchase (or not). But the name generates images and meanings that go well beyond this simple function. Consider *Armani* high heel shoes. The name of the manufacturer allows us, at a literal level, to identify the shoes as denotatively different from other shoe brands. But it does much more than that. It taps into a code of connotations that are designed to evoke images of artistry, craftsmanship, and superior quality to the shoe product. The name *Armani* thus transforms the shoe product into an "authored" work of shoe art, not just an assembly-line product for everyone to wear. Designer names for clothing and footwear evoke a similar range of connotations, evoking images of clothes and shoes as constituting *objets d'art,* rather than mere items of clothing or footwear. Designer names are thus crucial and must sound appropriate. New York designer Ralph Lifshitz changed his name to Ralph Lauren, for the reason that it was more pleasant-sounding. Similarly, the designer Pietro Cardin altered his name to Pierre Cardin, in order to give it a more fitting "French sound." So powerful is the brand name as part of a semiotic code that, on several occasions, it has been used by consumers as a metonym for the entire product type. Such names have lost their legal status as trademarks. Examples include *aspirin, scotch tape, cellophane, escalator,* among others.

The purpose of this essay is to describe various semiotic strategies used by manufacturers and marketers to bring a product to life, in a manner of speaking. It follows up on previous work (Danesi 2008) and complements the excellent study by Nuessel (2010) on naming strategies for energy drink products. Transforming a simple product, like a lipstick, into a brand entails "semiotizing" it (that is, giving it sense and meaning) by creating an appropriate name for it. As an example, consider a fictitious lipstick product to be marketed to thirteen-to-fifteen-year-old teenage girls. To convert it into a brand with a specific code of semiotic meaning, we will have to start by giving it a suitable name, say, *Kiss Stealer*. This opens up a whole array of meanings that are, arguably, consistent with what a pubescent young girl today might understand (romance, kissing, looking appealing, etc.). A lipstick product without a name, or with an anomalous name, will not sell in today's world.

Historical Note

The practice of brand naming emerged around 1880 in the US, when soap manufacturers started giving names to their products so that they could be distinguished from similar ones in stores. Among the first names used were *Ivory, Pears, Sapolio,* and *Colgate.* It is not known which of these was first. The *Ivory* name goes back to 1882 and is considered by most marketing historians to be the most likely candidate. It was Harley Proctor who decided to rename his generically named *White Soap* as *Ivory Soap*—an idea that seemingly came to him while he was reading a psalm in church. In December of that year, Proctor introduced the first true slogan into advertising, referring to his named product as "99 and 44/100% pure." The modern concept of brand was thus born. By simply coining appropriate names for their products, manufacturers quickly discovered that sales increased significantly. In some cases, the trademark itself was used as the brand name for the product. Such was the case with the *Parker Pen*—one of the first trademarks to be converted into a brand name in 1888 in Janesville, Wisconsin, by George Safford Parker. Parker simply decided to name each pen produced by his company after himself. Arguably because of this strategy, the Parker Pen Company became the world's largest producer of fountain pens in the latter part of the nineteenth century.

It was immediately obvious that a product with a name garnered itself a special type of recognition, leading (as far as early marketing documents can be accessed) to an increase in sales. In that era, various sophisticated persuasion strategies and techniques (the use of different fonts, of color ads, etc.) were established that manufacturers starting using systematically to promote their products. But without naming the product first, all these would remain largely ineffectual. A general law of marketing thus crystallized spontaneously—consumers perceive a product as something unique and possessing specific (desirable) qualities through the name it bears. Indeed the term *brand* is really a synonym for product name. Branding was, originally, the term used to refer to the searing of flesh with a hot iron to produce a scar or mark on livestock for identification or other purposes. The Egyptians branded livestock as early as 2000 BCE. In the late medieval period, trades people and guild members posted characteristic marks outside their shops, thus establishing the concept of *trademark*. Medieval swords and pottery, for instance, were distinguished by identifiable symbols on signs hung at the entrance of shops. Among the best-known trademarks surviving from that period are the striped barbershop pole and the three-sphere pawnbroker sign.

By the early 1920s, it became evident that branding was not just a simple strategy for product identification or differentiation, but the very semiotic fuel that propelled corporate identity. As Naomi Klein (2000: 6) aptly writes, "competitive branding became a necessity of the machine age," because the market was starting to be flooded by uniform mass-produced products. At the same time, the semiotic power of the name itself became rather conspicuous, embedding a product unconsciously into social life. Names such as *Nike, Apple, Body Shop, Calvin Klein, Levi's,* etc. have, in fact, become de facto cultural symbols recognized by virtually anyone living in a modern consumerist society. As Klein (2000: 16) goes on to remark, for such companies the brand name constitutes "the very fabric of their companies."

Semiotic Strategies

Why does naming a simple detergent, a toothpaste, an automobile, and so on create such a powerful effect? Undoubtedly, the answer lies in the ability of names in themselves to impart a life-giving force to things. In Hebrew culture, the ancient art of *gematria* was based on the belief that the letters of any name could be interpreted as digits and rearranged to form a number that contained secret messages encoded in it. The Romans, too, thought names were prophetic, imprinting this belief in their proverbial expression *nomen est omen* ("a name is an omen"). Clearly, there is something about names that resonates with all humans, at least unconsciously.

Decoding the onomastic strategies used by manufacturers and marketers is thus a key step into understanding why consumerist culture has become so emotionally powerful. As indicated elsewhere (Danesi 2008), brand-naming strategies can be classified into several generic categories that belie the underlying psychology of the onomastic process—*manufacturer names, fictitious character names, descriptor names, suggestive names*, and *symbolic names*. These are elaborated below.

It should be stressed from the outset, that even in relaying straightforward information, such as identifying the manufacturer (*Bell, Kraft*, etc.), indicating the geographical location of the company (*Southern Bell, American Bell*, etc.), describing what the product can do (*Easy On, Quick Flow*, etc.), and so on, brand names nevertheless create signification systems—systems that possess a broad range of culturally-relevant meanings. The name *Bell*, for instance, evokes meanings of "tradition" and "reliance" that familiarity with the name kindles. In effect, every brand name entails an unconscious signification system—or set of connotations—of one kind or other. It is this system that is used and reused for various marketing and advertising purposes. Indeed, the more connotations a name evokes, the more powerful it is and, as a consequence, the more possibilities it offers to the advertiser for creating truly effective ads and commercials. The higher the "connotative index" of a signification system, as it has been called (Beasley and Danesi 2002), the greater its market appeal.

Name Types

Below are just a few examples of how signification systems are generated by brand names:

Brand names	Signification systems
SuperPower, Multicorp, FutureNow, Quantum Corporation, Powerade, etc.	big picture, forward-looking, strong, powerful, contemporary, etc.
People's Choice, Advantage Plus, Light N' Easy, Choice Corporation, etc.	free-spirited, advantageous, egalitarian, common, friendly, etc.
Technics, Vagisil, Anusol, Proof Positive, Timex, etc.	scientific, structured, fool-proof, accurate, reliable, established, etc.
Coronation, Morning Glory, Burger King, Monarch Flour, etc.	conquest, eminence, majesty, nobility, blue-blood, etc.
Wash N Wear, Drip Dry, Easy Clean, Okay Plus, etc.	user-friendly, simple, uncomplicated, fine, etc.
General Electric, General Mills, General Dynamics, General Foods, etc.	all-encompassing, widespread, popular, accepted, comprehensive, etc.
Cheer, Joy, etc.	happy, bright, friendly, smiling, etc.
Pledge, Promise, etc.	trustworthy, reliant, secure, etc.

Manufacturer names

The manufacturer's name imbues a product with a code of connotations connected with a sense of reliability, trust, and artistry (according to product). Names such as *Armani, Folgers, Calvin Klein, Gucci*, etc. are examples of names that evoke this code. This semiotic strategy straddles all kinds of products, from cheese (*Kraft*) and coffee (*Folgers*) to automobiles (*Lamborghini, Maserati*) and designer clothes and cosmetics (*Gucci, Prada, Chanel*). In the case of products such as cheese or coffee, the name is a promise of quality and tradition, since the maker can be easily identified and its track record thus easily accessed. Much like instruments named after their makers, from the Stradivarius violin to the Steinway piano, brands like these ones suggest superiority and reputability, based on the fact that they have been around for a considerable period of time and thus have (presumably) withstood the test of time. Like wines, they are perceived to be of a vintage quality, hence they are also called *heritage names*. In the case of designer clothing, jewelry, perfume, and other lifestyle products, the manufacturer name can more appropriately be called a *designer* or *creator name*, since it evokes, instead, connotations of skill, elegance, high class, and the like. The same applies to automobile names such as *Ferrari* or *Maserati*. When people buy an *Armani* or a *Ferrari* product, they can feel that they are buying a work of art authored by a genius.

Manufacturer brand names are, in effect, eponyms, since they refer to a person whose name is on the product and is thus perceived as being the authorial source of the product itself. Marketing research shows that luxury items named after the manufacturer might even produce a cult of connoisseurship whereby the brand is the symbolic means by which consumers can aspire to attain (or maintain) a high class and lifestyle (Klein 2000; Wheeler 2003). Consumer discernment of brands is now a subtle form of imaginary social status climbing, based on the signification code of the name. Such names make it possible for anyone to climb a ladder of success (real or imagined) (Baudrillard 1983).

Fictitious Character Names

Products named after a fictitious character (*Mr. Clean, Barbie, Betty Crocker*) suggest specific kinds of personal qualities, such as cleanliness or else idealized portraitures of personality, represented by the character. For this reason, they are also called *portrait names*. *Mr. Clean* (a detergent) is, more specifically, a *cartoon character name*, also known as a *mascot name*. Another subtype of portrait name is that of a *human effigy* (real or fictitious). The *Betty Crocker* product, for instance, bears the effigy or portrait of a fictitious female.

Some of these names are based on real people. For example, *Duncan Hines* is a character seen on boxes of cake and brownie mix. Many assume that he is a fictitious character. But in actual fact, there really existed a Duncan Hines, who was born in Bowling Green, Kentucky, in 1880, becoming widely known, at first, for his newspaper ratings of restaurants. Around 1950, Hines agreed to let his name be used for products. Another example is the Wendy character of the *Wendy's* restaurant chain. Dave Thomas, the founder of the chain, used his own daughter's name (Wendy), even though the image on the logo is not a portrait of his daughter, but rather a stylized version of a young girl.

In sum, such names attribute a personal nature or human characteristics to a brand product, thus giving them, literally, a face that consumers can easily identify, much like the face of a friend or someone familiar. In fact, Betty Crocker, invented in 1921 by Gold Medal flour to serve as the logo of the company, became, according to a 1945 issue of Fortune magazine, the second most popular woman in America after Eleanor Roosevelt, having evolved into a mythic American character—an expert cook, a friend, and a mother figure. Played by various actresses on radio and television, Betty became a true icon of "ideal American womanhood." She appeared in movies and on television. Her countenance was shaped to have a combination of Caucasian features designed to present the perfect composite of the stay-at-home American woman. Twenty years later, a new portrait produced a new image—older and friendlier. Currently, her image has been updated to reflect yet a new image of American womanhood. She now resembles anything from a Latina female and a soccer mom to a female CEO. The Betty Crocker "makeover" is a perfect example of how brands must constantly be reshaped to keep in step with the times.

Descriptor Names

The descriptor describes the product in some concrete way (such as what the product allows users to accomplish with it). For example: *Frogurt* (= Frozen + Yogurt), *Go-Gurt* (= Go + Yogurt). It can also be a toponymic descriptor, identifying the geographical location (or country) from where the product originates or where a company is situated: *American Bell*, *Bank America*, *Western Union*, etc.

Most descriptors names, however, indicate what products can do: *Air Fresh* (air freshener), *Bug Off* (insect repellent), *Close-Up Toothpaste* (dentifrice), *Drip Dry* (spray), *Easy Wipe* (cleaning cloth), *Easy Clean* (cleaner), *Kleenex* (tissue), *Lestoil* (household cleaner), *Light N Easy* (mop), *One Wipe* (hygienic cloth), *Wash N Wear* (garments). Even in relaying seemingly straightforward information, descriptor brand names nevertheless evoke signification systems. They identify the product not as a simple product, but as something that belongs somewhere, is created by someone, or can do various things. And often the name is linked subconsciously to specific lifestyles. For example, in 1998 General Mills introduced a yogurt category called *Go-Gurt*. The name was designed semiotically for the pre-teen market for which it was targeted. With alliterative and entertaining flavor names such as *Berry Blue Blast* and *Rad Raspberry*, the brand was an immediate success, because, as Spiegel, Coffey, and Livingston (2004: 185) observe, the name informed pre-adolescents that they could eat the yogurt "on the go," and thus do it as they played sports, went skateboarding, and the like.

Suggestive Names

Suggestive names connect the consumer by allusion to certain lifestyles. Consider the name of the *Acura* car. At a literal level, the name is, clearly, suggestive of the word *accuracy*. But its structure is allusive to a combination of Italian (or Spanish) and Japanese words. The feminine nouns in the former language end in *-a* and certain Japanese words end in the suffix *-ura* (*tempura*). The brand name thus suggests, by extension, the perceived qualities of both cultures at once—artistry and scientific precision. Carmakers have used this strategy frequently: *Altima, Corsica, Elantra, Lumina, Maxima, Sentra*, and so on.

The code can take many forms. For example, using certain morphemes (such as suffixes) might convey scientific soundness. The brand names *AndroGel* and *ViraMax* for male potency products are two cases-in-point. In both names, the first part (*Andro-* and *Vir-*) refers to various gender qualities (*androgen* and *virile* respectively), while the suffixes evoke scientific connotations. Various brand names are created in similar ways, connecting them to a generic scientific code: *Panasonic* (televisions and stereos), *Proof Positive* (eye cream), *Technics* (stereo system), *Timex* (watch), and so on.

Some names are suggestive of the qualities of Nature, which is an appropriate onomastic fit since they refer to cleanliness or some natural process—*Aqua Velva* (aftershave lotion), *Cascade* (detergent), *Irish Spring* (soap product), *Mountain Dew* (soft drink), *Surf* (laundry soap), *Tide* (laundry soap), etc. When people buy *Moondrops, Natural Wonder, Rainflower, Sunsilk*, or *Skin Dew* cosmetics the suggestion is that they are acquiring some of Nature's beauty resources; and when they buy *Eterna 27, Clinique, Endocil*, or *Equalia* beauty products the suggestion is that they are getting products made with scientific precision.

Others suggest lifestyle preferences or needs. For example, car models are named to suggest countryside escape, wild west living, back-to-nature feelings, and so on—*Dodge Durango, Ford Escape, Ford Explorer, Jeep Grand Cherokee, Jeep Renegade, Jeep Wrangler, Mercury Mountaineer*, etc. Names constructed as hyperboles imply superiority, excellence, the big picture, a forward-looking attitude, and so on—*FutureNow* (marketing services), *Maxi Light* (skin cream), *PowerAde* (sports drink), *SuperFresh* (grocery store), etc. These also show the technique of blending words together or combining parts of words. The endings *-tastic* (as in *fantastic*), *-tacular* (as *spectacular*), *-licious* (as in *delicious*), *-rama* (as in *panorama*), among others, are found commonly in this category of brand naming (Cook 2004: 68): *Snack-Tastic* (snack product), *Pet-tacular* (pet grooming product), *Soyalicious* (frozen dessert), *Beef-a-rama* (food-tasting), etc.

Suggestive names are particularly effective, because they link products to human life schemes and cultural symbolism subconsciously. Cars named after animals (*Mustang, Jaguar, Cougar*, etc.) imply that animalistic qualities are entailed by driving the automobiles—a *Jaguar* brings to mind a large and powerful creature, a *Cougar* a fast and exotic animal, and so on. A previous car model named *Park Avenue*, on the other hand, suggested upscale-ness; one named *Cavalier* nobility; one named *Yukon* exploration; one named *Sonata* classical music sophistication, and so on. The names given to video games fit in perfectly with the mind of the game player, including an appetite for adventure (*Final Fantasy X*), ludic play (*PlayStation*), intrigue and excitement (*Grand Theft Auto*), free-for-alls (*Melee*), and so on.

Iconic Names

The iconic name is a subtype of the suggestive name category. There is, in fact, considerable overlap among these two categories. In semiotic theory, an icon is a sign that is made to resemble its referent in some way. The Apple Computer logo is an example of a visual icon, because it portrays its referent (an apple) visually. Alliterative names such as *Frosted Flakes* (cereal) are vocal icons simulating the sounds that eating the cereal are perceived to make. Similarly, the name *Ritz Crackers* assigns an iconic sonority to the product that is simulative of sounds that crackers make as they are being eaten. A classic case in the annals of marketing history, showing how this basic type of phonetic iconicity can be a brand's greatest asset, is that of *Smuckers* jam (named after the manufacturer), which appears at first to be a poorly-given name, but actually turns out to be a highly effective one. The slogan of the company plays cleverly on this initial perception: "A name like Smuckers, it has to be good." The name is indeed good because, as Neumeier (2006: 83) aptly puts it, it is "distinctive, short, spellable, pronounceable, likable, portable, and protectable." And, more importantly, it is iconic: *Smuckers* sounds like smacking lips, which, as Neumeier (2006: 83) goes on to point out, is the preverbal "testament to a yummy jam."

Another iconic strategy is matching the design of the product or its logo, emblem, or container to some property of the name. As Nuessel (2010: 103) writes about energy drinks, this type of iconicity inheres in designing the physical appearance of a product so as "to appeal to this group in terms of colors, images and container design." Thus, one finds containers which are descriptive of their names, as, for instance, a can with an unusual twist-off cap named *Jolt* and one with a grenade shape named appropriately *Bomba*.

One of the most famous of all iconic brand names is, of course, the *McDonald's* one, which is written in such a way that the initial letter resembles arches (iconically). Such names, which are recognizable through some feature of their lettering or layout, are also called *letter names*. Another classic example of such an iconic name is the *Coca-Cola* one. In this case, the name is written in a distinctive style (font, color, etc.), which also constitutes its logo. It is probably the most recognizable visual symbol in the entire world today. Letter names constitute a relatively large onomastic category. It seems that the blending of the purely linguistic with the visual is highly effective since it taps into two forms of memory—the verbal and the eidetic.

Another example of an iconic brand name is *Drakkar noir*, chosen by Guy Laroche for one of its cologne products. Together with the dark bottle, the name conveys images of fear, the forbidden, and the unknown. Forbidden things take place under the cloak of the night; hence the name *noir* (French for "black"). The sepulchral name *Drakkar noir* is clearly iconic with the bottle's design at a connotative level, reinforcing the idea that something desirous in the "dark" will happen by splashing on the cologne. The word *Drakkar* is obviously suggestive of Dracula, the deadly vampire who came out at night to mesmerize his sexual prey with a mere glance.

Metaphor

Overall, most of the above strategies can actually be put under the rubric of *metaphorical names*. Brand naming is, fundamentally, a rhetorical strategy, and thus the line between the various categories discussed above is really a fine one, since they could easily be considered to be tropological in the basic sense of that word. Many of the suggestive names above, for instance, are saliently metaphorical. Automobiles named after animals (*Beetle, Colt, Cougar, Viper, Mustang, Cobra*) are part of a long-standing perception of the automobile as a replacement of animals as transporters of people. This is why we still refer to the energy associated with motor vehicle engines in terms of "horse power." This rhetorical linkage reaches as well into other domains of meaning. A car model named *Breeze* suggests that the driver will feel a breeze by driving the vehicle and that driving the vehicle is "a breeze." A car named *Pathfinder* implies instead that it will allow its driver to discover a new path into unexplored regions. And a model named after a zodiac sign (*Aries, Taurus*) suggests character traits associated with that sign. In a phrase, metaphor allows carmakers to link automobiles with aspects of psychological and social life: upscaleness (*Park Avenue, Fifth Avenue, Catalina, Monte Carlo, Capri*), country lifestyle (*Outback, Villager*), social rank (*Viscount, Marquis, Diplomat, Monarch, Ambassador*), exploration or escape from city life (*Dakota, Montana, Yukon, Sierra*, etc.), social advantages such as protection, friendship, security, etc. (*Protégé, Sidekick, Escort, Cavalier*), the artistry and élitism associated with classical music (*Sonata, Tempo, Prelude*), world travel, car racing, and the alluring qualities of foreign worlds (*Seville, Grand Prix*).

Perfume and video game names are also often metaphors. The perfume named *Poison*, by Christian Dior, is an obvious one because, as Wolfe (1989: 3) aptly points out, it evokes a sense of "mystery, alchemy and the archetype of the sorceress." Names such as *PacMan, Pitfall, Pong* that were common in 1970s and 1980s (when video games came onto the social scene) have been replaced with new, trendy names, such as *GameCube*, which suggests the Rubik's Cube, and others that implicate new forms of intelligence tied to technology; *Grand Theft Auto*, which suggests intrigue, life on the margins, excitement, cool, James Bond, etc.; *Melee*, which brings to mind violent car racing, clashes, free-for-alls; and so on. As Gabriele Zamara (2018) observes:

Just what makes a metaphor such a powerful brand name is far more complex and fascinating than we think. The obvious is true. Metaphors make great names because they paint a simple, strong image in customers' minds. When you hear the name Amazon, you think big, impressive river. And you remember that river. Metaphors also dance around the obvious. They are not the first, most immediate or literal way to express a key idea. Metaphors have that special surprise factor. They are big and broad and continue to surprise over the lifetime of a brand because they easily shift to tell more than one story. It's the difference between the name Amazon and Online Bookstore; Amazon allows the business to grow in an infinite number of directions and change its focus time and time again.

Brand Logic

The term "brand logic" is now used in marketing to explain the logic behind naming products in ways such as those described here. This is indeed the correct term. The word *logic* derives from the Greek *logos* meaning both "word" and the "thought" it evokes. A product is something made in factories, in shops, etc. A brand, on the other hand, is a logical construct—a name evoking an unconscious system of thought. But the "logical reasoning" used is hardly deductive or rational; it is, rather, based on a figurative-suggestive sense of the meaning nuances built into words. The whole brand-naming process is essentially a "rhetorical act." As Zamara (2018) explains, the power of such naming acts lies in the ways in which metaphor invites us into its realm of meaning: "A suggestive or metaphorical name serves as that same kind of invitation. Not between two people, per se, but rather, between a brand and its audience. Amazon, Nike, Safari, Oracle, Kayak, Nest. They are strong names because they entice us to dig deeper and try to understand the story they start. They ask us to consider why the name of the world's largest river is being used to convey scale and scope, or why a bird's roost relates to a protective home automation system."

Symbolic Names

In early 2000 some carmakers started using naming strategies that were designed to appeal to a new generation of customers accustomed to an Internet or digital style of communication. *Cadillac*, for instance, announced a new model with the monogram name *CTS* in 2001. *Acura* also transformed its line of models with names such as *TL, RL, MDX, RSX*. Such names are now common. They can be called, simply, *symbolic names*. They involve the use of letters, numbers, acronyms, reflecting an "Internet-savvy" code: *X-Factor* (television show), *Toyota XR Matrix* (car), *iPad* (digital device), *X-Stick* (snack), *Xbox* (video game), *PS36* (video game), *2BFree* (clothes), *XM4Home* (radio system), *Spex Appeal* (eyewear), *Glam Gurlz* (dresses), *Hotpak* (heating pad), *Minds@Work* (digital equipment). These tap into a "text-messaging" style of writing words that is in step with the times (Frankel 2004: 106–7; Cook 2004). Actually, this strategy was used long before the Internet Age. Products such as *Cheez Whiz* (cheese paste), *Spic 'N Span* (cleaning liquid), *Weetabix* (cereal), *Kool* (cigarettes), and others were named in a similar way. The brand names *U All Kno* (after dinner mints), *Phiteezi* (shoes), and *U-Rub-In* (cream) actually go back to the 1920s (Cook 2004: 44). It seems to have always been a pattern within modern culture to use letters as symbols, suggesting a kind of inherent symbolism inherent within mass culture itself. Rock and rap musicians, for example, have always used it to name themselves— *Guns 'N Roses*, *Snoop Dogg*, *Salt N Pepa*, etc.

One of the most widely-used practices is the use of certain letters as symbols by themselves. Consider the letter X, which appears throughout brand-naming landscape. In the area of clothing and footwear, one finds (or found) brands named: *X-treme, MaxX, X-tech, X-Girl, X-Cape, XOXO*. In the field of electronic products, the following names can be (or were) found: *X-cam, Xybernaut, NeXT, XM Satellite Radio, Xbox, Xobile, Xincom*. In the domain of household products, foods, and drinks, one finds names such as *Xanath, Xellent Vodka, XuXU, Xyience, Xantax*. Indeed, X-named products are found (or were found) in every sector of the marketplace: *Xcite* (herbal Viagra), *X-Lite* (bicycle), *X-Terra* (vehicle), and so on. In a fascinating book titled *Sign After the X* (2000), Marina Roy has traced the history of X as a polyvalent sign, showing that it has had very little to do with phonetics at any period of its history, but everything to do with symbolism, standing for such referents as the sign for a mistake, the unknown, location on a treasure map, a symbol for Christ, the symbol for a kiss, and so on.

Today X stands for youth culture (*Xbox*), adventure comic heroes (*X-Men*), movies (*X-rated*) and virtually anything that is both forbidden (or mysterious) or exciting. Single letter symbolism does not stop at X. Another example is the use of lower-case "i," a practice introduced (to the best of my knowledge) into brand naming by the Apple Computer Company. Today it is used to name a vast array of products: *iCaps* (eye-care products), *iCom* (computer software), *iMac* (computer), *iMark* (eye shadow), *iPad* (digital device), *iZod* (shoes), and so on. Such names reverberate with technological chic, suggesting "imagination," "Internet," "ingenuity," and "intelligence," among many other things.

Alphanumeric brands are those that deploy numbers for either their phonetic qualities or their numerological symbolism: *2BFree* (clothes), *2CE* (computer software), *4 Ever Nails* (nail polish), *H2Optix* (eyewear), *XM4Home* (radio system), As Altman (2006: 70) points out, numbers used in naming practices are effective because of their various connotations:

> Think about the difference between a "blended vegetable drink" and "V8." From the name, you know that there are eight kinds of vegetables in every container. Heinz 57 explains on its Web site that in 1896 H. J. Heinz arbitrarily turned "more than 60 products into 57 Varieties." The magic number became world renowned and now is virtually synonymous with the H. J. Heinz Company.

At one level, alphanumeric names are clearly designed to appeal to the current generation. But at different level, they conjure up the same images of occultism evoked by ancient numerological practices. Consider the number 5, used famously in the *Chanel No. 5* perfume product. There are, of course, historical reasons for naming the product this way—*Chanel No. 5* was the fifth perfume created by Coco Chanel (so the story goes). But the instant a product is so named, our reaction to it is hardly literal. The number 5 was associated in ancient numerological systems to the pentagon and its mystical derivative the pentagram. The Pythagoreans ascribed the power of the feminine to this five-sided figure. Thus, it can be suggested that the *Chanel No. 5* unconsciously evokes the symbolism of the mystical feminine, of the perfection of feminine beauty, and so on.

As Gunasti and Devezer (2016) have shown, there are two dimensions involved in alphanumeric naming, which they call *link* and *alignability*. The former refers to the connection between the brand name and a specific product feature or the product as a whole; whereas the latter is about whether the preferences for a product can be aligned with the numbers included in the brand names in an ascending or descending trend. The *Chanel No. 5*, possesses both features—it is linked to the company as the fifth product in its production history and it is aligned with the ancient mysticism of femininity.

Symbolic brand names such as these are powerful because they cast a kind of magic spell on the product. From the beginning of time, names have been thought to have special magical powers. The newly fashioned symbolic brand name also seems to work an unconscious magic on modern-day humans, making them see, for example, products as necessary for success, beauty, adventure, etc. or creating distinctions between better or worse—be it in body, hairstyle, or general lifestyle.

Concluding Remarks

Naming a product makes it possible to refer to it as if it had a distinctive character or quality. Some of the most basic ways this is carried out have been described here. The underlying premise is that it is easier to remember things as words than to remember the things themselves. A word classifies something, keeps it distinct from other things and, above all else, bestows socially relevant meanings to it. Brand names stick to the mind, in the same way that the meanings of ordinary words do. They become a part of our semantic memory system. The name is so intrinsic to creating brand image that it is perhaps the reason why term *brand* is no longer used today just to refer to a specific product line, but also to the company that manufactures it and to the social image that the company wishes to impart of itself and of its products. Thus, the name *Coca-Cola* now refers not only to the actual soft drink, but also to the company itself, the social meanings that drinking it entails, and so on and so forth.

As the examples discussed here show, brand names are constructed to create signification systems or codes for the product. As Alina Wheeler (2003: 2) has observed: "Products are created in the factory; brands are created in the mind." By naming a product, the manufacturer is, in effect, bestowing upon it the same kinds of meanings that are reserved for people. The integration between brand-naming style and pop culture is part of a larger phenomenon that came into full force in the 1920s. In 1929, for instance, the Disney Corporation permitted Mickey Mouse to be reproduced on school slates. In the 1930s, the Mickey Mouse brand name and logo were licensed with huge success. In 1955 *The Mickey Mouse Club* premiered on US network television, further transforming the corporate brand into a symbol of childhood.

The histories of brand naming and marketing overlap considerably. The reason is a straightforward one—it is impossible to advertise and promote "nameless" products with any degree of efficacy. Brand names are signs that influence people's unconscious perception of objects as necessary referents of everyday life. Brand-name designers are, in a fundamental sense, our modern-day wordsmiths, since many of their name-construction strategies have spilled over into society at large. (see also Watkins 2014).

Author Profile: Marcel Danesi

Marcel Danesi is Professor of Semiotics and Linguistic Anthropology at the University of Toronto, where he directs the Program in Semiotics and Communication Theory. Editor-in-Chief of *Semiotica: the Journal of the International Association for Semiotic Studies,* from 2004 to 2019. Marcel is a past-president of the Semiotic Society of America. He edited the Toronto Semiotic Circle Monographs from the mid-1980s to 1990s before moving the series to its current home at the University of Toronto Press. Marcel has authored over 100 books and academic papers which consider the semiotic and anthropological aspects of emoji, popular culture, puzzles, crime, youth, and a range of other topics. Marcel recently gave a popular Ted Talk on emojis.

2

Strategic Semiotics

"No brand is an island." Laura Oswald, *Marketing Semiotics*

Chapter 1 introduced readers to the basics of brand semiotics, the meanings that define the brand's identity and cultural positioning. While brand meaning in and of itself is a powerful concept, brand meaning only grows value for the firm through a well-executed brand strategy that calibrates the brand to external market forces such as competitors, category trends, new technologies, and cultural change.

Management's decisions about everything from new product development and technology to pricing strategy communicate to consumers what the brand stands for, including the brand persona, value proposition, and its customer relationship.

Kodak's dramatic fall from the pinnacle of category leadership to bankruptcy illustrates the importance of this principle for managing brand equity. Blinded by their unchallenged leadership in the 35mm photo industry, Kodak failed to respond to growing consumer preferences for digital imaging devices, condemning the business to obsolescence. On the surface the case looks like a matter for new product research and development rather than semiotics. However, it wasn't for lack of digital expertise that Kodak failed. The company was already leading advances in digital imaging technologies for industries such as healthcare. The problem centered on Kodak's failure to adapt these new technologies to their trademark positioning as leaders in consumer photography, as aptly expressed in the historical tagline, "You push the button, we do the rest."

Rather than an R&D problem, Kodak's business crisis began as a crisis of brand semiotics. Driven by complacency, the company supported an outdated brand image that was communicated in management decisions across many facets of the business, including marketing that still commemorated "Kodak moments" in photo albums, in the vintage headquarters in Rochester reminiscent of Norman Rockwell's New York, and in the company's top-down organizational structure that blocked new ideas from moving up from junior management.

Kodak's marketing myopia (Levitt 1960) doomed them to bankruptcy. Rather than align ease of use with digital consumer technology, or even produce "Kodak inside" technology for the growing cellular phone industry, management milked the proverbial cash cow and ignored the external environment. Kodak was blindsided by

Laura R. Oswald, *Strategic Semiotics* In: *Doing Semiotics: A Research Guide for Marketers at the Edge of Culture.*
Edited by: Laura R. Oswald, Oxford University Press (2020). © Laura R. Oswald. © Rachel Lawes, Reading 2.
DOI: 10.1093/oso/9780198822028.003.0002

competitors such as Fujifilm, who undermined Kodak's value proposition by slashing prices on 35 mm film stock and developing easy to use, inexpensive digital cameras.

In the discussion that follows, readers discover how semiotics-based research can anticipate these kinds of problems by examining the impact of external factors such as competition, new technologies, and cultural change. Some readers may be surprised that semiotics addresses specific business issues such as this because they assume that semiotics is strictly limited to the way meanings are communicated in texts. In fact, brand strategy "speaks." Management's decisions about everything from new product development and technology to pricing strategy communicate to consumers what the brand stands for, including the brand persona, value proposition, and its customer relationship.

The discussion, exercises, and team project center on the play between code and performance in cultural brand management. Teams will learn to: (1) conduct a binary analysis of brand meaning; (2) decode the strategic dimensions of a product category; (3) define the brand's strategic positioning; and (4) map competitors on a double-axis grid, and 5) find a new cultural space for new product development.

Code Theory

Codes are cultural norms that account for the collective understanding of sign systems such as language, rituals, and brand discourse and perpetuate these systems over time. They are the scaffolding that supports the production of meaning and culture. Performance defines the act of manipulating these codes in the interest of creativity. More specifically, the mind creates meanings by filtering our sensory perceptions into discrete semiotic codes that articulate sounds into language, roadways into rules of the road, and populations into social segments. This sorting process translates into the distinct codes that structure communication, social organization, and consumption rituals that consumers learn in a given culture.

The Binary Structure of Meaning

Codes create meaning by structuring difference and distinction between elements of discourse. Saussure (2011 [1916]) claimed that difference and distinction actually form the essence of meaning production. For instance, we define white in terms of black, masculinity in terms of femininity, life in terms of death, and good in terms of evil, etc.

Codes also account for the variations in language and consumer behavior that differentiate one culture from the next and structure the reproduction of cultural systems over the long term. For this reason, the binary analysis is a fundamental analytical tool used by semioticians to articulate the broad cultural dimensions of a set of data, a market, or a product category.

While the binary analysis cannot account for the endless ways human experience and living culture perform these norms and codes, it is the first step in making sense of the marketplace. Because of its emphasis on difference and distinction, it is particularly useful for charting the strategic dimensions of a market and pinpointing where specific brands fall within these dimensions. The case example below walks readers through the basics of the strategic analysis of the personal computer category by comparing and contrasting the cultural positioning of the two brands.

Case Example: Decoding the Personal Computer Category

In the early 2000s, a tech company approached Marketing Semiotics to find out how to position a new personal computer brand that could compete with the category leader, IBM. Positioning new brands is similar to finding your way in an unfamiliar city—you need a map of the space and some landmarks to help you navigate your position on the map. The case analysis walks the reader through the steps involved in decoding and mapping the strategic dimensions of a market for purposes of positioning and brand strategy.

The Competitive Brand Audit

Though Apple was still catching up to IBM in terms of market share, it formed a counterpoint to IBM's high tech, corporate image by means of new, user-friendly technologies targeted to everyday users. The audit revealed recurring themes and symbolism over the years that reinforced the initial binary in multiple brand associations related to things like personality, mood, and relationship strategy. We began the research with a semiotic audit of major advertising campaigns going back five years for two main players in the category, IBM and Apple. We then compared and contrasted brand associations for Apple against IBM and identified a binary relationship between two brands and two cultural positionings.

The Paradigmatic Analysis of the Category

By listing the binary attributes of both competitors in a table (Table 2.1), we gained insights into the broad paradigmatic dimensions of the personal computer market. A paradigm is a system of meanings defined by a series of binaries that relate vertically to other elements in a set.

The table shows that IBM's high-tech positioning is supported by paradigmatic associations such as the blue/grey palette, the distant camera angle, and the absence of people. In contrast, Apple's rich color palette, the smiling faces of consumers, and close-up and personal camera angle support the brand's user-friendly positioning. Although the paradigmatic analysis may oversimplify the nuances and overlaps between the brands, it provides a roadmap for entering the category in the spaces that lie between the binary dimensions of the category.

Table 2.1 The paradigmatic dimensions of the personal computer market

Cultural categories	IBM/APPLE
Consumer behavior	Hi-tech/User-friendly
Mood	Serious/Fun
Culture	Corporate/Personal
Color scheme	Grays and blues/Colors
Consumer relationship	Cool/Warm

Brand Mapping

Brand mapping is useful for visualizing the cultural dimensions of brands and even identifying unmet needs in a product category. We choose two of the binary dimensions to create a double-axis grid. The intersecting axes form four quadrants, each of which maps the brand's association with two or more variables, as for example, [High Tech + Corporate] or [High Tech + Home Computing]. We then position the two competitors in the appropriate quadrants (Figure 2.1).

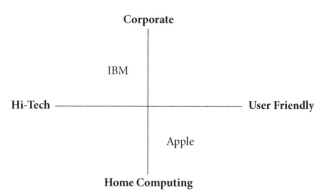

Figure 2.1. Positioning analysis: Apple and IBM. © 2018 Marketing Semiotics

A typical study would usually include multiple brands and explore multiple cultural dimensions of the category. In the computer example, IBM occupies a cultural space framed by "corporate" and "hi-tech," while Apple occupies a contrasting quadrant defined by "user-friendly" and "personal computing."

If we had included a third competitor in the mix, we would refine the analysis further. Samsung presents a strong competitor in the PC category today. Positioned as an advanced technology tool for corporate or home computing, Samsung could occupy two quadrants, the first defined by the variables [Corporate + Hi-Tech], the second defined by the variables [High-Tech + Home Computing]. Of course in today's market, where computer use has grown to 90 percent of American households, we would have identified a rather different set of cultural categories and several other players in the competitive field.

Exercise 2.1 Decoding the Product Category

Exercise 2.1 extends the Brand Audit exercise outlined in Chapter 1. It presents a simple introduction to the competitive analysis of brands in a product category.

Instructions

- Working in teams, students compare and contrast two (2) prominent competitors in a product category, as they will normally represent the broad cultural dimensions of the market, as in the Apple vs. IBM example. Keep in mind that at this stage we are looking for the broad brushstrokes of meaning that predominate across the data set, not the variations or nuances.

  Note: Students may reconstitute the same teams they formed for the exercises in Chapter 1 or form new ones. They may also continue with the same brand the team chose for the Brand Audit exercise in Chapter 1.

- Referring to the personal computer example above, teams choose a specific brand (other than sportswear) and two direct competitors in the same product category. The business press, such as finance.yahoo.com, provides ample information about key competitors in a given category.
- Teams perform a semiotic audit of each campaign regarding the brand messaging, color scheme, logo, and message.
- Comparing and contrasting the cultural positionings of all three brands, identify the key cultural binaries that structure meaning across the product category (i.e., Personal/Corporate, Power/Ease of Use, etc.)

Exercise 2.2 The Competitive Brand Audit

Teams select at least three advertising campaigns for three top competitive brands spread out over a minimum of five years. Teams may not choose sportswear brands.

Create a data log based on the sample in Table 2.2 located in the Appendix, including the date, title, and description of the ad.

Step 1: The Brand Audit

In Table 2.2, make note of the verbal, visual, and rhetorical cues that each brand employs to represent brand elements such as the consumer target and lifestyle, the value proposition, the brand relationship, and the mood or tone. Is there a story? Is age a factor? Lifestyle? Social demeanor?

Step 2: The Binary Analysis

Referring to the worksheet in Table 2.3 located in the Appendix, make note of several key brand attributes that recur over all the campaigns. Define the cultural category in which they belong. If the brand emphasizes a casual lifestyle, for instance, Lifestyle defines the category, and the binary code [casual/formal] defines the range of lifestyle choices available to competitive brands in the data. These kinds of codes structure meaning production in a product category.

Directions

- List three of the main cultural categories in column 1 of the grid.
- Deconstruct each cultural category into a binary under column 2. For the personal computer example, one could say that the binary [trust/expertise] relates to the Customer Relationship, the binary [anecdotes/facts] relates to the Tone, and so on.
- In columns 3 and 4, list the binary term that best describes each of the two brands.

Exercise 2.3 Brand

Instructions

Using information from the binary analysis performed in Exercise 2.1, teams will now map the cultural dimensions of the competitive set by creating a double axis grid, using the sample in Figure 2.2, located in the Appendix.

Steps

Choose two binaries and plot them on the brand map in Figure 2.2, located in the Appendix.

Key Learnings from Exercises 2.1, 2.2, and 2.3

Exercise 2.1 taught methods for decoding the cultural dimensions of a product category. Collecting sample advertising for three brands, teams learned how to use the semiotic analysis to identify strategic differences between each brand. Beginning with a semiotic analysis of messaging and visual semiotics of each ad, they compared and contrasted the three brands and distilled findings into sets of binary pairs that represent the cultural dimensions of the product category. The exercise prepared them for the more thorough competitive Brand Audit presented in Exercise 2.2.

In Exercise 2.2, students learned some basic semiotic methods for developing a simple communications analysis to a broader strategy for positioning brands against competitors. And in Exercise 2.3, students learned to map the strategic dimensions of a product category on a binary grid for purposes of mapping the cultural positionings of competitive brands and exposing "white spaces" in the category that represent opportunities for growing the brand's competitive edge.

Brand Positioning Basics

The exercises prepared readers for an extended team project that applies these methods to a business problem study to map strategic relationships between multiple competitors in a category. By means of this analysis, we are able to expose strategies for both clarifying brand positioning and exposing opportunities for and innovation by identifying "white space" on the map (i.e., cultural territories that reflect unmet needs and emerging cultural trends in a market).

When shopping for a high-ticket item such as a road bike, consumers assess the price-to-benefits equation of any given brand by comparing and contrasting it to other brands in terms of functional attributes such as price and technologies and intangibles such as design and brand image and reputation. The brand positioning defines the cultural space that each competitor has carved out in the category to communicate the brand's value with a specific set of consumers.

Another way of viewing brand positioning is to imagine a consumer running in a competitive race and they look about to assess how they measure up with the runners in their pack. Maybe age, fitness level, and brand use are important to their assessment. Are their cohorts older or younger, more or less fit, wearing Nike or another brand, etc.? Consumers filter the cultural categories of age, fitness, and brand use through a rudimentary binary analysis, ending up with a set of binary codes, including [older/younger], [more fit/less fit], [Nike/other brands]. They may even assess the fitness of the people wearing Nike versus other brands. Does it seem as if Nike users are more or less fit than users of competitive brands? In brief, consumers "decode" the market environment by means of binary thinking.

The semiotic analysis begins with a brand audit of each brand in the data set in order to identify the binary categories that shape the category as a whole, such as athleticism, lifestyle, and fashion, and also maps on a strategic grid the distinct cultural positioning of competitive brands in the category.

Case Example: Nike Sportswear

By way of illustration, I will conduct a brief strategic analysis of the key competitors in the sportswear category, beginning with a semiotic audit of three campaigns for Nike launched between 1988 and 2016. Due to copyright restrictions, the ads could not be reproduced here but I include online links to the ads in footnotes 1–3. Although a more realistic study would include dozens of campaigns in various media, including digital, the Brand Audit that follows paints a broad brushstroke of Nike's core positioning around sports performance, athleticism, and a motivational relationship with their target market.

Data Collection
The question is often raised concerning the scope of the sample for a semiotic study of this nature. I have found that a sampling of communications going back at least five years will provide a sufficiently rich snapshot of the brand positioning to establish the strategic parameters of a product category. However, in most cases I also take a cursory look at additional campaigns going back to the brand's origins. This perspective determines whether the brand has moved off of its historical positioning or how the brand has adapted to cultural change over the years.

Methods
Methods include the Brand Audit of historical advertising, looking for recurring codes related to the brand message and semiotic elements across multiple ads. Although I highlight three key examples in this analysis, I made my selection based upon an informal review of dozens of Nike ads going back over twenty years.

The Semiotic Analysis

Nike advertising reaching back to the 1980s represents a consistent brand message and positioning. They center the brand on the extraordinary performances of elite athletes in order to communicate its commitment to excellence, personal improvement, and pushing boundaries—both in sports and new product technologies. In many Nike ads, the legendary tagline, "Just Do It!" calls upon amateur athletes to get in the game as well, motivating consumers to reach farther,

and exceed personal expectations, in sports as in life. The ads exploit the transformative effects of rhetoric to further the larger than life spectacle of elite athletes
in motion.

"Air Jordan is landing," 1988
The 1988 ad both refers to the market launch of the Air Jordan brand and
the aerodynamic lift of Michael Jordan that resembles a bird or a plane
touching ground.[1] The brand positioning is rooted in a metaphor linking
Jordan and the brand along the lines of their aerodynamic attributes
(Figure 2.3). The hyperbolic representation of Jordan taking flight also suggests
that the new technology can add lift to even Jordan's performance. The analogy
also bridges the gap between the elite athlete and the average consumer by
means of a chain of metonymies linking Jordan to the shoe he wears, the shoe
to the Air Jordan brand, and the brand to consumers who buy into the brand
promise. These kinds of rhetorical webs essentially produce what we know as
the brand world.

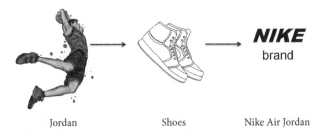

| Jordan | Shoes | Nike Air Jordan |

Figure 2.3. A rhetorical web

"The Bullet in the Chamber," 2012
The 2012 ad, "I am the bullet in the chamber," compares Pistorius's speed
to the ballistic force that drives a bullet through the chamber of a gun.[2] In a
reference to Superman lore, the metaphor infers that the runner, like
Superman, is "faster than a speeding bullet." Unlike basketball, running requires
not so much an aerodynamic lift as a projection forward of the body, which Pistorius,
a bi-lateral amputee, achieves by means of an extraordinary motion of his arms.
Nike's choice of a weapons metaphor drew criticism even before Pistorius himself was
accused of shooting his girlfriend, which prompted Nike to pull the ad from circu-
lation in 2013.

---

[1] Air Jordan Is Landing. https://yard.media/michael-jordan-la-construction-dune-icone-trentenaire.
[2] I Am the Bullet in the Chamber. https://www.businessinsider.com/nike-reacts-to-accused-
murder-oscar-pistorius-i-am-the-bullet-in-the-chamber-ad-2013-2

"Just Like Woman," 2016

The tagline for the 2016 ad, "Just Like Woman," is not a metaphor.[3] It makes sense only if the researcher recalls a Bob Dylan (1966) song with a similar name, "Just Like a Woman."[4] The Nike ad presents a powerful counterpoint to the woman in Dylan's song—sweet and vulnerable, "just like a little girl"—in the image of a tough and disciplined female athlete, Sophia Boutella. When references such as these are too obscure for the modern researcher, an on-line search of the phrase may provide the needed clarity.

By contrasting the tough, disciplined female athlete in the ad with Dylan's woman, the ad confronts a gender stereotype that barred women from competitive sports for many years. It recalls Nike's pioneering efforts to advance women's participation in competitive running in the 1970s, which became a platform for the brand's activist positioning.

Interestingly, in browsing through Nike advertising over the past ten years one notices contrasts between the metaphorical style used in relation to male athletes and the more prosaic, metonymical style used in relation to female athletes such as Serena Williams, described not only as "The Best Female Athlete," but the Best Athlete, period. Such insights often emerge in the Brand Audit research and suggest research directions that may not have been anticipated in the original plan.

In all three ads, formal similarities between the shape of the swoosh logo and the posture of bodies in the image. This figure reiterates the equation of the brand with the feats of the athletes. Jordan's body reaches up to the right toward the net; Pistorius' body winds up and moves forward toward the right. In the skateboarder ad, the parallel is even clearer, since a large logo is superimposed over the woman's body, aligning swoosh and pose in an unmistakable identification of Nike with powerful action.

The Brand Audit

The information in Table 2.4 summarizes findings from the advertising analysis. The table presents two dimensions of the brand discourse: the summary of each ad from left to right on the linear, syntagmatic axis; and the comparison of the three ads from top to bottom on the vertical, paradigmatic axis, which highlights semiotic codes that recur over multiple years and campaigns. The syntagmatic and paradigmatic dimensions of the brand discourse are marked by horizontal and vertical arrows on the grid. These kinds of visuals both help the researcher decode the brand discourse. The approach proves that researchers did not pull their strategic findings from their imaginations but drew conclusions from visible evidence in the data.

---

[3] Just Like a Woman. https://i.pinimg.com/originals/70/bb/9d/70bb9d76f0f38c5cc3e0e9fc384f8fef.png
[4] Bob Dylan. "Just Like a Woman." https://www.youtube.com/watch?v=dRLXZVojdhQ

Table 2.4 A brand audit of Nike

	NIKE 1988–2016	
1988. Air Jordan has landed.	Jordan, in a red Bulls uniform, takes flight toward the net, arms and legs expand in a V. Jordan is superimposed over a darkened cityscape at sunset.	*Metaphor: Jordan/aerodynamic machine or bird.Metaphor: Nike (swoosh) = action*
2012. I am the bullet in the chamber. Just Do It!	Pistorius, wearing a green and blue uniform, is shown in three poses in freeze frame winding up for the start of the race. The body pose resembles the form and dynamic of the swoosh logo, up and forward.	Metaphor: Pistorius/ aerodynamics of a bullet. Metaphor: Body in motion/Nike brand.
2016. Just like a woman.	A woman skateboarder lands an aerial kick flip on the right hand. Her legs bend forward forming a V. The body pose resembles the form and dynamic of the swoosh logo.	Metonymy: The tagline references a love song by Bob Dylan, the image belies the sweet, soft woman in the song. Metaphor: Body in motion/Nike brand.

The Brand Legacy

In addition to rhetorical devices, visual effects also influence our perception of the Nike athlete as larger than life. Athletes are posed against a blank or abstract background, moving them from the realm of real events to the realm of the super-natural. Their strong postures highlight the grace with which they perform super-human feats of power and speed. Jordan seems to take flight against the backdrop of a darkened cityscape. Pistorius gathers speed with his arms as he winds up for the start against a black backdrop; and the skate boarder lands on one hand against a stark white background. These formal effects reinforce Nike's association of athletics with pushing boundaries, realizing dreams, and working to overcome challenges.

A more detailed historical review of Nike advertising illustrates how the fundamental brand message has evolved in line with cultural change, the expansion of Nike's customer base, and the translation of the Nike ethos in messaging for social cause marketing. Drawing energy from high performance athletes, Nike's hopeful messaging inspires consumers to get into the game by getting into action. Their cutting edge sportswear technologies promise to give consumers an edge on the trail and the playing field. The dynamic form of the swoosh logo represents the Nike experience, and in the more iconic ads there are formal parallels between the logo's shape and the forward-moving poses of the athletes. The positive, action-oriented "Just Do It!" tagline inspires courage and hope, not only in consumer athletics but also in all aspects of their lives.

A Positioning Statement for Nike

The positioning statement is a brief summary of the brand ethos and personality that is sufficiently strong and clear enough to drive long-term creative strategy for the brand. By summarizing key findings from the semiotic analysis, we created the following positioning statement for Nike: "Nike is an inspirational, action-oriented brand that motivates consumers to live their dreams and cross the finish line."

The integration of the signs, symbols, and meanings we drew from the data form the brand system and account for Nike's unparalleled dominance of the sportswear category. A visual such as the Brand System grid in Figure 2.4 makes for a clear summary of the brand analysis for use in the final report.

1988–2016	Semiotics	Nike Positioning
	Just Do It!	
	Bodies in motion	Nike is an inspirational, action-
	Body/Logo match	oriented brand that motivates
	Dynamic visuals	consumers to live their dreams
	Elite athletes	and cross the finish line.
	Reaching height	
	Hard work	
	Personal victory	

Figure 2.4. The Nike brand system

In the concluding section of the report, one should also comment on any inconsistencies in the brand message over the years, any variations on the basic theme that warrant further examination, such as the rhetorical style of women-focused ads, and how the brand has responded over the years to cultural change.

Extended Case Example: A Strategic Semiotic Analysis of the Sportswear Category

We continue the brand strategy research process with a competitive analysis of multiple brands in a product category. The research includes a communications audit of key competitors, a binary analysis of the cultural categories occupied by the brand, and a positioning analysis of each brand. Before introducing the next team exercise, I will illustrate the process by extending the Nike case example into a strategic study of the sportswear category.

The Brand Audit

The competitive analysis begins with a communications audit of Nike's key competitors, Adidas and Puma. At this point in any project, it behooves the researcher to behave like a management consultant and find out some financial information about the brand and competitors.

We defined the competitive set in the sportswear category by referring to on-line financial data on Nike (O'Connell 2019). With revenues of $21.08 billion in 2017, Nike is far and above the leader in the sportswear category, followed by Adidas with $10.36 billion and third-place Puma with $2.41 (Statista 2018).

Furthermore, the relative share of market claimed by the three top brands has remained consistent since 2010. The brand analysis that follows will shed light on the reasons for Nike's dominance and the much weaker performances by competitors. This kind of market information can be found by searching in the business press or going to the site, finance.Yahoo.com

Adidas

In contrast to Nike, Adidas is a lifestyle brand that extends beyond sports to culture and fashion. Most advertising targets groups of young consumers with popular musician/designers such as Kanye West's Yeezy brand (Taylor 2018, Greenburg 2019). The message emphasizes personal creativity and style and culture bending rather than athletic performance. Adidas weaves sports into these discourses but cannot compete with Nike's dominance in the active-performance space. As a result, Adidas suffers from a lack of clarity, sometimes veering into Nike territory with ads that feature professional athletes at play in football or basketball with intense, performance-driven taglines such as, "Get explosive." Still other ads promote Adidas's commitment to social causes like climate change. Adidas's struggle to find a clear identity exemplifies the challenges posed by iconic brands that seem to have captured, like Nike, the spirit and meaning of the category as a whole (Table 2.5).

Table 2.5 Adidas: A simple brand audit

Language	Visuals	Rhetoric
2004–2015. Impossible is nothing.	*Historical photos of leaders who shaped the world: Mohammed Ali, Martin Luther King, Obama, etc.Focus on winning and leading, not sports.*	*Hyperbole, implied metaphor (i.e. if they can do it, you can too).*
Language	**Visuals**	**Rhetoric**
1980s. You don't have to be a tennis pro to look like one. 1989. I want, I can.	Models standing around in Adidas outfits with friends or an attractive woman. In contrast, the "I want" ad shows intense athletes in highly stylized images set to achieve their goals.	Metaphor—consumer/tennis pro. Metonymy—wear Adidas, look athletic. The "I want" campaign—hyperbole.
Language	**Visuals**	**Rhetoric**
2018. Yeezy 2018. Kyle Jenner models Adidas on social media.	The campaign shows the Adidas logo in black and white, the words Yeezy 2018 and Kanye West, the artist and designer, not the shoe. Kyle Jenner quits Puma, models for Adidas, and creates an Adidas clothing line.	Metonymy: wear this brand and and belong to Kanye's hip culture. Wear this and be famous like Kylie Jenner.

Paradigmatic Axis →

Syntagmatic Axis →

Puma

Although historical advertising reflects Puma's original positioning to competitive sports and winning performance, the brand was repositioned over the years and is now primarily a lifestyle and fashion brand targeted to more affluent consumers. Their advertising features rebellious youth and celebrities from the fashion and pop music industries such as Kylie Jenner (2017) and Emory Jones (2018). Although sports enthusiasts criticized Puma's choice of Kylie Jenner rather than an athlete to represent the brand in advertising, the campaign rings true for Puma's current positioning as a trendy brand for non-athletes. Like Adidas, Puma nonetheless crosses over into Nike's cultural space from time to time in advertising that harkens back to their roots in competitive sports. Nike's strong and consistent presence in this space nonetheless overshadows these efforts, which may explain why Puma diversified into fashion and leisure (Table 2.6).

Table 2.6 Puma: A simple brand audit

Language	Visuals	Rhetoric
1970s. Clyde Frazier: "Good reasons why I lace into Puma shoes," followed by language on product features.	Clyde shown ready to play basketball in Puma shoes.	The unadorned, straightforward style may add credibility to the brand endorsement.
Language	Visuals	Rhetoric
2017 "After Hours Athlete"	The video shows groups of young consumers in Puma clothing playing social sports such as bowling and pool.	Metonymy: Puma brings people together.
Language	Visuals	Rhetoric
2017 "Forever Fierce"	Kylie Jenner in stylish Puma sports gear shown jumping, running, and playing basketball. She left Puma for Adidas in 2018.	Metaphor and Metonymy—wear this and you will resemble Kylie's attitude and belong to her hip world.

Paradigmatic Axis ↑

→ Syntagmatic axis

In the next table (Table 2.7), I summarize key attributes of all the competitive brands in order to visualize where points of contrast and crossover may occur.

Table 2.7 The competitive brand audit

Brand	Semiotics	Positioning
Nike	Solo athletes poised for movement, dynamic swoosh design. Just do it.	Focused: Hyperbole, intense, mercurial, active. "Stop dreaming start working."
Adidas	Everyday activities—kids running to school, teens socializing; elite athletes; fashion and sex appeal.	Confusing: Fun and serious sport, everyday and history-making; advanced shoe technology blurred with fashion and sex appeal.
Puma	Culture-bending personalities, fashion, high-end style. Fast and sleek as a cougar, forever faster, cougar figure, athletes moving forward like Nike athletes	Inconsistent: Trend-setting style and luxury that banks on association with famous young celebrities. Puma swings also toward athleticism in ads that encourage persistence and the obsession to "go faster."

Decoding the Sportswear Category

As illustrated in the personal computer example earlier in the chapter, the semiotician decodes the product category by defining points of difference between competitors and articulating them into binary codes, such as sports/fashion. The codes structuring meaning in the category do not account for the nuances and complexities of individual brands, but provide a broad overview of the cultural dimensions of the category.

A Competitive Analysis

We begin with the market leader, Nike. In contrast to Nike, with its strong association with action and individual achievement, Adidas and Puma have wavered over the years between their origins in active sports and their more recent evolution into lifestyle brands that focus on fashion and personal appearance more than athletic achievement. Adidas differs from Puma by satisfying needs of young consumers for social belonging and trend-setting fashions, highlighting younger consumers in social interactions at work and play. More recently (2018), Adidas has encroached on Puma's cultural territory by identifying the brand with culture-bending celebrities such as Kendall Kardashian and Kanye West and including very high priced luxury brands into their portfolio, such as West's Keezy shoe, which runs between $300 and $600. They even enticed Kylie Jenner away from Puma and developed a Kylie sports clothing line.

Puma once distinguished itself from Adidas by targeting more affluent consumers and featuring celebrity spokespersons in advertising. Puma wants to be the brand to see and be seen in by trend-setting consumers, but as Adidas grows their stable of high-profile celebrities, it will struggle to maintain its current positioning.

Both Adidas and Puma not only suffer from a lack of differentiation, but from inconsistencies in their message from one campaign to the next, one year to the next. They dip into Nike territory from time to time with advertising that emphasizes athletic performance and intense competitiveness. They are literally "all over the map" when we try to position them in a given quadrant on a binary grid.

The Binary Analysis

In the next step, we outline the strategic implications of these contrasts by articulating them into binary pairs. I'll begin with the category, Consumer Behavior. Nike is committed to moving consumers into action. To define the binary pair for [action] we do not simply look for an antonym such as "inaction," but look to the ways other brands define that opposition. As fashion and lifestyle brands, Adidas and Puma do not specifically promote "inactivity," but orient their brands to consumers who use sports brands for the sake of appearance and social behavior (Croce 2018). For this reason, we articulate the Consumer Behavior category into the binary, [action/appearance].

As shown in the next table (Table 2.8), we focused on four cultural territories that appeared frequently throughout the data, including Consumer Behavior, Purpose, Value Proposition, and Brand Relationship. The selection of these territories was not determined by a rulebook in advance of the study, but emerged in the course of analyzing the data. Although analyzing the cultural codes that structure meaning in a product category is challenging, semiotics experts become skilled in the art of analysis through lots of practice and over time learn to identify the key territories for analysis rather quickly. Remember that the purpose of the binary analysis is to provide an overview of the cultural dimensions of the category. This preliminary stage of analysis establishes the basic norms that enable communication, whether in the form of marketing, cultural identity, or something else, to take place. As the analysis teases out tensions within the code system due to cultural difference, consumer agency, or creative play, it exposes the highly volatile and malleable nature of codes in the production of meaning. Furthermore, the limited set of binaries the analyst chooses to represent the category is chosen because these binaries recur with the most frequency throughout the data.

Table 2.8 A binary analysis of key competitors

Cultural category	Binary	Nike	Adidas	Puma
Consumer behavior	Action/appearance	Action	Appearance	Appearance
Purpose	Sports/fashion	Sports	Fashion	Fashion
Value proposition	Achievement/lifestyle	Achievement	Lifestyle	Lifestyle
Brand relationship	Coach/cohort	Coach	Cohort	Cohort

Brand Mapping

Once the researcher identifies the binary dimensions of the category, they map them on double-axis grids like the ones in Figures 2.5 and 2.6. This exercise illustrates how brands are positioned within the quadrants formed by the binary pairs. For example, Nike's association with Sports in Mapping A (Figure 2.5) does not distinguish the brand from competitors. In fact "sports" is not an intangible emotional attribute so much as a generic description of the product.

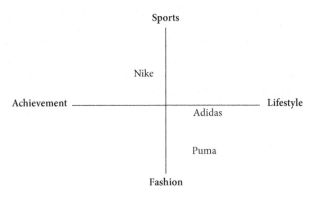

Figure 2.5. Mapping sportswear competitors—A

However, by framing Nike's cultural space between Sports and Achievement in Mapping B (Figure 2.6), we illustrate the brand's long-standing association with elite sports, performance, and "Just Do It!"

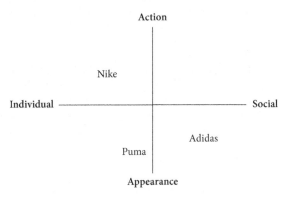

Figure 2.6. Mapping sportswear competitors—B

Likewise, when we compare and contrast Adidas and Puma based on a single attribute, Appearance, the brands blur together. However, if we frame the cultural spaces of each brand in relation to complementary attributes we clarify their points of difference (Figure 2.6). We map Puma in the lower left quadrant defined by the binary Appearance/Individual to account for Puma's focus on consumers taken in isolation. We map Adidas in the lower right quadrant defined by the binary Appearance/Social to account for Adidas's focus on consumers in social groups.

White Space

By pinpointing the relative positioning of brands in a competitive set, brand mapping not only charts the cultural dimensions of a product category but also exposes "white space" in the competitive environment that presents an opportunity for new product development. In Figure 2.5 the lower left quadrant framed by the binary, Achievement/Fashion, is empty. In Figure 2.6, the upper right quadrant framed by the binary, Action/Social is empty. By exposing white space in a category, the binary analysis provides insights for management to either reposition a tired brand or extend a brand into a cultural space that may represent an emerging trend or cultural phenomenon.

Brand mapping begins with market insights, gained either by advertising research or through primary research with consumers, or both. The semiotic analysis articulates brand attributes into binary pairs that distinguish one brand from another by creating double-axis grids. The mapping process enables management to visualize the relative positioning of competitors in consumer culture and adjust their own brands in response.

By articulating unoccupied "white space," brand mapping exposes unmet emotional needs in the marketplace that are not currently being met by competitors. The process was particularly useful for developing new product strategy for the Ford Escape in the early 2000s. Before the brand even had a name, Marketing Semiotics was tasked with understanding points of differentiation within the subcompact SUV category that included Jeep Cherokee, the Toyota Rav-4, and the CR-V. Ford originally conceived the brand as a smaller version of the Explorer, a very popular mid-sized SUV positioned to families and soccer moms. Ford targeted the smaller vehicle to women at either end of the cohort—new moms and empty nesters, whose families were naturally smaller than families in the middle of this life stage. However, findings from depth research with new moms and empty nesters prompted Ford to pivot from their original plan.

Ethnographic research revealed that women at either end of the family spectrum resisted being pigeonholed as "Mom" and displayed a strong need for self-expression and independence. In projective tasks they chose attributes such as /self, power, and performance/ over things like /social, safety, and efficiency/. The younger moms regretted the sporty Mustangs or BMWs they drove as single women and the older moms were looking forward to a life unfettered by the daily demands of dependent children. The older moms in particular wanted the vehicle for themselves, not for sharing with spouse and kids. We mapped these insights in ideation sessions using various combinations of the attributes consumers associated with the category. The mapping exercise helped us form a set of brand attributes for the Escape that redefined the category for consumers looking for the utility of the SUV but the self-determined power and excitement of a sporty sedan. The Escape was awarded Car of the Year by Consumer Reports several years running and has sustained its original positioning for almost two decades.

Case Example: Repositioning a Category Outsider

For purposes of illustration, let's imagine that a European sportswear company called NU is developing brand positioning and creative strategy for the global launch of a new sportswear line, provisionally called Brand X. Management is aware of Nike's dominance in this space and the lack of differentiation and clarity of Nike's competitors, Adidas and Puma. They also realize that NU has lived too long at the edge of the popular market and needs to gain momentum with a broader spectrum of consumers. They hire a semiotician to help them navigate the market and uncover a new cultural space for positioning the brand.

To pinpoint the cultural space for the new brand, we take into account three key factors. It must (1) sustain the brand's historical legacy and loyal following, (2) grow market share, and (3) leverage the brand's distinction from key competitors. The case walks readers through the steps taken to meet the project objectives.

Know the Brand

Since the primary brand sets the tone for any new brands in the portfolio, the first step in the investigation would involve a thorough audit of the NU primary brand, the organization, any business news, and its financial standing. The research then assesses the primary brand heritage—its loyal consumer base, narrative, and ethos, by performing an audit of communications for other brands in the portfolio, going back five years. The research compares and contrasts NUSport brand positioning with that of the category leaders Nike, Adidas, and Puma, and its relationship to local European sports brands.

Let's imagine that NUSport is a luxury brand that is positioned to athletes and amateurs in the high-end market. The brand originated in the 1960s as the chief provider of sportswear for European Olympic teams. It evolved into the brand of choice of affluent consumers who follow fashion but also take sports very seriously. Perhaps the strongest point of difference between NUSport and Nike, Adidas, and Puma is the brand's positioning to consumers who can afford to participate in more elite sports such as golf, sailing, or tennis, or have the distinction and savoir faire to choose unusual sports such as curling, climbing, or cycling.

Although the brand boasts a very loyal group of category insiders who shun the mass appeal of the major brands, the current target is aging and their elitism has become unfashionable. NUSport developed Brand X to expand market share by appealing to younger, more engaged consumers while remaining true to its heritage as a brand for consumers at the edge of sports culture.

A New Positioning for NUSport

In our review of Nike, Adidas, and Puma, we identified some key cultural binaries that structure the meaning and value of brands in the mass sportswear category, including [sports/fashion], [achievement/lifestyle], [action/appearance], and [individual/social]. Our analysis also revealed white space in the quadrants associated with [action/social] and [achievement/fashion]. We now map these binaries on a multivariable grid that superimposes one binary over the other. This process forces us to blend meanings from various cultural categories in order to identify a new cultural space and positioning for NUSport (Figure 2.7).

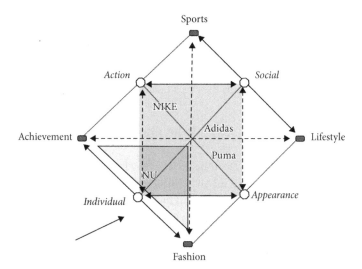

Figure 2.7. Finding a new cultural space for the NUSport brand

To clarify a distinct cultural space for NUSport in the category, I begin by superimposing Map A over Map B. This method provides a more nuanced representation of the cultural dimensions of sportswear. We positioned NUSport in the lower left area of the map associated with achievement, individualism, and fashion. As the brand of choice of affluent, highly achieving and individualistic consumers, NUSport has an opportunity to grab market share from Nike by satisfying the needs of consumers who take sports and achievement seriously but resist "running with the crowd." NUSport can also draw share from Puma by creating exceptional sportswear designs that revive NUSport's reputation for distinctive styling for sports and after-sport.

Extended Team Project: The Strategic Semiotic Analysis

The extended team project brings together the various skills and methods learned throughout the chapter. The project begins with a historical review of advertising for three brands, in a competitive set within a category chosen by the team. Teams choose a product category other than sportswear, identify the top three competitors based on market share, perform an audit of all three brands, decoding the cultural dimensions of the category, and mapping competitors on one or more double-axis grids.

Study Design

Project proposals usually include a summary of various aspects of the study design and approach, including a brief description of project objectives, the scope of research and specifications for the data set, staffing or team composition, and logistical details concerning the timing and location of the research. In the following example, I suggest language that can be used to describe the various stages of a project.

Objectives
The purpose of this study is to develop a positioning statement for brand X by performing a semiotic audit of historical advertising. The analysis will also track the consistency of the positioning over the years and observe how the message has adapted to cultural change over time.

Scope and Data Set
Research will focus on a sampling of three to five historical advertising campaigns covering at least a five-year period. Included in the data set will be a review of very early campaigns going back to the brand's origins in order to assess the brand's evolution over time.

Teams
Students form new teams for the study and identify a leader to present findings to the whole group at completion of the exercise. For the sake of efficiency, teams should assign to each participant a portion of the work and coordinate.

Timing
The exercise may require several hours. For a traditional university class schedule, we recommend dividing the time between the classroom setting and take-home assignments. For a professional workshop, we recommend leaving a window of two hours minimum to complete the basic elements of the exercise.

Project Steps

1. Teams select a brand (i.e., the "client") and identify two key competitors, in a category other than sportswear. For each brand in the competitive set, teams collect a sampling of major campaigns dating back at least five years.
2. Using the worksheet in Table 2.2, located in the Appendix, identify each campaign by date and title, summarize the semiotic elements of each ad, such as the tagline, brand symbolism including logo, color scheme, design elements, theme, story, and rhetorical style. Make note of recurring patterns in the data and their implications for the brand meaning.
3. Using the worksheet in Table 2.3, located in the Appendix, identify the key cultural binaries that recur in all three campaigns. The binary analysis defines the cultural dimensions of meaning in the product category.
4. Using Figure 2.2, located in the Appendix, map the binaries on a double-axis grid and plot the brands in the proper quadrants.
5. Teams write a positioning statement for the brand based on research findings.

Concluding Remarks

The team project engages teams in an extended team project that applies the methods employed in the sports brand case study. Due to the complexity of the work, the exercise could be used as a midterm activity that summarizes a broad range of skills reviewed in the first two chapters of the book. When I have taught this process to undergraduate and graduate students at ESSEC Business School and the University of Illinois, I commonly receive feedback that the branding principles and methods learned in this exercise either gave students an advantage in their job search or helped them advance in their current business.

Appendix

Table 2.2 Grid for Recording Advertising Data

Data set—Three historical advertisements		
Year	Title	Summary description

Table 2.3 The binary analysis grid

Cultural category	Binary	Brand X	Brand Y
Consumer behavior			
Brand relationship			
Semiotics			
Other			

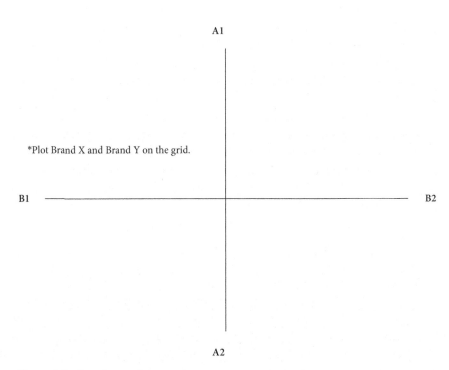

*Plot Brand X and Brand Y on the grid.

Figure 2.2. Brand mapping exercise

Reading 2
Semiotics, Humans, and Technology

Rachel Lawes
Lawes Consulting Ltd, London

A PhD in social psychology in the late 1990s introduced me first to semiotics and then to the market research industry in London, which in those days was unfamiliar with semiotic method. A turning point was the publication of a paper called "Demystifying Semiotics" (Lawes 2002) which supplied a simple, accessible account of what semiotics reveals about brands and consumers. It broke new ground and kept me busy supplying semiotic insight to marketers all over the world from that day to this. During that time, I have seen semiotics rise from obscurity and become quite widely available. As a result, it is subject to the same trends and market forces as other kinds of business, including a move towards technology and automation. In this chapter I argue that technology-driven semiotics has not yet surpassed the capabilities of the human analyst, but there is a promising future if we apply technology to semiotics more creatively.

The Rise of the Machines: AI and Machine Learning Appears in Semiotics

Artificial intelligence and machine learning are areas where we are making rapid progress, and in business and academia there is an understandable eagerness to be the first to transform normal activity using AI. This inevitably involves a degree of quantification. Quantification can sometimes find a useful role in semiotics; the cognitive semiotics of Lund University in Sweden is a reasonable and circumspect application of quantification to what must be essentially a qualitative discipline. However, in applied semiotics as we encounter it in market research, there is a rush towards automation which is driven partly by the struggle for research suppliers to get ahead in a competitive marketplace. As a business community, we are hurrying to develop products which automate semiotics, but they are still at an early stage of evolution and functionality is limited. We commercial semiologists are still at a stage of using technology to sort and group words or visual images according to easily-detected contrasts found within a discrete data set, a process that resembles transformative semiotic analysis less than it resembles the descriptive or reactive exercises that we regularly give focus group respondents. Organize brands and packs into groups. This one seems premium, that one looks sporty.

When simple sorting exercises are automated and used in place of the ability of the human semiologist to interpret rather than merely describing, errors and oversights may result. AI is not particularly skilled at even quite simple tasks such as differentiating among faces or distinguishing adults from children. It is quite unable to tell when a photographer has deliberately omitted something from a photograph, is telling a joke or is alluding to local politics, yet these are areas where human analysts excel because we are sensitive to detail and context and we have expansive interpretative resources.

There is a role for technology in helping us think, this being the part of the job that most semiologists value but it has not been invented yet. I make some suggestions regarding innovation at the end of this chapter, but first I want to discuss some of the many interesting and necessary features of competent semiotic analysis which can only be accomplished by humans at this time.

Human Manoeuvres in Semiotics: A How-To Guide

There are several semiotic puzzles—that is, puzzles of detecting meaning in samples of human communication—that only humans can solve. While these are quite numerous, they can be grouped into categories. In the paragraphs that follow, I identify three of the most well-populated categories, namely context, absence, and misleading appearances. I offer practical how-to advice for the reader who would like to excel in the type of semiotic analysis that humans do well.

Context

Every semiotic sign has its context. Each word that you are reading now sits within the context of this chapter and this book. The context supplies the words with meaning. An image of an apple changes its meaning depending on whether you encounter it in a grocery store or on the lid of your laptop. A bell ringing in the context of a school communicates that it is time for a break or to change to a different lesson, but the same sound coming from a religious building is a call to prayer. Humans are very sensitive to context and this is necessary for accurately determining the meaning of semiotic signs. Here are two business cases where human sensitivity to context becomes important.

Examples: Context
A food brand distinguishes variants within a range using arbitrarily-assigned colours. The meaning of the colour of any pack is set by the use of colour

throughout the range and not by the colour itself. Consumers learn that the salt-and-vinegar potato chips come in a green pack, salt-only chips are in the red pack and cheese-and-onion is denoted by blue, even though there is nothing about salt, vinegar, and so on which dictates these choices. The potato chip manufacturer is free to introduce other colours into the range and even swap them around and consumers will still be able to figure out the code as long as no colour in the series is repeated. This common, everyday aspect of communications is a problem for forms of automated semiotic analysis which want to tie meanings to colours in the style of a dictionary, so that red must mean "power" and green must mean "nature." This type of abstracted, de-contextualized coding system simply does not work when so much of the meaning of colour is awarded by the context in which it is found. Meanwhile, consumers locate their favourite flavour of potato chips without a problem.

A fragrance brand is marketed in an ad that reinforces its message with visible signs and symbols which are borrowed from nineteenth-century painting. The overall meaning of the ad somewhat relies on the viewer's ability to detect that these signs and symbols had another context before they were used to sell fragrance. In this case, the ad mimics not just any nineteenth-century painting but a particular tradition that existed to tease the imagination of European audiences who enjoyed fantasizing about travel and foreign cultures. This type of complexity in a visual message is a problem for automated systems because their interpretative resources are only as good as the person who programmed them. If the developer doesn't know about traditions in nineteenth-century painting that live on in the collective memory of European consumers, then the software cannot know of it. I have seen ads which were clearly derived from Orientalist painting tagged as "exotic." This is about as far as automated analysis can go. It cannot interpret visual messages such as ads which are obvious references to art movements if the person who wrote the software is unaware of those movements.

How to analyze context
1. Assemble a data set
As you are a human with an ability to process many different kinds of data simultaneously, cast the net wide. Don't stick to the ads and packaging of your client and their competitors. Don't stick to visual images—other semiotic signs are just as important, including words, sounds, physical properties of objects, built environments, and all matters of design and custom.

The places you go to collect these data and your sampling criteria will depend on the project. Let's say for example that you are interested in a sport such as sailing. Your data will certainly include the marketing communications of sports brands that make equipment and clothes for sailors but you will also want to include a wide range of other culturally produced materials which depict or refer to sailing. These could include conversations among groups of sailors or fans. They could include sailing-themed social media. They could include the communications of training bodies and competition organizers. If your client's budget allows it, go to physical locations where sailors congregate. Record your observations.

2. List some signs

List the semiotic signs that seem to be somewhat unique to sailing and that merit further investigation. Visual signs could include flags that are used as maritime signals, action photos of boat races, photos of sailing club dinners. Linguistic signs could include a tendency that you've noticed in conversations among sailors to return to a theme of self-reliance, with associated metaphors, descriptive terms, moral values, and even folklore. While looking at the data, you also notice odd linguistic habits, uses of archaic or rarefied phrases such as "top notch." Physical signs could include the architecture of sailing club houses, which leans towards being functional rather than decorative, notwithstanding features such as picture windows and asymmetrical peaked roofs which mimic the sails of yachts.

3. Determine their meaning

For each semiotic sign that you've identified as interesting, consider how the meaning of the sign is determined by its context.

The shapes depicted on sailing flags are what semiologists call symbols. They are not "pictures of" anything, they are abstract, graphical devices. Each symbol has only an arbitrary relationship to its meaning. One flag has a cross which outside a church could mean "Christianity," in a retail park could mean "pharmacy" and on a different flag could mean "Sweden" or "England." Your sailing flag means none of these. It is part of a unique maritime code and its meaning derives from within the code. The cross means "stop what you are doing and await directions." Ask whether the semiotic signs you are looking at are part of a closed systems of meaning.

A lot of advertising and packaging is designed by people who would rather have been artists, so it is no surprise when ads refer to famous art works, movements in art, bits of art theory. If you are looking at ads or at other data which you think may contain some art content, inspect them for evidence. If something is present, it will not be ambiguous but you will need the interpretative resources (such as knowledge of the history of art, design, or cinema) to know how to look for these kinds of semiotic signs and trace their origins.

If your search for images of sailing throws up an art print called *La Baule* by Charles Allo, would you recognize it as a 1930s travel poster? Do you know why travel and tourism were important in the 1930s? Cultivate and use this type of knowledge. Your ability to detect historical references, both visual and verbal, and give them an informed reading is one of the things that separates you from a robot.

You collect a range of images tagged "sailing" from social media. You notice that even though the images predictably have in common boats with humans on board, the humans are not all the same. Some have windswept hair, facial expressions that look almost as though they are fighting something, and high-visibility outfits in waterproof materials, zipped up to the neck. Others have hair that would be in keeping with a L'Oréal commercial, are wearing bikinis, and are doing yoga poses. It is apparent you to that the word "sailor" does not adequately describe the variations among the humans in the images.

Absence

Among the many puzzles that humans are good at solving, one involves noticing where elements in an image or text are out of place or missing. Noticing when images have had something removed or added, offering a mediated depiction of reality, becomes vitally important in an age of fake news and widespread ability with Photoshop. Consumers have become very alert to indications that something is wrong. A short Google search while writing this chapter uncovered: a photo of a British politician at an event, in which she has Photoshopped a rival out of the scene; a photo of Kim Jong-Un outside a hospital in bright sunlight, in which he and his men cast no shadows; a photograph of 42-year-old singer John Mayer, in which his face has no wrinkles.

Here are two business examples where the human ability to notice absences becomes useful in semiotics.

Examples: Absence
A new, premium shopping mall is built in the Netherlands. The designers resist the aesthetics of shopping malls elsewhere in the world by cutting unnecessary and decorative elements out of the interior landscape. Most surfaces are metallic grey. Retailers keep their wares and promotions firmly inside the store, leaving clear the wide corridors that sweep through the mall. The external signs on shops are small, uniform, and subdued. Visitors from countries where malls are like circuses (for example, the United States, Malaysia) wonder why this mall resembles an aircraft hangar. However, shoppers who are local residents regard the mall as a demonstration of good taste. Software which automatically detects the features of images is designed to pick out features which are materially present. It cannot identify when items are not present, nor can it tell you which groups of viewers will see the environment as complete while others detect deficiencies.

A company that owns a brand of frozen vegetables is refreshing its packaging. It looks at competitors and notes variations in the way that products are depicted on pack. Some competitor brands use high-definition photography. They appear to be photographs of vegetables which exist in material reality and are products of nature. Some use what seem to be computer-generated images of vegetables: the peas are glossy, perfectly spherical, and uniform. Still others use crude, hand-drawn, empty circles which are recognizable as peas only because that interpretation is encouraged by on-pack text. Shoppers regard the latter brands as honest, ethical, possibly organic, and suitable for children. They derive this meaning from the crude, hand-drawn images, not because of what they include but because of what they leave out. The packs are part of a semiotic tradition called "naïve representation" in which images and text are made to look like the work of children (or perhaps an adult idea of children). The images look like the work of children because children characteristically produce drawings which include the bare essentials necessary to getting a message across. They don't aim for photo-realism. Image-sorting software can detect that some images of vegetables are more detailed but it has no means of interpreting a meaningful stripping-out of detail.

How to analyze absence

1. Assemble a data set
Assemble some data as described above. Let's imagine that your project concerns homewares such as cushions and decorative throws—I did a project like this for a British client, which generated data such as photos of domestic interiors, video clips filmed in store and recordings of conversations. Inspect your data and look for absences, reductions, deletions, and removals.

2. Look for binary oppositions
Begin by looking for binary oppositions. This is a fairly easy step to learn in semiotics and most qualitative researchers will quickly recognize when participants on this project start to talk in terms of summer versus winter or "making a few changes" versus "redecorating." Additionally, you might find that there's a binary opposition between "patterned textiles" versus "textiles which are blocks of plain colour," which can be detected by noting the absence of patterns as well as the presence of the blocks. As a human researcher, you are sensitive to the culturally and historically specific idea that "less is more" and you also know about competing aesthetic traditions where "more is more." If the client on this project is making seasonal homewares and Christmas decorations, they will want to know that minimalism and Christmas are hard to combine well. Even though "less is more" is a sound motto most of the time, Christmas in English-speaking countries tends to be a Victorian fantasy, resulting in dense patterns, bows and lots of other decorative features.

3. Observe consumers detecting missing pieces
The homewares company pays a social media influencer to feature their product, in this case, duvet covers. The influencer posts a carefully arranged photo and titles it "my morning routine." In the photo she sits on her bed, displaying the

duvet. To her and her sponsor's surprise, it gets an angry response from her followers. As you examine this situation, you detect that some of the ire of the followers is focused not only on what is present in the image but also what is missing. The duvet and the model's pajamas are free from wrinkles. There is no coffee in the cup from which she is sipping. The model's hair is carefully styled so that not one hair is out of place. Actual morning routines produce visible evidence which is conspicuously missing in this highly produced image.

Misleading Appearances

A third group of semiotic puzzles for which humans are well-equipped concerns misleading appearances. It serves them well as consumers for many reasons. For one thing, the rise of digital retailing has taught consumers to be alert to counterfeit goods and to product descriptions which don't match the accompanying photos. For another, people in many cultures enjoy humour in the form of sarcasm and puns. Advertisers, too, take the opportunity to make consumers feel clever by showing them messages which contain multiple and sometimes contradictory meanings. Here are two business examples where the ability to see through misleading appearances becomes useful in semiotics.

Examples: Misleading appearances

A jeweller, De Beers, is looking for creative ways to sell engagement rings. Its agency (Miami Ad School, 2018) develops a print ad that says "It's just a stone, technically. She can say no, theoretically." Human analysts (and consumers) can easily recognize this as irony: the words and their meaning seem opposed. The consumer is expected to infer that a diamond ring is far more than "just a stone" and as a result the recipient will find that, in fact, she cannot say no. A sophisticated automated system may be able to recognize "it's just a stone" and "she can say no" as negative statements but cannot cope with the built-in ambiguity of "theoretically" and "technically." This is because the ambiguity of those two words is where the humour and insight of the ad resides. The statements in the ad are simultaneously true and false.

A food company is launching a new brand and is designing packaging. It believes that its target customer will enjoy something retro. The company is aware that to consumers there is a difference between "retro," "vintage," and things which are merely dated. To remain on-brand, the packaging needs to be retro. The brand owner is not sure how to pin down the difference between "retro," "vintage," and "dated." They decide to hire a semiologist who assembles a set of key semiotic signs and design guidelines relatively quickly and easily. The semiologist has not found any technology so far which adds any speed or efficiency to this process because it involves detecting complex relations among semiotic signs which usually would not occur together, conveying a sense of intentionality in design. The target customer who encounters the food packaging looks for the meaning of some signs, which are "vintage" or even "dated" to be subverted by other signs or design gestures which are self-consciously modern or witty. The appearance of self-consciousness is essential for "retro" to work, yet it is too subtle an appearance to be detected by technology.

How to analyze misleading appearances

1. Assemble a data set

Assemble some data. For the sake of a fresh example, assume that your project concerns the fashion brand Supreme. You are in the happy situation of having been asked to suggest ideas for items which it can sell as accessories. You take a look at its existing range of accessories and here is what you find:

- An inflatable blimp, $175
- A Pilot marker pen, $50
- An inflatable pillow in the shape of an Uzi submachine gun, choice of green or orange. $120

All these are limited edition items. Previous accessories by Supreme have included cough drops, a short ladder, two steps high (red, $350), and a single house brick. The brick is not available for purchase because it sold out the same day that it went on sale in 2016. Supreme bricks then quickly turned up on eBay, priced at up to $1,000 per brick.

2. Confirm normal appearances

It's clear to you that these items are a considerable distance away from what clothing brands normally regard as accessories. You check the inventory of another men's clothing retailer. Your sense of normality is confirmed as you see that "Accessories" means belts, gloves, hats, watches, scarves, sunglasses, ties, wallets, and bags. All of them can be worn on the body and in conjunction with the garments which are the retailer's main offering.

3. Ask critical questions

Return to the Supreme accessories and ask these questions.

- Are any of these items ironic?
- Is there a conflict between the expected use or meaning of an item versus the execution of that item within the Supreme range?
- How about those Uzi-shaped pillows?

The Uzi is a formidable weapon. It fires 600 rounds of ammunition per minute and has been used in military service around the world since 1954. It has been somewhat glamourized by rap music, along with the AK-47 assault rifle and Beretta pistols, but glamourizing these items depended on taking their force and power seriously. Rappers have not represented the Uzi as something soft and cuddly. Yet here is the Supreme version, an Uzi pillow. The mere existence of the object seems to upset or subvert the idea of the Uzi (especially given the improbable, gaudy colours and the fact of the pillow needing to be inflated like a child's balloon). At the same time, the Uzi causes problems for the idea of a pillow. Who wants to cuddle an Uzi? What conventional standards of interior design would recommend decorative cushions in the shape of lethal weapons?

Are any of these items a simulation? Alongside the inflatable Uzi which is in fact a simulation rather than the real thing, you particularly notice the blimp and the brick. The dimensions of the blimp are not specified but it looks to be considerably smaller than an actual airship and has a thread attached to the top, presumably for hanging it from the ceiling. It accurately mimics the shape and proportions of a blimp. It doesn't fly. In simple language, it is a fake. The house brick, too, is useless. At $1,000 each, nobody will be using these to build a wall and, in any case, only a tiny number went on sale. Acquiring one is difficult enough. Acquiring several, or enough to build something, is out of reach. As such, the Supreme brick is more a brick-like object than a real brick.

Do these items, or this range of items, depend for their meaning on self-conscious and reflexive ideas? The brick is conspicuous in its self-aware uselessness but your eye also settles on the Supreme-branded Pilot marker pen. It closely resembles the Pilot 43300 Jumbo Permanent Marker which retails at about $10 or $5 when purchased in a multi-pack. The Supreme version, which appears to be the same pen except for the Supreme brand mark, is priced at $50 and only comes in one colour. It seems to you that the price tags almost guarantee that a consumer could not buy one of these items without colluding in an elaborate joke about the pointlessness of consumerism and people's willingness to pay over the odds for branded items, even and especially when the discrepancy between price and value are deliberately called to their attention. Supreme deeply flatters its audience as part of an in-joke about fashion and marketing, while at the same time taking their money.

Continue your semiotic analysis to find out what else items in the range have in common. It strikes you that most are quite masculine. There is military hardware (gun, airship) and tools that one would use for a construction job (brick, ladder). It occurs to you that the Supreme range has things in common with children's toys. Children like toys which simulate items that they aren't allowed to handle in their original form, such as guns and work tools. Are the Supreme items toys for adults? You're now in a position to start recommending items for the new range.

Envisioning the Future: What Semiotics Really Needs From Technology

The point of this chapter is not to exclude technology from consideration as a tool for semiotics but to appreciate the vast range of things that human semiologists can do, including making sense of things which are simply absent. Early attempts at automating semiotics are a long way from being able to recognize and decode gestures such as exclusion, deletion, misleading appearances, simulations, and self-conscious irony. Humans—including consumers—are proficient with all of these things. The question then arises of whether researchers in semiotics need to turn their backs on technology completely, except as an interesting quirk of human behaviour and a researchable topic in its own right. That is, can technology rise to the level of being an analytic resource and not just yet another example of cultural material which it remains to semiologists to decode?

A New Tool: Video Games

I think there is a place for a new tech product for marketers which has yet to be invented. There is a category in which technology is performing as a tool for thinking and it is available in mass culture. That category is video games, in which I do a lot of semiotic thinking and also journalism. Here is my wish list for a tech product for practising semiologists. It is a list of things that video games already do and that the market research industry could adapt to make a better tech tool.

- Offer immersion: absorbing activity in a self-contained universe.
- Facilitate storytelling and imagination.
- Facilitate exploration of social problems, moral dilemmas and questions of how to live.
- Offer opportunities to make and build things that last and can be shared with other users.
- Allow users to express multiple personalities and identities.
- Show awareness of historical and cross-cultural specificity.
- Compare the player's responses and actions with those of other users.
- Differentiate between a normal state and an enhanced or a reduced state. In games, these are temporary conditions known as buffs and de-buffs.
- Satisfy multiple styles of play, allow users to set their own objectives.
- Make the player feel that they are increasing their skill over time.

It's noticeable that previous attempts to gamify processes such as exercising and dieting have not been particularly successful and this is perhaps because they have focused on the wrong things such as unlocking "achievements" which have no real value. This may be a problem, also found in automated semiotics, of importing mechanisms which are easily visible while ignoring aspects which humans find more compelling. I anticipate that in the future, semiologists working in applied research will be able to develop tools which learn from games; a category of tech products which is known to help people think creatively. This is also a way for technology to make itself useful in consumer research, by helping the semiologist to co-create with research participants.

Examples: Video games

Here are some examples of games which help their users to do the things on my wish list.

Minecraft (Mojang Studios) is a creative game in which users build anything they want using virtual blocks. It has resulted in spectacular feats of architecture which have been shared with millions of other players. Semiotics would benefit from a version of *Minecraft* where the bricks could be semiotic signs.

The Sims franchise (EA Games) invites users to simulate homes, neighbourhoods and various social problems such as economic struggle and divorce. It has lasted 20 years because players use it to craft rich narratives which are personally meaningful. The practising semiologist could use something like this to simulate consumers and their activities such as shopping and decorating their homes.

World of Warcraft (Activision Blizzard) is a titan of a video game which enjoys universal awareness among gamers. It is a multi-player adventure in which the player spends most of their time fighting (monsters, other players) or preparing to fight. Players become expert in the matter of buffs and debuffs which facilitate or restrict combat. In a video game for semiologists, a buff could be "client has a generous budget" or "the brand has an existing base of loyal customers" while debuffs could be "an unpopular merger has forced a rebrand" or "brand assets can't be changed."

A game like this would externalize our semiotic thinking processes. It would record our processes rather than dictating them and it would expand our analytic abilities rather than shrinking them. As any gamer will attest, there are games which are led by creativity and insight and then there are games which are led by advances in technology. Games which are led by technology usually have sharp graphics and they run fast, because they can process a lot of data very quickly, but they tend to deliver a soulless experience to the user because they lack originality and ignore the reasons why people play games. Analogously, human semiologists need technology when it supports and facilitates rather than suppresses all the aspects of semiotics which only humans can accomplish, and which I have outlined here.

Author Profile

Dr Rachel Lawes is president of Lawes Consulting Ltd, London. She applies her expertise in semiotics and social psychology to brand strategy research for major brands in Europe, North and South America, Asia, and around the world. Rachel has authored over 40 marketing industry publications and conference papers and her work has appeared in the *British Journal of Social Psychology,* the *International Journal of Market Research,* and *Clinical Therapeutics.* She directs and delivers masterclasses for the Market Research Society in the UK, in Discourse Analysis and Advanced Qualitative Methods. She holds a PhD in social psychology from the Discourse and Rhetoric Group of Loughborough University and is a former Principal Lecturer in Marketing at Regent's University London. Her new book, *Using Semiotics in Marketing* is published worldwide by Kogan Page in 2020.

3

Design Strategy

"Design matters." Laura Oswald, *Creating Value*

Introduction

Design is a semiotic system, a technology, and a commercial practice that shapes to a great extent the ways consumers sense, experience, and understand objects, events, spaces, and processes in the marketplace. Some writers have used the term "semiotic engineering" (Souza 2005) to describe the design process because it involves the deliberate actions of molding and organizing phenomena to influence human behavior.

Although design performs an esthetic function to create beautiful, pleasing things and environments, it differs from fine art in several ways. Fine art is valued for its unique, one-of-a-kind creativity, its ability to transcend the mundane, functional aspect of things, and the force of its impact on the hearts and imaginations of the individual spectator. Design, on the other hand, weaves the esthetic priorities of art into functional forms that help consumers build stuff, organize processes, and navigate the world of things and information.

Whereas artwork occupies the sacred spaces of museums and galleries, design lives in the day-to-day encounters between consumers and the marketplace. The conceptual artist Duchamp highlighted this distinction by moving ready-made objects such as a chair and a urinal from their everyday surroundings and putting them on display in the museum (Howarth and Mundy 2015). By isolating art from life, art works traditionally stand for transcendence, original creativity, and spiritual rapture. In contrast, design brings transcendence, creativity, and spirituality to the street where life unfolds. Although design may reflect the unique creativity and originality of the designer, good design is also iterable—it can be copied indefinitely in mass-produced goods, consumer experiences, and programs. The serial esthetic of Andy Warhol (1962), as exemplified in the canvas painted with row after row of Campbell's Soup cans, forms a commentary on the infinite replicability of designed objects in the age of consumer culture (Reder 2015).

The present chapter focuses on the basics of design research oriented to the principles and methods of semiotics. The discussion and exercises walk the reader through practical application to marketing arenas such as product packaging and service design.

Laura R. Oswald, *Design Strategy* In: *Doing Semiotics: A Research Guide for Marketers at the Edge of Culture.*
Edited by: Laura R. Oswald, Oxford University Press (2020). © Laura R. Oswald. © Dr. Laura Santamaria, Reading 3.
DOI: 10.1093/oso/9780198822028.003.0003

Design in Cultural Perspective

Design forms a kind of interface between perception and culture because it engages consumers at two levels: (1) the individual's sensory response to things as pure shapes, colors, and other esthetic elements; and (2) the individual's cognitive response to things as signs and the cultural codes that connect thought to the social world. The moment we think "tree" when we perceive a tree-like object in our line of vision, we have moved from the realm of pure sense perception to the realm of semiotics. In the next sections, I review some basic concepts related to the way we think about design, human experience, and culture.

From Phenomenology to Semiology

In a sense, the experience of designed things builds upon a kind of phenomenology of perception that accounts for our ability to sense things and capture their meaning in consciousness. Phenomenology orients consciousness to an ideal of pure subjectivity based on the dialectical closure between sense perception and thought, impervious to the effects of culture and social organization (Figure 3.1). Whereas the phenomenology of perception may account for transcendent flights of the spectator's imagination in front of a work of art, I propose a *semiology*[1] of perception, which takes into account the cultural codes that determine to a great extent how designers construct spaces that conform to industry standards, category trends, or the human factors associated with technologies. The design experience is defined by a play between these codes and consumer performances in their day to day encounter with constructed objects, technologies, and public spaces.

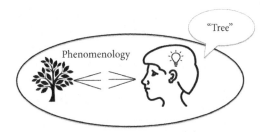

Figure 3.1. The phenomenology of perception

[1] The term "semiology", in contrast to "semiotics", defines the general epistemological dimension of the discipline, i.e. a world view centered on meaning production rather than, for instance, metaphysics.

Beyond Phenomenology

A close reading of Figure 3.1 reveals the limits of phenomenology to account for the role of meaning production in the construction of consciousness. The mind translates sense perception into thoughts by giving things a name. By means of the term /tree/, the mind seizes the object of perception as meaningful (Figure 3.2). By joining sense perception to thought, semiotic codes such as language implicate subjective experience in the shared, collective consciousness of a culture.

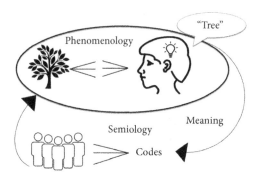

Figure 3.2. The subject of semiology

The Subject of Semiology

By inscribing sense perception with meaning, language and other semiotic systems contribute to the construction of consciousness. As a result, they also implicate individual subjectivity in the cultural systems structuring the collective consciousness. Like language, design is a code system that articulates sense perception into the meanings and functions we associate with goods.

A Multi-Coded System

Design stands at the intersection between the personal and the social by leveraging multiple code systems—hence the complex role of design in producing technologies, processes, and consumer experiences. These code systems transcend the creativity of the individual designer and account for the infinite iterability of a given design scheme across the mass market, in daily events such as brewing coffee, navigating the mall, or searching the Internet. Furthermore, however innovative, the designer's personal creativity is reined in by the system of cultural codes and norms that transcend the individual. Even one's personal experience of social space is culturally coded and determines our comfort level with the disposition of social actors in a given setting.

For example, the cultural anthropologist E. T. Hall (1966) discovered that cultural norms structure the experience of personal space and can produce vastly different experiences of social proximity, depending upon the personal intimacy and culture of origin of the social actors. We expect close friends and family members to get up close and personal with us. The same degree of physical closeness from a colleague or acquaintance may generate discomfort and even stress. Cross-cultural encounters are ripe for misunderstanding when the parties to a meeting do not share the same proximity codes for social proximity. Since North Americans like to keep their distance from others in conversation, they may be shocked when their South American colleague gets too close. It goes without saying that such cultural tensions could spoil everything from a blind date to a business negotiation.

Consumer-Centered Design

There exists a variety of schools of thought on the role and function of design for consumers. The two most influential approaches are Human Factors Design (Sanders and McCormick 1987) and User Experience or UX Design (Brown 2009).

Human Factors Design changed the way engineers think about design by focusing on ergonomic factors that influence the ways humans interact with things, tools, technologies, and processes. Human Factors research observes interactions between people and things in order to test the functionality and usability of new products, develop technology solutions, and improve workplace functions.

UX Design is a growing field devoted to improving human life through innovative design thinking. Rather than centering research on specific goods or processes, UX Design research develops solutions to human problems ranging from food distribution in underdeveloped countries to managing patient treatment protocols, multi-tasking in the kitchen to moving people through a transit system. In some cases, the UX design process may not involve products at all. The researcher may investigate the way a product evolves from production and consumption to disposal, and may even include marketing factors such as branding and advertising.

Semiot-EX Design

In contrast to Human Factors and UX Design methods, marketing semiotics research frames consumer-centered design in the cultural codes responsible for the shared aspect of design experiences across a market. I call this Semiot-Ex Design, design centered on consumers' performances of cultural codes. The semiotician begins the discovery process by decoding the design context, such as the service and product categories, the organization culture or work process at the workplace, or the design expectations that consumers associate with a technology, including computers and cars. By establishing these underlying norms at work in an environment, the semiotician observes how these codes both regulate consumer experiences in the market and evolve and change in conjunction with emerging trends in the culture. Whether mobile devices actually gave rise to mobile consumer culture or consumer lifestyles created demand for mobile technologies, the semiotician pinpoints opportunities for growing value by evolving a design scheme in line with cultural change.

The Design of Things

The codified aspect of design creates a play between the designer's creativity and cultural norms that dictate consumer expectations about the meaning, value, and experiences they associate with design forms. The designer's task involves mastering the design codes related to the brand's value proposition and quality, while executing these codes in creative ways that please the eye, stand out at the point of purchase, and deliver positive consumer experiences.

Packaging Semiotics

Take packaging design for example. A semiotic exploration of the salty snack aisle at the supermarket demonstrates how specific design codes regulate the meaning and perception of the value of products at the point of purchase. At first glance, one notices that some packages are brightly colored and flashy, while others are muted and discrete, or employ earth tones rather than primary colors. The containers may include bags, boxes, and novelty packs. Where an art director would see endless artistic creativity across the shelf, the semiotician looks for the underlying semiotic codes that structure the design schemes across the category, because these design schemes relate directly to the meaning and value consumers associate with various brands.

Processed, Natural, or Organic?

For example, is the product made from healthy, all natural ingredients? Or is it a fun and flavorful processed food product that may not be as healthy? Maybe it's organic? All of these food categories are associated with specific design codes that consumers learn through repeat exposure over time, in the same way that we all learn language.

Based on my own experience with package design, there are clear-cut distinctions between the design codes on processed, natural, and organic brands. Processed brands employ bright colors, flashy paper to grab attention, and include a complicated panel of chemical ingredients. Natural brands employ earth tones, higher quality paper, and list a few simple ingredients. The packaging on organic brands may resemble natural brands, with the addition of the dark green and brown accents and the USDA Organic badge.

A Semiotic Strategy

It is important to spell out to clients in advance that the semiotician is not a creative artist or a magician who drums up design ideas by means of ideation or artistic inspiration. (More than one client has asked me how long it would take me to "work my magic.") The meaning and value that consumers associate with specific design codes determine in advance what one can or cannot use on packaging in order to communicate the brand's value proposition. If the designer chooses the wrong set of design cues, they risk confusing consumers and undermining the brand's value in the market.

For this reason, a packaging design project must begin with a thorough audit of specific colors and proprietary symbols associated with the brand heritage, as well as packaging for similar products across the category. The audit reveals both the code systems associated with each grouping of brands. Once the semiotician has matched a set of codes with a specific value proposition (i.e., muted/bright, shiny/matte, flashy/discrete), they can recommend elements of an overall design strategy that serves the functional, strategic, and esthetic functions of effective packaging.

A Luxury Design Strategy at Apple

The design codes consumers associate with specific product categories influence the meaning and value of brands in a product category. However, marketers sometimes draw inspiration from contrasting and even incongruous product categories to reposition a brand or develop innovative design strategy. For example, Apple was traditionally positioned as the experts in consumer technology targeted to consumers seeking ease of use and convenience in their home computers.

Over the years, as new product innovations moved Apple to the leading edge of consumer culture, management took the risk of repositioning Apple as a luxury brand. Since the cultural attributes consumers associate with luxury include leisure, fantasy, beauty, status, and high price, Apple's strategy moved against the tide of technology's current associations with functionality, industry, and competitive pricing. Their sleek product designs, their culture-bending digital devices, and the cutting-edge modernity of their new retail sites reflected the brand's luxury strategy and distinguished the brand from its more function-driven competitors. Furthermore, by limiting the sale of new products, management adopted a luxury strategy of scarcity to generate competitive shopping and invite fans to stand in long lines for the privilege of purchasing the latest generation of a device. Apple essentially changed the culture of consumer technology.

The new strategy called for package design that aligned with the packaging on European luxury brands, including the high-quality paper stock of the box, the rich white color, and layer upon layer of wrappings that invite comparison with unwrapping a gift. The design scheme thus exceeds its function to protect and display the product and prolongs consumer anticipation and discovery of the treasure inside. These kinds of intangible brand attributes contribute to the 80 percent profit margins enjoyed by the luxury sector and provide a rationale for the high price of Apple products.

Exercise 3.1 Using Design to Reposition a Long-Standing Brand

Thus packaging design is not simply window dressing for the brand but drives brand awareness, the perception of quality, and positive brand experiences in viewing, handling, and using the product. In the present exercise, the reader is guided through all phase of semiotics-based package design research. Teams choose one of the following case examples for their projects: (1) "Moving Candy into the Snack Space" or (2) "Repositioning a Tried and True Soap Brand." In the interest of brevity, I have listed the steps involved in the semiotic analysis under option 2. The instructor is at liberty to adapt this exercise to any number of brands, product categories, and learning objectives.

Option 1—Moving Candy into the Snack Space

If the team chooses Option 1 for analysis, please follow the steps detailed in the Option 2 case study topic that follows. Mom's Candy Brand is a global confectionery company that has treated consumers to quality chocolate treats for over 100 years. In view of declining sales in confectionery and the growing expansion of the snack food category, Mom's wants to develop a new product format and packaging for their chocolate treats that would move the brand into the snack aisle. Decode the packaged snack category and find ways to reposition packaging for Mom's by aligning it with snack-like formatting and packaging.

Case Topic: Option 2—Repositioning a Tried and True Soap Brand

The following exercise walks the reader through all phases of a semiotics-based package design project for a global personal care brand under the pseudonym, Mr. Soap. The project leads students through the research design, data collection, semiotic analysis, and concept development for designing the product container in preparation for the launch of a new body wash.

Background

Mr. Soap is a long-standing American brand that is known for its no-frills image and its legacy as the bar soap used by the military during World War II. Sold at supermarkets across America in blue and white paper wrapping, Mr. Soap is popular with athletes for its strong deodorant properties and low price. In recent years, Mr. Soap has relied increasingly on institutional accounts with hospitals and schools to sustain market value due to changes in consumer culture. Consumer preferences for fancy liquid soaps, body washes, and facial cleansers have out-paced the market for plain bar soaps.

To staunch declining revenues, Mr. Soap developed Brand B, a new line of trendy body wash products targeted to women who purchase personal care products at the supermarket and shop for intangible benefits such as scent, skin care, and overall pleasure. The new product line will drive the overall reposition-ing of Mr. Soap in a more contemporary, upscale direction. Management also wishes to renovate the brand's overall messaging while preserving Mr. Soap's long-standing equities in consumer trust and quality. The packaging design for Brand B will play an important role in moving forward the new agenda.

Project Objectives

The Mr. Soap Company hires your team to develop a design strategy for Brand B and propose specific design concepts to send to the design team. The research team must make recommendations related to two key questions:

- Should Mr. Soap market the new brand on the supermarket shelf alongside their bar soaps, or should they place it in a kiosk with the specialty items near the health and beauty department?
- Should the package design of the new brand extend the blue and white design scheme of the old brand, or create a new look, or some combination of the two?

In your report you must provide a rationale to support your recommendations, including reference to your semiotic research findings with photos of specific brands.

Research Design and Approach

Working in teams, students develop a research approach and design that includes methods and steps for achieving project objectives. The project design, scope, data collection, and analysis will be guided in a clear understanding of Brand B's positioning, consumer target, and value proposition. Teams will support their findings and recommendations with product samples or photos drawn from the data.

Background

Write a concise brand strategy statement for the Brand B body wash line that describes the consumer target, the brand positioning and value proposition, the pricing strategy, and the brand's relationship to the primary brand, Mr. Soap. The brand strategy statement will guide your approach.

Research Scope

Define the scope of research. For example, will you limit research to supermarket brands or collect samples from brands at other retail outlets such as specialty boutiques? Will you only examine body wash packaging or include a wider sampling of soap, body, and bath brands?

Data Collection

Collect samples of product at the supermarket and any other stores in your data set, making sure to represent a variety of package designs across the sector. To determine when the sample is sufficiently representative, perform a semiotic analysis of the broad formal dimensions of fifteen packages, and sort the packages into groups based upon their common styles. Then collect fifteen more packages, analyze them, and classify them in the same groups. If you find exceptions to the current groupings, create a new group, and keep doing this until you find no new styles. Keep in mind that to qualify as a grouping, it must include three or more examples.

Collecting samples of product is the best way to deliver a detailed semiotic audit of the data. However, for purposes of this exercise, teams may substitute photos for the actual packs, making sure to photograph all the details on the package, including pricing and ingredient panel.

The Semiotic Analysis

1. Make a visual and photo snapshot of the soap, bath, and shower section of the supermarket and compare and contrast the design scheme on Mr. Soap's original brand with the design of newer brands in the category. Do you

observe an overall theme or design trend on the shelf? How does Mr. Soap measure up in comparison?

2. Perform a semiotic analysis of visual and formal elements on packages in the data set. Refer to Table 3.1 in the Appendix for a list of design dimensions to guide the analysis. Avoid going into too much detail with the analysis. For purposes of this classification exercise, the analysis must focus on the broad brushstrokes that characterize multiple design schemes from multiple brands.

3. Data Sorting
   - In this step teams will classify the data into discrete cultural categories defined by their similar design schemes. (Each classification may include body wash and other soap brands.) Identify each group by a number or description (i.e., "fun" or "functional," etc.).
   - Make note of correlations between the overall design scheme associated with each group and product attributes such as price and product claims related to ingredients, health benefits or consumer pleasure. For example, is there a design code that applies specifically to all low-priced brands; to healthy brands; or to fun and pleasurable brands? Could shoppers spot the healthy brands by means of specific design cues and so on?

Design Concept Development

- Based on your knowledge of Brand B's strategic dimensions, in which cultural category would you classify the brand? Would you mix and match elements from several cultural categories? Explain your answer.
- Based on your knowledge of Mr. Soap, explain how would you adapt Brand B's general design scheme to Mr. Soap's historical legacy? Include reference to specific design elements.

Recommendations

- Write a design strategy statement for Brand B, providing a rationale for your strategy based on the brand's positioning, its association with design codes you observed in the data, and its suitability for sustaining the primary brand's equities in consumer trust and quality. Based upon your conclusions, would you market Brand B on the supermarket shelf alongside Mr. Soap products, or place it in a kiosk with the specialty products?
- Develop specific design concepts for the brand related to formal elements such as shapes, colors, and materials. Based on your conclusions, would the design concepts for Brand B extend the blue and white design scheme of the old brand, create a new look, or some combination of the two?
- Using Photoshop, or even PowerPoint, create visuals that illustrate as closely as possible how you envision the execution on your design concepts. These

kinds of prompts bring your presentation to life and also provide direction for the company's design team.

Key Learnings from Exercise 3.1

- Students learned how to design and execute research for developing design strategy;
- Students acquired the ability to think strategically about design matters by learning to:
  - Write a brand strategy statement that guides the design process;
  - Understand the role of codes in structuring the meaning and cultural positioning of packaging design;
  - Classify packaged goods in a product category according to their design schemes;
  - Position the design scheme of a new brand in relation to these design classifications;
- Students also developed design concepts that satisfy the dual need to differentiate brand extensions from the parent brand while also retaining the primary brand's most valuable equities.
- Teams created visuals for illustrating design concepts for the client and the design team.

The Design of Environments

Service design integrates a complex variety of semiotic systems related to brand communication, the consumer experience, and the practical matter of moving consumers through a service space for purposes of shopping, choosing, and purchasing goods.

A New Paradigm for Fast Food Service

The following case study illustrates how semiotics-based service design solved a business problem by decoding the service category, identifying emergent codes in the category, and developing recommendations for revising the current design plan. A global fast food chain was showing declining profits and favorability in face of increased competition from competitors in the emerging market of quick food service, which refers to shops that serve cold foods prepared and packaged in advance and sold in refrigerated display cases. In order to gauge the impact of the service experience on brand performance, the client commissioned Marketing

Semiotics to decode the service design in their restaurants and recommend changes for improving the customer experience.

Research Design

Following a basic principle of semiotics-based research, the research design took into account the effects of three basic contexts on the meaning and experience of the client's service sites, including the brand's legacy and positioning, their direct competitors, and broader category trends. The project was designed in four phases:

- Data Collection
- Competitive Analysis—The Cultural Paradigm and Strategic Difference
- Cultural Analysis—Category Trends and Emergent Codes
- Reporting

The data set included multiple visits to the client's restaurants, competitor sites, and venues typical of the emerging category of quick food service venues, a growing category of quick serve prepared sandwich outlets, including branded shops such as Prêt à Manger, sandwich displays in supermarkets, and quick food kiosks in malls and train stations.

The semiotic analysis began with an assessment of fundamental structural elements common to fast food service generally, including architectural elements, furnishings, and merchandising. All the restaurants in our sampling moved customers through a street-facing entrance through a dining area toward the cashier counter in the depth of the restaurant. The counter forms a structural and cultural barrier between the spaces of food and beverage preparation behind the counter and the consumer spaces in front. The absence of food and beverage displays in the consumer spaces of the restaurant prohibits impulse purchases and limits consumer control over the purchase experience.

The traffic flow from the entrance to the cashier counter moves through a dining area furnished with tables and chairs, counters with stools, and a condiment kiosk either in the middle or to the side of the store. The decor includes branded signage and merchandising messages about new products and specials.

In addition to identifying the structural elements common to all forms of fast food service, we also observed customers in the stores and conducted short interviews with them after their purchases. We offered a cash incentive to customers who were willing to be interviewed at their tables during their lunch.

In contrast to fast food service, quick food service is not bound by the regulations that limit consumer access to the preparation of hot fast food. Quick serve shops offer cold prepared sandwiches and other foods that are often packaged off site and sold in refrigerated display cases in the consumer spaces in front of the cashier counter. This design scheme gives consumers greater flexibility in their ability to select and examine packaged foods before making their choice.

Reimagining the Fast Food Consumer Experience

In comparing and contrasting the client's design strategy with other fast food franchises, we noticed the relative mobility of the furnishings and the flexibility of traffic flow, the effects of signage and merchandising on consumers' attention as they moved from the entrance to the cashier counter, and the relative openness of the cashier counter and the accessibility of the people and events located behind the service counter.

We took into consideration the food safety codes that regulate restaurant service protocols. Hot fast food must be prepared out of the reach of consumers and packed and served immediately after preparation. Cold prepared sandwiches, on the other hand, can be prepared and packaged in advance and conserved in refrigerated displays accessible to consumers. However regardless of the type of venue, the trend toward more consumer control of the service experience prevailed.

A Semiotic Solution

In the course of the research, we noted a shift in the design strategies at work in competitors' restaurants that brought more clarity and flexibility to the customer experience. Although fast food service is to a great extent regulated by government regulations that limit consumer access to the spaces of food and beverage preparation and service, the client's competitors designed service spaces that encouraged consumer engagement and creativity in the service experience. They provided movable rather than fixed furnishings, simplified attention-grabbing merchandising, provided greater clarity and flexibility in the traffic flow, and lowered the cashier counter to expand visual access to the cashier and the food preparation in back. In the next phase of research, we discovered that these new trends originated in the emerging category of quick food service.

The quick food category, which included cold pre-packed meals, offered consumers more freedom and variety for moving about the shop, serving themselves and interacting with the cashier. The center of control was moving from store management to the consumer.

Client Recommendations

In contrast to this trend, the design strategy of the client's brand called for a rigid, tightly controlled service experience. Consumers had to navigate furnishings fixed to the floor, which formed a strictly controlled line of traffic from the entrance to the cashier counter, communicating discipline rather than creativity. Distracting merchandising displays were placed or hung from every available space, emphasizing the brand's selling strategy rather than a comfortable, welcoming relationship. A raised shelf about eight inches high ran end to end of the transaction counter, punctuated by openings that provided access to the cashier. The structure formed a symbolic barrier between consumers and the transaction space behind the counter. Furthermore, the beverage service behind the counter blocked views of the kitchen and the food experiences that consumers associate with the brand.

In the same way that spatial proximity affects our experiences of personal encounters, the organization of elements in a service environment affects how consumers move within the space, experience distance or closeness to the store environment, and these experiences even influence consumers' purchases decisions. By comparing and contrasting the client's service scheme with their competitors, we noted that our client's design strategy maintained tight control over the customer's encounter with the service space. In brief interviews with customers after purchase, we found that the closed, inflexible service design diminished consumers' willingness to break out of their routines and order a new menu item, to the detriment of the brand. Furthermore, the rigid structure, the cluttered merchandising presence, and the low visibility of the spaces behind the counter communicated distance and distrust, a message that was at odds with the brand advertising, which communicated a friendly and open brand personality.

Outcomes

The client responded quickly to our recommendations for improving the customer experience not only of the space but with the brand. Within months of the study, they lowered the counter top, improved visibility at the cashier counter, opened up the view of the kitchen, removed the clutter of merchandising messaging, and clarified traffic flow from the entrance to the cashier counter in order to simplify the purchase decision, speed up the ordering process, and improve customer enjoyment.

Team Exercises

The following exercises walk the reader through three phases of the design semiotic analysis.

Exercise 3.2 Collecting Data

1. Visit a small shop—a boutique, a quick serve restaurant, a workout space (spinning or yoga, etc.). Using the grid shown in Table 3.2, located in the Appendix, note the architectural features, the placement of the cashier counter and display areas, the furnishings, decor and merchandising signage, and their effects on traffic flow and consumer attention.
2. Take photos to record the visit.
3. As you explore the space, consider the impact of the service design elements on your experience of the space. For example: Are they welcoming? Do they distance you from the brand? Do they encourage you to explore or do they limit your movements?
4. Draw a floor plan of the shop, including rough measurements of the distances between important elements in the site and the placement of all movable and immovable objects.

Exercise 3.3 The Strategic Semiotic Analysis

1. Visit at least two other examples of shops in the same service category as the shop in Exercise 3.2. Referring again to the Fieldwork Guide in Table 3.3, add the two new shops to the table and fill in the other two columns with your observations about the various design elements at the site.
2. By identifying common elements across all three sites, try to generalize your experience into a statement about the overall service paradigm represented by these stores (i.e., define the boutique experience, the quick food service experience, the workout space, etc.). Include in your statement a concise description of the overall service style and relationship to the consumer, as well as a summary of the overall consumer experience elicited by the design strategy. Be precise and do not use general descriptors such as good or bad.

Exercise 3.4 Innovation Strategies

1. Having defined the paradigmatic dimensions of the service category you studied in Exercises 3.2 and 3.3, now visit another specialty shop from an entirely different product category. Compare and contrast the service design strategies of both types of shop.
2. Are you surprised by the common elements they share?

3. Now it is time to play with the codes structuring differences between two types of service site by mixing and matching design elements. Does the new shop suggest ideas for innovating on the design strategy of the first group of shops? For example, if the team is marketing personal care items for a supermarket, would a visit to a bath and body care boutique suggest ways of improving your supermarket display?

Key Learnings from Exercises 3.2 through 3.4

The three exercises in this section instruct students in some very basic methods used in design semiotics research. Exercise 3.2 included practical steps such as site selection, conducting on-site observations, organizing field notes, and taking stock of the effects of the design elements on consumer behavior. Exercise 3.3 sharpened students' observational skills by asking them to compare and contrast three shops in the same service category in order to discover the design elements that they have in common. These kinds of shared design elements define the cultural codes that distinguish one service category, such as the boutiques, from another, such as a department store. At the same time, the comparative analysis reveals how various brands interpret these codes in unique ways to differentiate their sites from competitors in the marketplace.

Exercise 3.4 encouraged students to consider ways that observations of peripheral service categories can inspire innovation and change for the category under investigation. By juxtaposing design styles from two distinct service types, such as fast food restaurants and cosmetic boutiques for instance, the researcher may discover ways to enhance and modernize the design strategy of the brand under investigation. And Exercise 3.4 situated the brand study in context with a peripheral category in order to reframe the data in a fresh context. This methodology serves to stir creative thinking about the current state of design in a given product or service category and developing a new, innovative design strategy.

The extended case study that follows illustrates how Marketing Semiotics put into play these methods and principles in order to reinvent the very nature of pick-up service and develop a new cultural space for the Domino's Pizza brand.

Extended Case Study: A Culture-Driven Design Strategy

In 2011 Domino's commissioned Marketing Semiotics to develop a service design strategy to support the company's repositioning initiative and improve consumers' enjoyment of their pick-up sites. Their move reflected shifting trends in pizza delivery caused by growing consumer mobility and advances in digital technologies that enabled consumers to order from their phones as they moved about in cars, public transit, and on foot. Cultural change had diminished the value of Domino's heritage positioning as the "Pizza Delivery Experts" and a brand promise of, "30 minutes or it's free." By means of semiotics-based research, analysis, and prototype development, we developed a new service paradigm for pizza pick-up that not only exceeded design objectives but ultimately drove the repositioning of the Domino's brand to the "Pizza Theater" strategy.

Background

Domino's original positioning as "the best home delivery" service was relevant in the 1960s world of suburban living, nuclear families, and stay-at-home moms. The company invested little in their pick-up service because the center of family life was the home rather than the family car. Delivery service made sense. As late as 2011, Domino's service sites were unadorned transaction sites characterized by white walls, a Coke machine, florescent lighting, and a cashier counter framed by a light soffit above and a bright red countertop below. The only visual representations of the brand in the waiting area included Domino's logo and the tagline, "The Pizza Delivery Experts" on the soffit above the counter, a small raised menu board on the countertop, and white tile flooring. Some photos of pizza and dessert specials hung on the walls.

The view behind the counter was completely devoid of branded signage. The back area was furnished with an order desk, stacks of pizza boxes, a cluttered desk, and the back of the stainless steel oven, trashcans, and empty cartons. The scene was devoid of appetizing views of the pizza since the ovens opened onto the back of the store, where service staff quickly packed it in the take-out boxes. Furthermore, the service staff at all the Dominos sites avoided direct eye contact with customers except to ask for payment. Turning away from the customer, they focused instead on kneading the dough without exploiting this potentially exciting element of pizza preparation for the customer experience. Some uncomfortable red metal chairs adorned the waiting area. Domino's was not alone in this approach to the pick-up service, since it also prevailed at competitors' franchises.

Prior to our involvement in the study, Domino's had rolled out a redecorating scheme in test markets that refurbished the decor with colorful signage and plastic accessories in bright red, yellow, and blue. The effort brightened up the place but did not alter the fundamental purpose, functionality, or consumer experience of the service space. What was needed was nothing less than a complete overhaul of the current interpretation of pick-up service for the category.

Study Design and Approach

To achieve this goal, we needed to understand the underlying codes that structured service design across the pick-up service spectrum. In our quest to answer the question, "What is pick-up service?" we expanded the research scope beyond the take-away pizza category itself and included a broad range of pick-up sites, including food service, including fast food restaurants, donut, cupcake and yogurt franchises, coffee shops, as well as other venues that whose business relied on pick-up service, including post offices, UPS stores, and dry cleaners.

Data Collection

We centered research in Chicago Semiotics and Los Angeles. Chicago was not only the economical choice because researchers were located there but also it has a strong market for pizza. We chose Los Angeles for the breadth and depth of its fast food and take-out options.

We prepared a list of addresses and maps of roughly two dozen sites in each market using client data and information we found on the Internet. A Fieldwork Agenda (Table 3.3) can be found in the Appendix. It serves to manage the timing and organization of the site visits. To facilitate on-site research, it is useful to hire a car service to drive researchers safely and securely from one site to the next. They can quickly navigate unfamiliar locations, handle parking in high-traffic areas, and even provide details and new information about the location. Although clients may balk at the added cost, a car service is ultimately more economical because it shortens researchers' time in the field. In Los Angeles, I relied on the services of my favorite limousine driver, who not only found the locations on our list but also directed us to local attractions that were not on our list.

The Semiotic Analysis

All the food service pick-up sites shared some basic cultural codes related to the disposition of service functions, customers, traffic flow, and transaction counter. The counter divides the service production areas in the depth of the site from the consumer areas in front. Consumers enter the site at the front of the store and line up to be served. Much of the consumer distress and frustration we observed stemmed from the lack of consumer agency and control associated with standard pick-up service.

By including such a wide swath of pick-up categories in our data set, we found that pizza pick-up lagged behind design trends across the board that were leaning toward consumer enjoyment, convenience, and engagement. Rather than a functional site for performing transactions, pick-up sites such as McDonald's 2005 flagship restaurant, Sprinkle's Cupcake and Forever Yogurt franchises are short-term destinations that deliver choice, pleasure, and a positive brand relationship by means of design features such as an open cashier counter, visual engagement with the food, and in the case of Sprinkle's and Forever Yogurt, personal access to products. At Forever Yogurt, consumers can sample the product and serve themselves from spigots installed in the walls. Sprinkle's customers have the option of shopping from an automated food service kiosk in front of the store where they select and purchase fresh cupcakes by inserting their credit cards in the machine, much like ordering beverages and snacks from a soft drink machine.

The McDonald's Example

McDonald's flagship store in Chicago, refurbished in 2005, provided an object lesson in consumer-centered pick-up service. The low, uncluttered cashier counter communicated openness and created a welcoming interface between consumers and service staff. The food preparation and kitchen areas were exposed, which communicated transparency and trust and invited consumers to enjoy eye pleasure as they waited for their meals. Menu boards highlighted appetizing visuals and healthy salad alternatives in clear, simple, terms and flat screen video monitors entertained consumers in the waiting and dining areas.

Every surface in the McDonald's space, including the trash cans and washroom doors, were inscribed with branding visuals that aligned with the basic decor themes throughout the store. Furthermore, the decor was not limited to brand logos and the brand's telltale red and yellow color scheme, but included a more muted, modern color palette, patterns, and design elements that reflected management's efforts to raise the bar on fast food service. In addition to flat screen plasma television screens to entertain consumers, the flagship store included luxury touches such as imported Italian lighting fixtures and designer leather seating. The result was a bright, inviting, forward-looking, and self-indulgent experience, both in the service queue and dining areas. The modern esthetic extended to the overall design of the stand-alone building, which aligned well with Chicago's long-standing commitment to excellence in architecture.

Beyond Food Service

Since we aimed to deconstruct the very notion of pick-up service, we included a range of other pick-up scenarios in the data set. We identified a design scheme at post offices, UPS and Federal Express centers, and dry cleaners that paralleled the layout of food pick-up service: an entry opened onto a line leading toward a service counter in the depth of the site. Even in these traditionally humdrum, functional service environments, the design included self-service kiosks in the wait area that offered things like greeting cards and office supplies. At one Chicago post office, there was even a concierge on staff who greeted customers at the front door and guided them through the visit. Apparently even the U.S. Postal Service has responded to competition from commercial delivery suppliers by improving convenience and consumer engagement at their sites.

Owner-Operated Pizza Venues

The data set also included owner-operated pizza pick-up service that offered limited seating for dining in. These venues expanded upon the emergent codes of greater consumer control and pleasure by turning the oven around to expose the sights and scents of the pizza coming out of the oven. There was also a spectator area where consumers sit up at a ledge in the kitchen area peer through a window at the cook kneading and tossing the pizza dough. This bit of pizza spectacle both entertained customers while they waited, engaged them in the service experience, and communicated brand transparency and trust. The owner-operated venues also included personalized features such as a corkboard on the wall for posting neighborhood events, photos of local celebrities and restaurant memorabilia, all of which anchored the business in the community encouraged loyalty.

Concept Development: Pizza Theater and the Semiotics of Spectacle

The Domino's case exemplifies how semiotics-trained researchers draw upon theory to solve strategic marketing problems, whether they involve design, communications, or consumer behavior. Building upon cues in the service environment that suggested parallels with the theater, I drew insights from my academic research on the semiotics of performance. By drawing parallels between the disposition of spectators in front of a stage and of consumers in front of the service counter, I reoriented the pick-up service to a space of pleasure, fantasy, and fun. The analysis inspired the pizza theater concept that ultimately drove double-digit growth for the company in a very short time.

Through the Looking Glass

In the early stages of research, I was struck by the way the counter, the light soffit, and the walls framing the transaction experience resembled a window opening onto the food production area in back. In Domino's redecorated shops, some chunky, brightly colored plastic materials drew attention to the frame as a kind of window into the food preparation area in back (Figure 3.3).

Figure 3.3. The service counter at Domino's. © 2011 Marketing Semiotics

The window is not simply a structural element for setting aside the service area from the wait area. It defines an underlying trope for the disposition of spectator and representation in spectacle. The spectating disposition is governed by cultural codes that put into play a dialectic between the here and now of the spectator facing a canvas, a cinema screen, or a spectacle, and the imaginary of the scene within the picture, the cinema frame, or the theater proscenium (Metz 1981; Oswald 2010). Hence the service window has the potential to be a magical looking glass into the brand world.

The window as trope transcends the here and now of the physical space and invites the consumer as spectator to project their imaginations into the scene viewed through the frame (Figure 3.4). We thus developed the theater metaphor into a design scheme for reimagining the pick-up space as spectacle, entertainment, and a stage for the brand story.

We then defined architectural elements in the site in terms of their role in staging this imaginary performance. The consumer's space in front of the cashier resembles the audience; the counter itself articulates the stage, and the spaces behind the counter resemble the space of the brand story.

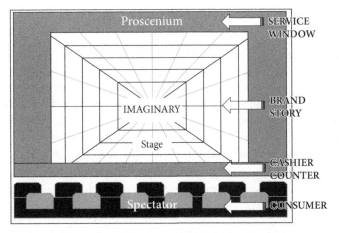

Figure 3.4. The spectating disposition. © 2019 Marketing Semiotics

Outcomes

Once we defined the space behind the counter as the brand story, the rest of the work entailed defining how to bring to life the pizza spectacle by reorganizing the space to put pizza on center stage. We gathered ideas from the service sites we observed in the field to develop design strategy for branding the food preparation area, breaking down visual barriers between the consumers and the pizza, and training staff to engage with consumers and take advantage of the entertainment value of kneading and tossing dough.

In conclusion, by reinventing pizza pick-up service in line with cultural change and category trends, we employed semiotic principles and methods to transform Domino's retail sites from bland way-stations for making transactions to branded destinations for satisfying consumer pleasure and engaging them in the brand story. We basically reinvented pick-up service by decoding the concept of pick-up service, combing the marketplace for emerging trends in pick-up service, and drawing inspiration from semiotic theory to reimagine the pick-up service experience.

Extended Team Project

The following team project reviews basic elements of the semiotics-based service design research. The scope is flexible enough to allow the instructor to expand or contract the project into a midterm evaluation or a simpler exercise.

Sample Case Topics

Option 1—Bringing Healthy Foods to the Mall

A quick food service brand, "Amy's Kitchen," is designing an on-the-go service kiosk for the atrium of an upscale mall. Amy's stands for healthy alternatives to fast food, serving high-quality, natural cold sandwiches, snacks and beverages, and hot coffee. Amy's will offer limited seating near the kiosk without interfering with the path of traffic moving through the mall. The design concept must communicate the brand's commitment to contemporary consumer needs for healthy takeaway products and also improve upon the convenience and service experience of the functional coffee bar.

Option 2—Finding a New Cultural Space for a Convenience Store

A convenience store franchise named after the pseudonym "All Rite" is seeking to improve the store experience in order to encourage consumers to spend more time in the store. They hope that by spending more time consumers will broaden the scope of their product choices. Contemporary trends in retailing had also raised consumers' expectations of the service experience that contrasted with the drab, uninviting atmosphere of convenience stores. Over the years, management had failed to keep pace with consumer-centered trends in retailing, drab store environments with their cheap, functional display cases, florescent lighting, and bad coffee, discouraged customer loyalty and prompted consumers to limit product choice to snacks, cigarettes, and soft drinks.

Management hires your team to develop a new service design strategy that aligns with changes in the grocery store environment at large, aligns with changes in supermarkets, and improves the shopping experience. Management hopes that by turning convenience stores from functional retail outlets to destinations, the design scheme will encourage consumers to spend more money on a wider range of products than before. Please follow the steps below as you plan your team's work

Steps for a Service Study
  I. Background
 II. Objectives and Scope
III. Project Design
IV. Data Collection
 V. Analysis
      a. Decoding the Category
      b. Conceptual Insights
VI. Write-Up and Power Point Presentation

Chapter Conclusion

The chapter introduced the reader to the basics of design semiotics as applied specifically to packaging and service site design. Multiple exercises and a team project instructed students in the practice of design research and concept development. Multiple exercises and an extended team project enabled students to learn firsthand how to apply semiotic principles to design research, think strategically about design in context with competitors, the category, and consumer culture.

Although discussion focused primarily on packaging and service site design, the methods and principles apply to the design of a wide variety of market channels across the marketing mix. Thus, the instructor may expand upon the current examples to include cases related to new product design, consumer-centered design experiences, and organizational alignment.

Appendix

Table 3.1 A guide to packaging semiotics

Design features	Category A	Category B	Category C	etc.
Form—rounded, squared, etc				
Shape—cube, cylinder, etc.				
Material				
Color scheme				
Other				

Table 3.2 Guide to service design research

	Site X	Site Y	Site Z
Architectural features			
Cashier counter placement			
Furnishings and placement			
Traffic flow			
Other			

Table 3.3 Fieldwork agenda

Market	Date – Time	Address	Notes

Reading 3

It's All About *Con[text]*: A Design Semiotics Approach for Managing Meaning-Value in Innovation Processes

Dr. Laura Santamaria
Loughborough University London

One of the most frequent questions I have been asked by clients throughout my years as a consultant is *"where shall we go next?"* Driven by a constant need to develop new products and services, companies become obsessed with finding out what customers want, and lost when it comes to tackling the process. Where does one start?

Innovation is a risky journey. Both start-ups and established brands encounter a diversity of risks throughout during the innovation path—technological, organizational or financial challenges can delay or halt progress to materialize good ideas. However, the biggest risk to be faced is market failure. Although one can never be fully certain about success, minimizing this one is key.

For successful introduction of new products, services, or technology into the market, it is imperative that the offer meets the needs, tastes, and preferences of the potential customer. After all, innovation is about value creation. However, value is a highly subjective matter—one that hinges heavily on relevance.

Beyond features and functional benefits, what does the overall offer mean to the customer? What *significance* and symbolic function does it has in their lives? Highly The most desirable offers are those that fulfil people's social and psychological needs and help them express who they are. And the more relevant and conducive of a person's sense of identity, achievement, improvement or advantage, the greater value they the customer will assign to it. These meanings are important "symbolic assets" to generate relevance and value, and therefore it is essential to be able to identify, manage, and use them strategically during the innovation process.

Understanding People

In a saturated market, developing relevant and desirable offers requires a fine understanding of the factors that shape people's choices. So, before committing limited resources to development and production, it pays off getting to know people at the deepest level you can dig into. But…is innovation driven by the demand or proposition? What comes first? This longstanding dilemma has led to a proliferation of innovation approaches based on quick, iterative trial-and-error cycles such as Lean, Open, Agile, and more recently, design-led innovation. Design Thinking, Service Design, and User Experience (UX) approaches are rapidly gaining popularity due to their focus on people's needs, behaviors, and preferences as the starting point for innovation (Brown 2009).

Naturally, these human-centered innovation processes start with user-centered research. Target customers are explored through qualitative methods, including interviews, ethnography, shadowing, and cultural probes to draw insights. More research follows in the form of iterative cycles of—rough to elaborate—prototype building and testing, and constant pivoting of the value offer until we get it right (or funds run out, whatever comes first!). More often than not, these efforts generate feedback to improve functionality and usability features, which leads to incremental rather than radical or disruptive innovation (Norman and Verganti 2014).

The problem is that, while these well-tried and tested methods work better than traditional market research to identify customer needs and behaviors, they still face limitations when it comes to pinpointing more subtle, intangible and nuanced aspects. Often, important symbolic and sociocultural meanings that influence people's decisions and value judgements are missed out, because these aspects are more difficult to capture by direct observation or consultation with users. In fact, unless we dive into the sociocultural context of innovation, what we see by observing behaviors is only the tip of the iceberg. Individuals don't exist in a vacuum.

I would argue that a person's conscious expression of their beliefs, preferences, and behaviors responds mostly to certain unconscious underlying assumptions related to "views of the world"—or frames—to which they conform or confront. It is these socially agreed, tacit rules which "invisibly" bind people together into social groups or "tribes." If we don't have this data, we can only claim to know people on the surface. In order to dig deeper, we need to zoom out from the focus on the individual behaviors, and learn about the normative of the groups they affiliate with. We need a helicopter view of the vernacular—the social markers common in the group and the context we are launching into.

It is here that marketing semiotics can make an interesting addition. The methods complement other human-centered approaches (Figure R3.1) focusing on context "deconstruction"—i.e. uncovering the "normalized" meanings that users are often unable to articulate, because these operate largely at subconscious level (Oswald 2012). The aim of this kind of research is to identify the social signifiers—"implicit" norms, meanings or codes that mark status and belonging—drawing insights from the analysis of discourses and popular culture (media, advertising, music, film, etc.) using a mix of semiotic, cultural studies and ethnography methods (Figure R3.1).

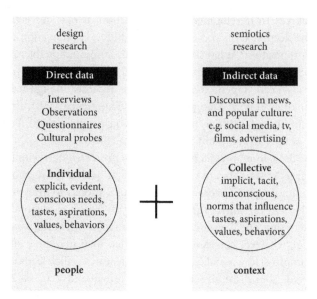

Figure R3.1. Human-centered design meets sociocultural research

Marketing semiotics offers great potential to obtain strategic intelligence by identifying emergent cultural themes (e.g. values, aesthetics, practices, and trends) that have a strong likelihood of spreading into the dominant or mainstream culture. Conducting this type of research at the earliest stages of innovation can save valuable time and resources, sometimes shortening the cycle of trial-and-error iterations dramatically. It can also prevent the emergence of ill-defined value propositions that struggle to attract a critical mass of customers. However, these methods have been mostly confined to the field of advertising, and their value to inform user-centered innovation approaches has been overlooked.

Creating Value by Design

The first big challenge in developing meaningful innovation is to obtain good insights. The next one is to translate them into good design—i.e. to figure out how an idea might add value to people's lives. While it is well-acknowledged that design creates value (kudos, desirability, identity, and legitimacy) it is less known *how* this value is created, systematically.

Three elements are key to develop desirable innovations (Figure R3.2):

- Utility (functional aspects)
- Usability (ergonomic aspects) and
- Pleasurability, which, in essence, refers to the subjective and emotional value of an experience (symbolic aspects).

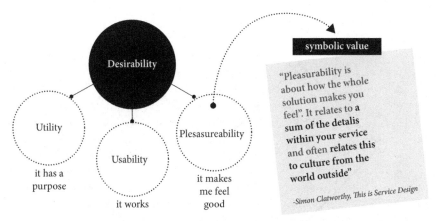

Figure R3.2. Designing desirable innovations. (Adapted from Clatworthy 2012)

The first two domains are the traditional concerns upon which the design discipline is grounded. Designers also develop an ability to intuitively apprehend the cultural meanings expressed through aesthetics that appeal to particular user groups. By virtue of their practice, they "frame" innovations by association with those meanings—or "codes" (du Gay et al. 2013). One could argue that a largely unconscious part of the design process implies curating and managing certain "symbolic assets" (sociocultural references and narratives) over others, in the quest to create innovations that are appealing, relevant, and meaningful for the intended target user group. Just as meanings do not merely add value to the functional dimension of goods, but indeed create brand value, these symbolic assets are essential to the value of design, because the degree of mastery in which we use them can *enhance* or *limit* an innovation's potential to be seen as a legitimate and, preferably, a highly desirable choice.

Although designers work with symbolic assets all the time, fulfilling this role successfully seems to be highly dependent on the designer's intuition and experience in addressing people's social needs (identity, belonging, and aspirations). We can always rely on heuristics, working our way through the process through trial and error, or we can be more strategic and smarter about the way we identify, interpret, and manage symbolic assets to create value.

Framing and Managing Intangible Assets, by Design

To tackle the meaning aspects throughout design innovation processes I developed *Con[text]*—I call it a "design semiotics meta-framework" useful for identifying,

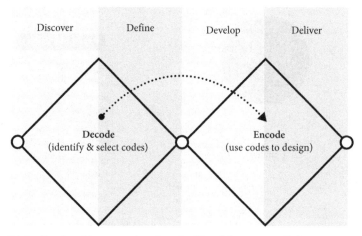

Figure R3.3. *Con[text]* integrated within the "Double Diamond" design process

mapping and curating valuable symbolic assets to construct value for existing or new customer groups. Inspired by the cultural studies "encoding–decoding" model of communication (Hall 1980), the approach consists of a series of methods grouped in two phases:

Phase 1 – Decoding. Decoding is about understanding the context of innovation. That is, mapping and organizing cultural codes and meanings by category, target audience, their global and local signifiers, and locating cultural positioning of competitors.

Phase 2 – Encoding. Encoding is about elaborating more precise guidelines for strategic innovation framing. That is, curating the most favorable cultural themes and codes identified in Phase 1, and utilizing them to frame the offer intentionally to create desirability and relevance (Figure R3.3).

Con[text] works aAs a meta-framework, *Con[text]* that can be adopted applied alongside other specific innovation processes. In Figure R3.3, it is situated it within the popular double-diamond Design Thinking, design and innovation process (Design Council 2005) where *decoding* encompasses the first diamond (discover-define) and *encoding* the second one (develop-deliver). In other words, *decoding* is about "designing the right thing" and *encoding* about "designing things right" (Nessler 2016).

In the next section, I present a case study to illustrate in more detail how *Con[text]* was used as a strategic approach to grow customer base by meaning innovation. Market opportunities were identified by structuring and facilitating context exploration, and the perceived value of the offer was increased by intentionally repositioning its meaning and communicating in a way a wider audience would appreciate.

Crop Drop Case Study

The case illustrates the semiotic process applied of to enhance competitive advantage and scaling-up a social venture through meaning innovation. Crop Drop (www.cropdrop.co.uk) is a social enterprise that operates a vegetable box scheme in the London borough of Haringey. The start-up is part of a larger network of growers and distributors dedicated to local and sustainable food production and supply. At the point of intervention, Crop Drop had been operational for two years, and they had developed a small but loyal core customer base. However, they struggled to find a direction to reach a wider group. The owner was quite knowledgeable of the local context and had explored most other traditional methods to understand customers (e.g. surveys, focus groups, and feedback questionnaires). This made it a great case for using Con[text] to dig into deeper aspects such values, norms and aspirations, and spot areas of opportunity for growth.

Phase 1—Decoding (Context and User Research)

The first working session with the client involved some initial conversations to familiarize with the business and identify priority issues. We went through business front and back operations, communication materials, customer feedback, existing business and marketing plans. Then, the client was introduced to the principles and commonly used tools in service design—e.g. service blueprint, customer journeys, stakeholders map, and user personas. Con[text] was presented as "a strategic approach to better understand users and business context." We explained how the approach differs from conventional market research (e.g. surveys, focus groups) and what could be obtained (deeper insights into what influences customers' choice).

Setting up sociocultural context research

The aim of the research was to map the cultural codes (within the business operational context) and identify the best codes symbolic assets to reposition the offer to appeal to a wider customer base. To this end, we gathered a "data set" of materials related to the food business sector, including news clippings, photos, adverts, website screenshots, book covers, magazines images, billboard ads, pictures of products, packaging, delivery vans, etc. These served as the basis for analysis, using some of the methods shown in Table R3.1.

Table R3.1 Semiotic/cultural analysis methods applied to context research

Method	Description	Function
Binary Oppositions	A pair of concepts that relate in direct opposition (i.e. clean/dirty). It breaks cultural and categories into two opposite sets of codes.	Normally a good place to start the code-mapping process, see opportunities for innovation, resolve trade-offs and cultural contradictions.
Semiotic Square (Greimas 1984)	Paired concepts analysis based on Jakobson's distinction between contradiction and contrariety.	Useful for accessing deep structures informing the communication and perception of meaning—i.e. the underlying connections with structures of power and logic.
Themes & Metaphors	A snapshot of the cultural landscape frozen in time, and the active codes present at that particular time. Searches for key metaphors and themes present in the category by dividing it up.	Good for locating developing themes, and cross-fertilization with themes from other related categories.
Cultural Archetypes (personas)	Rooted symbols and cultural archetypes such as gold, America, home, work, family, etc. Received wisdom, "what everyone knows" and "goes without saying"	Useful for building narratives and associations with deep-rooted cultural values and traditions. Normally used in storytelling material, film, novels and popular culture.

Mapping global meanings (binary oppositions)

We started with a category analysis at its broadest level. The aim was to locate the main associations, myths, trends, and generic assumptions related to food consumption as a social practice. To make these cultural assumptions explicit, we went through the materials asking the question: *"what is food about?"* Two broad overarching themes emerged: *nutrition* and *pleasure*. We found that, at one end of the spectrum, food was being represented as nutrition—its most *factual* level, a necessity for human survival. On the other hand, food was also associated with the *pleasure* derived at an emotional, visceral level, from satisfying that need. We also observed that in some representations people were *alone*, while in other situations they were depicted *together* with others—e.g. couples, families, friend's gatherings. This observation led us to break down the category into these four themes: *alone–together, nutrition–pleasure*.

Locating perceptions and meaning (semiotic square)

We then decided to take a closer look at how meanings were being constructed around these themes, and their relationship to people's attitudes and aspirations. What did these different representations evoke? What basic tensions or needs did they tap into?

Broad Category Analysis

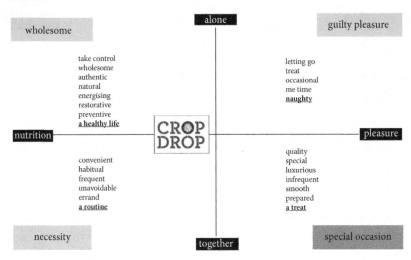

Figure R3.4. Broad category analysis axis

To map these positions, we formed an axis of opposite logical relations with the four themes drawn from the previous step (nutrition–pleasure, together–alone). We then picked four stereotypical examples (relevant to the UK) of the themes in each quadrant, to illustrate the notion contained within it—i.e. "*nutrition-alone,*" "*nutrition-together,*" "*pleasure-alone*" and "*pleasure-together.*" Guided by these stereotypical representations and asking "*it feels like…*" each quadrant was labelled. The concepts were further elaborated into more detailed descriptions of the characteristics associated with each concept (Figure R3.4).

This method (based on Greimas' semiotic square) was useful to locate which broad areas of meaning were being used by different brands in the sector. Placing Crop Drop within this axis helped us consider how their value proposition was probably perceived from the point of view of potential customers, in relation to other market offers. To identify Crop Drop's position, we referred back to the brand's promises communicated through marketing materials.

The analysis revealed areas of opportunity and challenge. On one hand, by offering "convenience" the brand was ruling out (by opposition) any associations to the "pleasure" side of the spectrum. Moreover, the "convenience" space was occupied by global suppliers such as mainstream supermarkets, and this placed the brand in direct competition with them—a clear disadvantage for a small business.

On the other hand, Crop Drop sat firmly in the "wholesome" foods position due to the characteristics of the product and ethos of the company. Without a

Sub-Category Analysis
Wholesome foods

Figure R3.5. Subcategory analysis using the global–local spectrum

doubt, this was an area of opportunity that resonated well with their customer base and growing market trends. As a next step, we decided to zoom in and explore the "wholesome" subcategory in more detail.

Mapping the "wholesome" subcategory (global–local spectrum)

Crop Drop was being promoted as a "local" business, as opposed to the "global" ones—e.g. supermarkets. So, to explore the *Wholesome* subcategory at deeper level, we placed the different competitors along a spectrum ranging from the *global* (widespread or mainstream) on one end, to the *local* at the opposite end (Figure R3.5).

We used visual references (representations of offerings) instead of logos or just the brand name. The purpose here was to pay close attention to what the visual references evidenced. We noticed that the global offers were built on *convenience* value propositions by communicating mass reach (e.g. home delivery, self-service collection points, large vehicles loaded with a wide variety of supply, suppliers present in every town's high street). These suggested that the "large system" takes care of our basic nutrition, however, it is impersonal and built to deliver generic quantity. The local offers, in contrast, were built on *specialty* value propositions—communicating that a product is crafted, artisanal, made by members of the local community.

In a globalized society, it becomes relevant to observe how these frames and counter-frames are represented, and how value is created by tapping into meanings implicit within both positions. In this example, for a group of customers holding holistic living lifestyles in high esteem, a local product would naturally afford higher value than a global one, due to an association made between "local" and "quality and personalization," two highly appreciated characteristics coherent with their value/belief system.

Exploring the implicit meanings of the "Local" label

For the purpose of framing (i.e. managing meanings and symbolic associations embedded in copy and visual communications), it was important to make evident the implied meanings of positioning the business as "local." Concepts such as this

Exploring implied meanings
What does it mean to be a 'local' provider?

Haringey's **local** veg box scheme.

Crop Drop is rightfully claiming to be local supplier. Standing for local means, by opposition, not global. Both words also trigger a network of associated concepts that people have come to acquire through past experiences, hearing other people and the media.

These associations are triggered by visual symbols or words, instantly and almost always unconsciously.

If is therefore useful to make them explicit, so we can deal with them in a systematic manner.

Global	Local
Artificial	Natural
Present	Future
Individual	Collective
ordinary	Luxurious
Common	Special
Affordabel	Expensive
High-tech	Low-tech
Immediacy	Nostalgia
Familiar	Rare
Habitual	Infrequent
Mass-produced	Artisan
Prepared	Raw
Smooth	Rough
Unoriginal	Authentic
Quantity	Quality

Figure R3.6. Related "local" and "global" associations

are often used as shortcuts which contain wider meanings or values, as discussed above. This is because words, as well as conveying meanings on their own, are also part of larger networks of related meanings. Thus, with a single referent (a word or image), related associations—which may have been acquired through past experiences, word of mouth and the media—are triggered instantly and unconsciously in our minds.

To unpack the network of associated meanings for "local" and "global," we used the "binary opposition" method once again. This time, we placed the opposite concepts at the top, and listed all the implied, connected meanings under each overarching concept (Figure R3.6).

Having explored the category and identified global and local expressions of the meanings relevant to Crop Drop, we were ready to move into understanding potential customers in more depth.

Extended User Research

We started by conducting some secondary research to gain insight into the neighborhood population. The guiding principle was to identify which households might be willing to eat vegetables on a more regular basis, but also open to accept an unconventional range, as the produce on offer implied being resourceful and creative with cooking. After consulting some statistics, four customer types were profiled, using both demographics and illustrative "persona" types (Figure R3.7).

Figure R3.7. Potential user group, represented with visual stereotypes

"Young Progressive Families" were considered a good match to Crop Drop's value proposition, as this group represented a natural progression from their current customer base, the "Singles and Young Couples." We selected this group for further exploration.

Personas and Lifestyle Codes Mapping (Stereotypes)

"People like us do things like this" – Seth Godin, *This is Marketing*

Stereotypes are widely used both in marketing (customer profile) and design (user persona). Personas are descriptive examples of typical target groups who have similar aims, motivations and behaviors, and can be elaborated at different levels of complexity (Massanari 2010). Empathy in human-centered approaches is key, and personas are "imaginary friends" that help us keep the process anchored on their preferences and needs. Based on the basic persona profile (Figure R3.8, left), we used images to map some of the popular lifestyle choices within this target group (Figure R3.8, right).

We selected brands and social practices that these users prefer, because these carry the symbolic assets that define their social identity. The collection of images is considered to contain some of the key *"signifiers"* or cultural codes, which bind

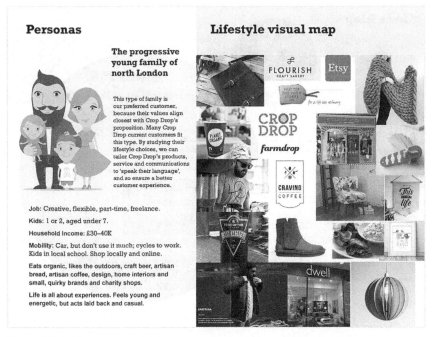

Figure R3.8. User persona incorporating a visual map of lifestyle choices

them together and as a social group, but also set them apart from other groups by means of a differentiated *aesthetics, appreciated values* and *common practices,* expressed through this particular normative (Bourdieu 2010).

Identifying these meanings is important because to be perceived as relevant, any innovation intended to appeal to this group must "fit" within this frame—i.e. it must be coherent with other choices and semio-aesthetic expression of this group.

By understanding these codes, it was possible to begin drawing some strategies and guidelines to frame Crop Drop's offering to fit more closely to this group's expectations and aspirations.

Producing guidelines for design

The visual references mapped alongside the personas were analyzed, deconstructing them and classifying them into three categories: *Aesthetic Codes* related to matters of style and taste, *Popular Lifestyle Practices* related to what is normal and enjoyable for people in this group to do, and *Appreciated Values* associated with how the group defines "quality of life." These were illustrated with explicit examples so that they can serve as reminders of how each "theme" was manifested in this particular context (Figure R3.9). In this way, the most powerful and

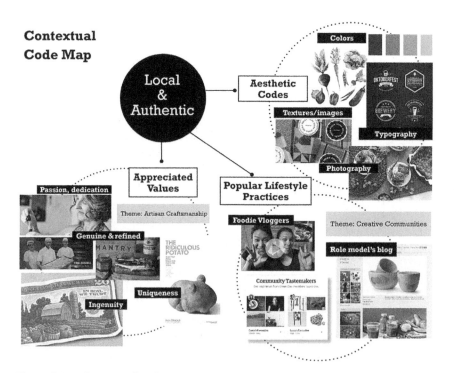

Figure R3.9. Contextual codes summary map

User Experience Design Guidelines

Local is good
But to make it feel special, it is best to lean towards craft and artisan, and away from 'farm', rough and raw.
Codes: Elegance, nostalgia, rarity.

Speciality
Introduce some 'gourmet' feel to the brand to convey 'premium and quality' aspects. Look at artisan bread, coffee, beer and chocolate brands for references.
Codes: black, craft paper, beige and red/orange, mustard yellow, retro/vintage-style typefaces.

Pleasure
Be emotional and evocative rather than factual. Appeal to the senses, make it tempting, delicious, fun, wholesome but special. **Watch trends in vegetarian restaurants images and communications. Show a balance of cooked and raw.**

Authenticity
Promote intrinsic values. Reinforce relationships over health and environment. Your value is **not in the box of veg, it's in the experience of learning new ways of being together.**

Figure R3.10. Summarized user experience design guidelines

relevant signifiers for this group became evident as tangible assets, and were ready to be used for framing and designing the user experience (Figure R3.10).

Phase 2—Encoding

Crop Drop is a typical case of product-service system innovation where the product items, the branding, communications and the experience of the service all interfere with each other in terms of how the innovation's value is perceived (Ceschin et al., 2014). In order to improve the service credibility and appeal, we proceeded to "reframe" its value in line with the insights identified throughout the Decoding phase.

Enhancing value by Deciding the brand repositioning meaning innovation
Before proceeding to design, we needed to identify a new, desired—and achievable—brand position. Going back to the axis tool to map category positions, this time we used four factors that seemed to shape the "wholesome" category in particular (Figure R3.11).

- *Limited Choice vs. Wide Choice*—Due to its proposition as a local produce supplier, Crop Drop offered quite limited choice of vegetables in comparison to other competitors operating in the same space.

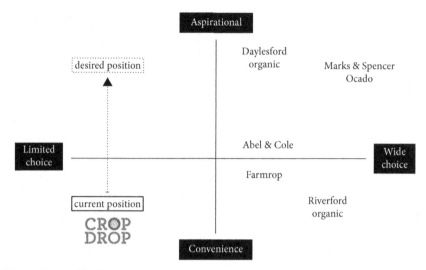

Figure R3.11. Market repositioning exercise

- *Specialty vs. Convenience*—However, their range could be considered quite "special" because it varies with the seasons. So, the weakness could be turned into an opportunity depending on how the offer is framed—"limited choice" or "a special selection of quality vegetables."

In this category, the *specialty* space is inhabited by aspirational brands. These brands appeal to customers' senses and emotions by using certain aesthetic associations that communicate trust, inspire and elevate people's everyday ordinary experiences. It is the *symbolic value* of the brand as expressed through semio-aesthetic associations that makes them aspirational. Therefore, people are willing to pay more for products which are perceived not as *ordinary*, but *extraordinary*. Although, Crop Drop was built on aspirational values, some of the signifiers used to translate the value proposition into design did not fit the user group's expectations and ideals of "quality" and "specialty." To do that, it became necessary to reposition the brand out from the "convenience" space (the global offers), and towards the "specialty" end of the spectrum by reframing the value proposition using the right signifiers.

Language framing
As a first step, we looked at the communication materials. To appeal to a wider audience, we decided to craft the messages around a well-being rather than an

Table R3.2 Aligning language with the new positioning

	Existing proposition	Reframed proposition
Strapline	"Local food for people, not profit"	"Live the seasons"
Main message	Crop Drop	Hello Winter
Sub text	Crop Drop veg-box scheme makes it easy for you to buy ethically, eat seasonally and cook with the best quality vegetables	Eat in tune with the season. Feel stronger, be the change.
Main text		Big changes can start with small steps
Highlight		Winter's local best

environmental discourse. Table R3.2 illustrates some of the changes introduced (Table R3.2).

Crop Drop's original strapline was "Local food for people, not profit." Due to its campaigning tone, it could be argued that this statement proposes a specific ideology—that food supplying must not be a "profitable" activity, a stance and assumption which might resonate with certain audiences whose values align to the socio-political implications of this ideology. This, in turn, might exclude other user groups whose interests, for example, could be to start incorporating seasonal and local ingredients into their diet for health-related reasons. On one hand, it adds value by proposing a "non-corporate" approach to food retailing; on the other, it subtracts value by implying a certain "amateur" approach. However, if that same statement is framed with an aesthetic that is in line with other "reputable referents"—i.e. aligned to the user group's lifestyle choices, then Crop Drop's value proposition appears much more appealing and trustworthy.

It is worth clarifying that there is no right or wrong framing, but when used strategically, the frame should be constructed according to the objectives to accomplished (Wolsko et al. 2016). Because framing predisposes the user, affecting their perception of value, receptivity, and appreciation, it is paramount to be aware of the effects and implications of choosing certain framing options over others.

Visual reframing

Figure R3.12 illustrates an example of the material used to promote the business over a period of two years. The new design (Figure R3.13) which evokes crops and "land" using warm and emotional references was constructed using the signifiers drawn in the Contextual Code Map (Figure R3.9). Figure R3.14 illustrates how the codes identified during the analysis were strategically implemented.

The website (Figure R3.15) was also reframed and redesigned (Figure R3.16) incorporating the aesthetic codes, but also allowed us to work with codes related to the users' *appreciated values* and *practices*. These translated into:

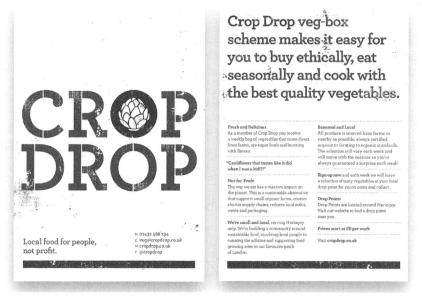

Figure R3.12. Example of publicity material before reframing

Figure R3.13. Example of publicity material after reframing

- Ample display of visual imagery of fresh produce and tantalizing, cooked meals;
- Homepage company video incorporating a short presentation of the company, to communicate company values at an emotional level;
- Featuring the owner prominently, to make the experience feel much more personal and welcoming but also to reinforce a sense of "dedication, passion and love"—characteristics of small business owners and craftsmanship;
- Featuring suppliers more prominently, to communicate transparency and collaboration;

Logo
Played down and embedded, rather than prominent

Message
Positive and welcoming, reinforce 'embracing the season'

Typography
Friendly (open, lower case)
Informal and vintage (cursive)
Refined (Roman style)

Colour
In line with brand, but enhanced for reference to artichokes and purple carrots

Paper
Craft stock

Print style
Reminiscent of manual and old-style printmaking

Illustration style
Pattern, flat, woodcarving style to convey authentic and handmade. References to nature's bounty and crops

Figure R3.14. Example of how codes were used for reframing

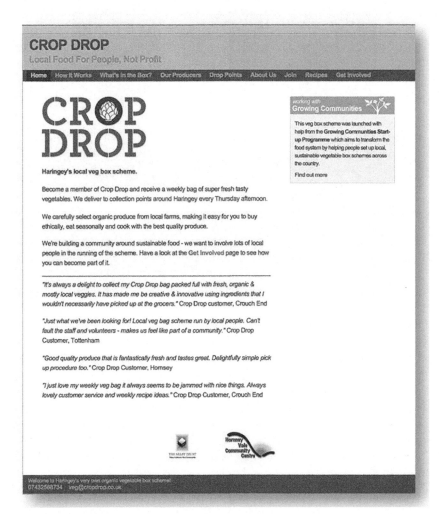

Figure R3.15. Website before reframing

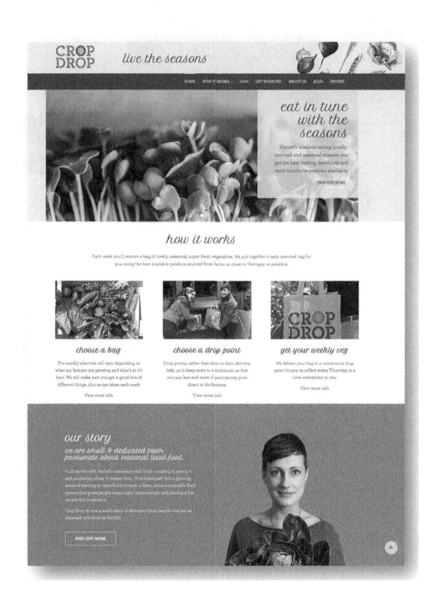

Figure R3.16. Website after reframing (www.cropdrop.co.uk)

- Blog and social media feeds provide a sense of community, participation, openness, and keep adding to the site fresh and relevant content;
- A Recipe section, where recipes are tagged by season and type of produce, so that users can easily find inspiration

Process evaluation

The case study evidences the value of *Con[text]* for facilitating a more systematic approach to meaning making in innovation processes. This approach provided good support for elaborating sociocultural insights and, as a result, both the designer and the customer became more aware of the assumptions, biases and tacit norms that affect the perceived value of the service. It also illustrates how these intangible aspects—values and perceptions—can be identified during the research process and negotiated more strategically.

Although the process may appear to be "just a repositioning and redesign," the difference is in that the dealing with meanings (constructing symbolic value) became a conscious, intention-driven activity, informed by strong research.

The designer reflected:

> Before the intervention, my practice was intuitive, and my confidence to deliver was based on heuristics and assumptions. Having to follow methods made me design in a different way. There were much clearer guidelines, I was better able to explain what I was actually doing, and ground it on research, which also helped to keep the conversations focused on the user, rather than assumptions based on personal taste and preferences of the development team.

Crop Drop's marketing team commented:

> We now feel better equipped to understand potential customers aspirations and expectations. This exercise has opened our eyes, especially about communicating benefits that are more relevant to them (rather than a set of service features), in a way that feels natural to them.

In Conclusion

Methods such as *Con[text]* can be very powerful when used alongside human-centered or other innovation approaches, opening another dimension for creativity and novelty by exploring ways to create value with symbolic meanings through meaning innovation. The most salient benefits are:

- Vernacular iInsight

Using semiotics methods to explore the sociocultural context of innovation enlarges the research focus from a user- to a context-centered approach, generating better understanding of both users and context of innovation. This served as a basis for repositioning the service within the category, expanding the offer to a wider range of customers, and improving competitive advantage by sharpening the value proposition framing.

• Richer persona insights

Mapping the persona profiles lifestyles visually alongside the personas was a fundamental step for gathering a valuable "data set" that contains the normative codes (aesthetics, practices, and values) that regulate a particular group, and understanding the key symbolic assets being used for understanding how the potential target group constructs their social identities. This is a fundamental step to gather a valuable "data set" for extracting the codes (aesthetics, practices, and values) that regulate this particular group. This method expanded insight elaboration beyond "user needs" (which tends to focus on users as individuals) and reinforced an understanding of what binds the user groups together. It enabled drawing a richer picture of users as "members of communities" The by providing a method provided a structured way to observe and interpret sociocultural aspirations and attitudes, enabling us to draw a richer picture of users as "members of communities."

• Strategic management of symbolic assets

Considering that the way in which an offering is framed has great influence on its perception of value, it is important to understand which unconscious biases we are triggering via representations and signifiers. Framing cannot be done casually, because it has a deep influence on purchase decision. In this, the Contextual Code Map (Figure R3.9) and User Experience Guidelines (Figure R3.10) served as clear criteria to follow for framing insights by design.

In summary, *Con[text]* offers a useful design semiotics construct to guide research and structure meanings in innovation, helping to make sense of the relationship between the value proposition, users, and the culture(s) they are immersed in. By developing stronger capacity to observe, analyze, and use symbolic assets, one can adopt a more strategic approach to innovation, creating products and services that bear greater resonance with users.

Author Profile

Laura Santamaria is Deputy Associate Dean for Enterprise and Director of the Design and Culture Program at Loughborough University London. Her research focuses on critical, meaning-making aspects of innovation. Laura has an extensive background in design practice, having held roles in new product development, design management, marketing, brand and communications strategy within the UK corporate and non-profit sectors since 1993. She is also co-founder and director of *Sublime* magazine, and marketing consultancy YourBusinessLondon.com

4

Consumer Semiotics

"Consumers do not always mean what they say or say what they mean."
Laura Oswald, *Creating Value*

Structural semiotics has origins in the dual disciplines of communication science and anthropology and evolved over the last century by means of the gradual weaving together structural linguistics and developments in the social sciences. Though Lévi-Strauss (1974) [1963]) drew direct parallels between linguistic concepts such as code theory and cultural production, Saussure ([1916] 2011), the founder of structural linguistics originally insisted on the social nature of language, and his contemporary, Emile Durkheim ([1893] 1997) drew inferences from linguistic theory to understand social organization and human behavior.[1]

In spite of semiotics' long relationship with the social sciences, many commercial semioticians devote their practice to the analysis of texts such as advertising, popular media, and cultural phenomena, to the exclusion of consumer research. Some practicing semioticians even advertise that semiotics does not apply to consumer behavior. However, a cursory look at the academic literature makes it clear that the object of semiotics is not limited to formal texts, but applies to a wide range of human experiences, including social organization (Hodge and Kress 1988), cinema spectating (Metz [1976] 1981), the flow of traffic in the mall (Oswald 2015), and animal behavior (Sebeok 1972). Furthermore, in the course of twenty years of consulting to blue chip companies, it is clear that the object of semiotics is not limited to textual analysis, but also applies to a wide range of marketing factors including consumer-centered design strategy, cultural branding, and media planning.

The Semiotic Paradigm

As Eco claims, "semiotics is concerned with everything that can be taken as a sign. A sign is everything which can be taken as significantly substituting for something else" (1976: 7). Thus, the object of semiotics includes anything that performs as a

---

[1] The weaving together of linguistics and social research continued to thrive throughout the twentieth century, from the work of Jakobson and the Moscow Linguistic Circle on literary theory and poetics and of late Russian Formalists such as Bakhtin who tied narrative structure to the discourse of resistance, to the Prague Structuralists in pre-war Czechoslovakia who identified performative dimensions of literary discourse that emphasized the effects of subject-address and reference on reader engagement.

Laura R. Oswald, *Consumer Semiotics* In: *Doing Semiotics: A Research Guide for Marketers at the Edge of Culture.*
Edited by: Laura R. Oswald, Oxford University Press (2020). © Laura R. Oswald. © Christian Pinson, Reading 4.
DOI: 10.1093/oso/9780198822028.003.0004

signifier for a meaning that transcends the thing itself, as when a seating arrangement at a corporate meeting represents power relations in the organization or when a red octagonal sign inscribed with the word "Stop" communicates "Stop or risk a citation."

Text and Context

Moreover, by extending the marketing semiotic paradigm to consumer research, I propose a more holistic approach to applied semiotics than the proponents of "social semiotics" (Hodge and Kress 1988), who position consumer semiotics as a distinct discipline and epistemology because it accounts for the role of the social context on meaning production. However, due to advances in semiotics and poetics since the 1970s (see Benveniste 1971 [1966]; Derrida 1976, 1983 [1972]); Eco 1976; Oswald 1989), it has become common practice to embed the semiotic analysis in the context of the message, whether the object of analysis involves formal texts or consumer behavior (see Arnould and Thompson 2005). This practice is fully compatible with poststructuralist semiotics across the research spectrum.

Take, for example, the meaning of the American flag. As a universal symbol taken out of context, the flag evokes the cheery clichés that abound in popular American culture, such as Mom, Mickey Mouse, and baseball. However, if we take the perspective of consumers in a hostile corner of the world, the flag evokes dark and threatening associations and may even provoke violence. The principle that context shapes meaning applies whether one analyzes the flag symbol in a film text, a public space, or a consumer event.

Rich Data

Although the field of semiotics invites multiple applications, including textual analysis and consumer semiotics, the main difference between them concerns not so much their theoretical focus, but the relative complexity of each medium of analysis. Where formal texts are fairly stable sign systems, consumer behavior is dynamic and changing; where formal texts consist of words, images, and stories, consumer behavior also includes performative elements such as gesture, facial expression, ritual behavior, and movement in social space.

Practical Applications

Text-centered semiotics is useful for creating a broad snapshot of the cultural and strategic dimensions of a product category or mass market, as we illustrated in the previous chapters. However, the dynamic, multivalent aspect of consumer research has the potential for more complex data, leading to richer insights. Since consumer semiotics draws insights from the dynamic and unpredictable resources of consumer behavior, it provides access to the effects of nuance, ambiguity, cultural difference, and local norms on meaning production. These kinds of insights not only move brands to the cutting edge of innovation but also expand our knowledge about the ways that consumers engage with the marketplace. If the research objectives call for a high degree of complexity, I usually adapt a two-pronged methodology that includes textual semiotics and consumer research.

In general, consumer semiotics is a form of qualitative research that employs many of the tools used by the research generalist to gain insights from consumers. In this chapter, I review the semiotic dimensions of consumer behavior, the basic methods and techniques of qualitative research, and the distinct advantages of consumer semiotics to develop rich consumer data, produce verifiable insights, and in general to make sense of consumer motives and market behaviors. Though the tools available to the qualitative researcher are abundant (see Merriam 2015), I focus here on two of the most common forms of qualitative research, focus groups and in-depth interviews. I devote Chapter 5 to semiotic ethnography, which is the most common application of semiotics to consumer research.

The chapter includes three main sections, including a review of the semiotic dimensions of consumer behavior, a summary of the basic methods and moderating techniques used in qualitative research, and application of semiotic principles and methods in qualitative research. The chapter also walks the reader through the application of semiotics to qualitative research in team exercises and short projects.

Consumer Semiotics

Consumer behavior is charged with symbolic significance (Sherry 1987a & b, 1990, 1991; Oswald 1999) and provides a rich terrain for semiotic study. Gestures, social interactions, the disposition of possessions within the home, or the performance of cultural rituals such as meal preparation all constitute semiotic systems. Even when qualitative research is conducted in a research facility, the researcher has access to nonverbal messages communicated in the respondent's voice, facial expression, and gestures as well as the anecdotes they reference in the course of an interview. The meanings signified by nonverbal communication may even conflict with consumer speech and betray their deep-seated insecurities or beliefs. For instance, a housewife we interviewed at home claimed that she served only natural, fresh foods to her family. The foods we found in her refrigerator, which were neither fresh nor natural, contradicted her statements.

Consumer semiotics accounts for the signifying practices consumers perform to make sense of an event, form an identity, organize into groups, and move through public space. It accounts for the cultural codes that shape thoughts and meanings in a given market as well as the various ways consumers interpret these codes in daily life. Semiotics also accounts for the malleability of codes which enable consumers to twist and bend them in the course of participating in language and culture.

The Codes We Live By

The mind creates meanings through a sorting process that articulates sensory perceptions such as sounds, visuals, and other experiences into binary contrasts, such as loud vs. quiet, forward vs. backward, or large vs. small. The dialectical structure of language and thought in Western culture (Saussure 2011 [1916]) and (Jakobson 1990 [1956]) accounts for the binary structure of the semiotic codes that structure meaning production in speech, social rituals, and other forms of social behavior. Consumers acquire these codes through prolonged participation in a given community. Codes are steeped in culture and account for distinctions between language, cultural rituals, and symbolic representations from one community to the next.

Codes not only structure language but also shape our interpretation of things like traffic signs, our participation in social groups, our genealogical ties, and our performance of daily rituals, such as dining out. The binary analysis forms a cornerstone of semiotics-based consumer research because it defines and refines our understanding of the deep-seated beliefs and norms driving consumer behavior, from syntax to the Rules of the Road. Though the binary analysis is the first stage in the semiotic research process, the following stages take into account the ways consumers and consumer cohorts perform and personalize these norms in day to day life.

In brief, codes are binary structures that produce meaning by leveraging the difference and contrast between elements of cultural discourse. The binary approach to meaning production is deeply rooted in the metaphysical orientation of Western thought. Take gender, for instance. Like all cultural categories, gender difference is not a simple function of nature but a cultural construct—a binary system that structures social life in terms of an underlying contrast between the notions of /femininity/and/masculinity/. The binary principle prevails even when we deconstruct the male/female binary into more nuanced interpretations of gender such as queer or homosexual because we are hard-wired to define phenomena by means of contrast with something else. Furthermore, consumers express gender distinctions through cultural norms such as fashion, stereotypical behaviors, and social roles.

Highly formal cultures have more rigid rules about gendered behavior than informal ones. In post-WWII America, the dress code reinforced the culture's more rigid interpretation of the male/female binary. Men "wore the pants"—in more ways than one—and women wore skirts. The housewives in my family even wore dresses, stockings, and high heels to perform household chores, a practice that was reinforced in advertising for household appliances such as vacuum cleaners or refrigerators. The model's dress conforms to a cultural ideal that positions women in terms of her physical beauty and fashion sense.

Exercise 4.1 Consumer Observations—The Dress Code

Since codes structure the norms that organize social behaviors, from language to shopping, the only way to expose the codes structuring meaning in consumer research is to trace recurring patterns of meaning over multiple groups or interviews. Although the single interview can yield information about the motivations of a single individual, it is only when those findings recur across multiple interviews that they indicate the presence of a code.

In the following exercise, students decode the social and personal meanings of dress choices of the class by finding a consistent style or styles that prevail across all students. The exercise aims to sharpen awareness of the codes structuring dress choices, to organize findings into codes, and summarize the general conclusions of the findings. This exercise could be applied to a variety of code systems, at the discretion of the instructor.

The work begins within each team with simple descriptions of all team members. This initial analysis enables the researcher to define a few variables related to dress that the researcher will use to organize the analysis of dress in the broader population of the class.

Steps

- Working as a team, students do an accounting of the dress styles of team members. This initial analysis helps to establish the variables.
- Begin by describing in detail the dress choices of each member of the team.
- Create a rudimentary table for classifying your observations into cultural binaries (Figure 4.1).
- Apply the binary analysis to the dress codes that you observe in the rest of the class.
- Define the overall dressing trends in the class (i.e., formal/informal), which ones are more/less popular, and how the dress codes represent the social conventions and mood that prevail in the classroom. Is the general dress code casual or corporate? Do certain individuals stand out for their fashion tastes? How about color codes—do they run to bland or bold? and so on.

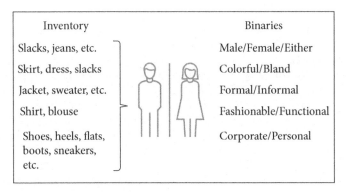

Figure 4.1. Decoding consumer dress

Key Learnings from Exercise 4.1

Exercise 4.I challenged students to sharpen their skills of observation by noting details about the dress of their classmates. They then practiced analyzing dress as an expression of cultural codes rather than personal taste alone. They performed a rudimentary binary analysis of the cultural dimensions of dress in the classroom.

Code and Performance

Product categories are cultural systems inasmuch as they represent the set of values, meanings, and benefits that consumers associate with a specific group of products. Product categories such as Consumer Packaged Goods (CPG), Automotive, or Consumer Technology, are each structured by a system of binary codes related to rational attributes like Price (i.e., Premium/Mass), Value Proposition (i.e., Processed/Natural), or Demographics such as Age (Youth/Adult), Gender (Male/Female) or Region (East/West Coast, North/South, etc.).

The qualitative attributes consumers associate with specific brands further segment the product category. These attributes relate to the distinct tastes, preferences, and behaviors of their target market, as well as the emotional positioning of each brand related to things like esthetics, lifestyle, and symbolic "personality." The brand perceptions, shopping behaviors, and driving rituals of luxury brand drivers form a culture unto themselves. The brands that enjoy the greatest market share form a competitive set. For example, in the automotive market, BMW, Cadillac, Lexus, Volvo, Audi, and Mercedes form a competitive set of luxury automotive brands.

Although semiotic codes provide the broad guidelines for meaning production and other social behaviors, codes are highly malleable, and it's their flexibility that enables us to navigate the world. For example, Western societies have loosened the gender codes related to fashion. Women and men mix and match garments that were traditionally classified in terms of the male/female binary, such as pants or jewelry.

CODE	PERFORMANCE	
Masculine/Feminine	Masculine	Feminine
On/Off	On	Off
Go/Stop	Go	Stop
Hot/Cold	Hot	Cold

Figure 4.2. Text and performance

Throughout the day, consumers "perform" cultural norms to meet their needs. From the Hot/Cold functions on the water faucet to the On/Off functions on the laptop, consumers adapt these binary codes to their tastes or to the occasion in order to make sense of a situation, organize their social lives, or accomplish a task, such as eating a meal. Consumers adjust water temperature to the preferred temperature by manipulating the faucets. We can set our computers to the Sleep functions at various intervals rather than having to choose strictly between the On and Off settings. Although our shared response to a Stop sign at an intersection is critical for organizing traffic in a safe and orderly manner, drivers perform this ritual in a variety of ways: drivers may brake abruptly or gradually depending upon their brakes, their attentiveness, or their personal style (Figure 4.2).

These examples illustrate how consumers constantly manipulate cultural codes throughout the day in language and other semiotic behaviors. They play within the tensions between the rules that we live by and the specific demands of the moment.

Qualitative Research Basics

Semiotics-based consumer research is rooted in classic qualitative research methods. In the following section, I review the basics of qualitative research design and implementation and walk the reader through the application of learnings to the practice of qualitative research.

From Surveys to Qualitative Methods

Customer surveys have been used in marketing since the nineteenth century and are characterized by simple, closed-ended questioning such as short answer, either/or, and ranking tasks that do not invite discussion. Surveys yield quantitative data about measurable factors such as the demographic profiles of users, frequency of use, brand preferences, or product likability. The survey format limits access to subjective factors such as consumers' unmet needs, emotional states, or motivations for choosing one brand over another. The surveyor is skilled at asking questions in a dispassionate manner that avoids influencing consumers' responses.

However by the 1950s, growing competition in the marketplace revealed the limitations of survey data to differentiate brands from one another, anticipate emerging consumer needs, or develop relevant and appealing advertising. Even if a company has introduced an entirely new product or technology, such as microchips or fast food service, they will soon encounter competitors vying for a share of the new market. To stand apart from competitors, brands have to claim a distinctive cultural positioning in consumers' minds by offering intangible benefits, communicating them in protected, proprietary symbols and service experiences; hence, the importance of qualitative research for brand equity management.

As brand consultants such as Interbrand Group (2018) have shown, a company's ability to develop and maintain their brand's distinctive market positioning has measurable impact on the firm's financial performance. Using a mix of research methods, Interbrand actually ranks the financial performance of the top 100 global brands (2018) by quantifying the value of the brand's intangible assets.

On-line and Mobile Qualitative Research

In addition to the traditional modality of personal interactions, there exist a variety of options for conducting qualitative research virtually or through mobile applications. To simplify the discussion of semiotics and consumer behavior I will not include a detailed discussion of these modalities here. The principles discussed in this chapter have applications to a variety of research technologies. Furthermore, whether the study calls for longer or shorter-term engagements, or whether they make use of on-line panels or mobile apps, remote, technology-driven methods still require a moderator and some sort of design or interview protocol.

The more important decision relates to the rationale for choosing direct or remote research methods. Based on my own experience, the decision should not be based solely on budgetary concerns, in many cases the on-line panel costs the same as traditional research. On-line research is particularly useful for accessing respondents who are spread all over the map, or who are located in remote areas that would be difficult and costly to reach. If given the choice, I prefer direct contact, since the written panel limits data to language, and even video panels block access to the visuals beyond the frame of the lens.

To understand the full spectrum of options currently available, I recommend contacting an expert at a trusted research facility that specializes in remote research.

Focus Groups

Focus groups mark an early development in qualitative research. The focus group methodology was developed in the 1940s by Columbia University sociologist Robert K. Merton (1964). Merton discovered the importance of guided discussion with consumers for revealing the "why" and "how" beneath the facts reported on surveys. Focus groups brought consumers into the conference room to understand the motivations behind their statements, decisions, and opinions.

Focus groups are guided discussions moderated by a research expert. The standard size of the group runs between six and eight respondents recruited through a database and lasts between ninety minutes. In contrast to surveys, focus groups consist of open-ended questions that elicit discussion and spontaneous remarks from the group. In contrast to surveys, which rely on consumers' verbal replies and may even be administered over the phone, focus groups structure direct interactions between the group and the moderator. Although focus groups do not probe the depths of consumer emotion like in-depth interviews, they provide access to the meanings communicated in nonverbal messaging in consumers' facial expressions, gestures, and interactions with other group members.

As the term suggests, focus groups structure discussion along the lines of narrow topics related to practical things like product use, shopping behaviors, brand perceptions, or political opinions. For example, the sample Focus Group Guide in the Appendix assesses consumers' purchase experiences at the car dealership and gauges their opinions of a new software application for shopping, negotiating, and purchasing the vehicle on-line.

The tight format enables the moderator to deliver answers to key questions in the course of the research, so the report does not call so much for deep analysis as a simple summary or "top line report" of what was said in the groups. The best moderators are able to generate spontaneous discussion while steering discussion back to the key topics of inquiry. Clients can observe the groups from the back room through a two-way mirror, reinforcing the idea that focus group moderation resembles a performance in front of an audience.

From my experience, clients often expect to find answers to their questions by the time they leave the focus group facility. The semiotic researcher must manage the client's expectations because the full benefits of semiotics-based research are not necessarily observable from the back room. These insights are often derived from the analysis phase of research and the semiotician's ability to expose "the meanings beneath the meanings" (Floch 2001 [1990]) of consumer statements.

Due to their limited scope, focus groups are not the methodology of choice for the semiotician seeking to broaden the semantic repertoire of brand associations. One can boost the creative potential of groups by incorporating projective tasks, such as an image sort, into the design. For instance, to prepare for the group, respondents may be required to bring from home an image from a magazine that reminds them about the way they feel at the car dealership. The exercise breaks the ice by enlisting consumers' anecdotes about their experiences shopping and purchasing a new vehicle. I discuss projective exercise in more detail later in this chapter.

I usually turn to focus groups to supplement findings from text-based semiotic studies, whose broad lens on mass market communications overlooks the effects of things like regional and ethnic difference and consumer creativity on brand perceptions. For example, our study of branding for paper diapers (Oswald 2012, Ch. 1) found that Pampers brand led the category with its ownership of the Good Mother myth. The P&G brand seemed impervious to competition, since competitors would either have to do the "Good Mother" better than Pampers or end up in the unfortunate position of the "Bad Mother." Through a semiotic analysis, we deconstructed the Good Mother/Bad Mother binary and identified a new cultural space defined by Real Mothers who were "good" but not perfect. We followed up with focus groups in order to gain insights about the ways real mothers handle the fun and foibles of baby care. By means of individual anecdotes, shared laughter, and creative exercises, the women knocked Mom off the pedestal, infused her with love, and used humor to forgive her imperfections. Drawing from these insights, the client positioned its diaper brand to real moms and imbued their creative strategy with humor.

The In-Depth Interview

In contrast with focus groups, the in-depth interview, or IDI, is more exploratory by nature, tapping into the emotional states, moods, and motivations that shape consumers' market behaviors. While the individual interview has been in use for over a century to form opinions about consumers, patients, or business personnel, it has evolved in the 1960s in response to the growing interest of social scientists and market researchers in consumer psychology. The interview guide is designed to gain insights related to the emotional states, motivations, attitudes, and experiences of respondents to a research question. The interviewer moderates the flow of this exchange in order to keep the respondent on track to meet the overall research objectives.

As demonstrated in the Interview Guide in the Appendix, IDI's include closed and open-ended questions that enable the moderator to weave consumer spontaneity and emotional response into the key marketing objectives of the study. If management wants to understand the mood states of consumers in response to a diet and fitness program, the interview guide will include questioning related to respondents' health, diet and fitness routines, and their general attitudes toward diet and exercise. The moderator may employ projective exercises such as picture sorts, storytelling, or sentence completion, to probe more deeply into emotional states and unconscious thoughts that respondents associate with diet and fitness. They may focus on body image issues or emotional triggers that either encourage or discourage the respondents' commitment to these activities.

The Reliability Factor

Although it would appear that the subjective nature of qualitative insights would not lend them to generalization about a population or market, in fact if respondents have been carefully screened according to project specifications, there is a remarkable degree of commonality among consumers' responses across multiple interviews and markets. When we interviewed chronic pain patients in three markets, respondents were recruited from the telephone book to avoid bias. Nonetheless most of them even chose the same images from a picture sort exercise to describe their pain experiences.

A Note on Consumer Recruitment

Clients often determine recruitment specifications based upon findings from prior research, including large segmentation studies and on-going nationwide consumer diaries. For the recruiter this means passing all potential respondents through an attitudinal algorithm that screens out respondents that do not correlate with prior research. My experience has shown that these kinds of screening specifications greatly increase if not interfere with the recruitment process because the prior studies are imprecise or inaccurate.

For example, to recruit respondents for a large, multi-market study of upper-middle class drivers for a $60,000.00 SUV, a large automotive company included in the screener a segmentation algorithm that asked if the buyer sought vehicles that "made them look like a working-class person." To pass the algorithm and participate in the study, respondents had to answer, "Yes"—they wanted the vehicle to look "working class." For the most part, consumers naturally answered "No." The question proved a barrier to completing the recruitment due to a flaw in the segmentation study.

On another occasion, prior to the widespread use of digital imaging, an international photo imaging company was recruiting for a multi-market ethnography to gain insights into the African American market. Management used findings from a prior, nation-wide diary study of film use among African Americans. The diary study found that African Americans used less than one roll of film per year. Therefore management specified that students in the new study had to use less than one roll of film. Once again, the specification "less than one roll" proved a barrier to recruitment in all three markets. There was clearly a reporting error in the diary study.

In order to complete both of these studies, the moderator had to challenge management's use of prior research to screen respondents. In both cases, the research exceeded management's expectations for deep cultural insights about their consumers. These examples illustrate that the best qualitative moderators have the confidence gained through experience to take control of the research process in order to meet client objectives.

Semiotics in the Qualitative Research Toolkit

An important measure of brand strength consists of the scope and depth of the meanings consumers associate with the brand name and logo (Aaker 1991). Strategic qualitative research not only appraises current brand strength but also plays a role in growing the brand's value by boosting the scope and depth of a brand's associations. Marketers draw from these insights to develop marketing campaigns and products and new service experiences.

Theoretical Grounding

Since competitors are all seeking the same kinds of information about the market-place, the choice of research is particularly important. The strength of any given research approach or moderator is judged by its ability to expose hidden truths, make new sense of the obvious, spot emerging trends on the horizon, and sense shifts in consumer culture. Semiotics-based consumer research is geared to this type of investigation because semiotic methods are designed to look beyond the meaning of individual phenomena to the underlying codes responsible for meaning production.

Furthermore, by bringing semiotic theory to bear on the analysis of data, in my own work I consistently solve problems that the client could not solve using other methodologies. I often find myself referring mentally to a theory or academic source to shed light on research questions I encounter in the field. For example, I was conducting in-depth interviews with two-dozen 21 to 35-year-old SUV drivers and binary contrast began to emerge between drivers who personified their vehicles as extensions of themselves and drivers who did not. While Group A personified their vehicles as "a reliable friend," "a member of the family," or even "my husband," Group B referred to the personal benefits they received from the vehicle's functions and technologies.

In other words, both groups of consumers personalized the vehicle, but Group A used metaphor, a rhetorical device that associates two disparate terms on the basis of similarity [vehicle = friend], while Group B used metonymy, a rhetorical device that associates two terms on the basis of cause to effect [vehicle function > my happiness]. Regardless of their brand, drivers in Group A filtered their vehicle perceptions through the lens of creativity and emotion; those in Group B filtered their perceptions through the lens of rationality and logic.

Since this binary emerged on a regular basis from one interview to the next, it triggered a reflection on a seminal qualitative study by Jakobson (1990 [1956]), which suggests that populations divide along the lines of their personal preferences for using either metaphorical or metonymical associations in thinking about things. In interviews with aphasic patients at various stages of language loss, Jakobson asked them to make associations with a table knife. Group A associated the table knife with similar instruments, including a dagger and a fountain pen, which shared common formal attributes. Group B associated the table knife with other table utensils in a contiguous set, including a fork and a spoon (Figure 4.3).

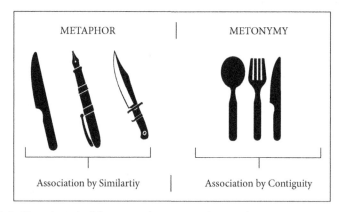

Figure 4.3. Two rhetorical figures and two mental operations

Jakobson's theory prompted me to probe for evidence that the metaphor/metonymy binary extended to other driver behaviors. I discovered that it extended to their brand perceptions, their evaluation of advertising, their experiences with the car dealer, and even purchasing after-market accessories. We recommended a two-pronged approach to marketing and sales of the client's SUV brand in order to embrace the worldviews of both groups of drivers. In other words, my training in semiotic theory provided a framework for moving the research forward, developing sharper insights, and translating them to actionable recommendations for marketing.

Tools and Techniques

This section reviews some of the techniques semiotics-based researchers employ to expand the scope of consumer insights, verify the truth of consumer statements, and tap into their creative imaginations.

Narrative Analysis

Although focus groups and in-depth interviews both provide access to the meanings communicated in facial expressions, gestures, and social interactions with the moderator and other group members, for the most part the insights we gain from groups and in-depth interviews derive from consumer narratives rather than the researcher's direct observation. Narrative makes sense of the random events of daily life by weaving them into a sequence held together by temporal, logical, and emotional connections. By means of narrative, consumers bring coherence, linearity, and logic to market behaviors such as choosing a brand, responding to a promotion, returning a purchase, or shopping for a car.

The researcher trained in semiotics examines not only what respondents report but also the manner in which they relate one event to the next, justify a purchase or return, or explain the social dynamic behind a shopping event or the thinking leading up to a diet slip-up. They notice if respondents adapt the roles of people they describe in their narrative, recreating the emotional tenor of a social interaction by imitating the other's style, or if they simply report an event with cool detachment. These nonverbal messages often create a subtext to consumer statements that go to the heart of consumer attitudes and motivations. The best moderators recognize the subtext and probe respondents until they tease it out and bring it to the surface. They may use this awareness to form questioning for other interviews or groups in the project.

Consumer Diaries

Since the moderator cannot verify through direct observation the veracity of the respondent's narrative or the accuracy of their memories, they may ask respondents to note daily behaviors related to the research in a journal or a daily diary. The exercise proves that consumers do not always say what they mean or mean what they say, not so much because they are intrinsically dishonest, but because mental obstacles such as poor memory, wishful thinking, shame, or denial may filter out unpleasant truths about themselves, such as the number of times they slipped up on their diet. The daily diary is a very common component of fitness programs because they focus consumers on the here and now of their behaviors rather than relying on memory. The skilled moderator will identify any disparities between consumer statements and the daily diary and probe for emotional or social factors that motivated these differences.

Moderating Strategies

Consumers employ narrative to give form and meaning to their experiences in the marketplace. However respondents do not entirely control the narrative. The moderator is responsible for eliciting associations and consumer stories to build a data set for semiotic analysis. The moderator plays a role in moving the consumer narrative forward by steering the discussion, probing for deeper insights, and highlighting tensions and contrasts between consumer speech, the narrative subtext, and any journal entries respondents may have prepared prior to the meeting. Laddering (Reynolds and Gutman 1988) is a moderating technique for moving the tone of the narrative from the rational realm of product attributes to the psychological realm of consumer motives. The moderator can modify the laddering technique by following a thread of free associations from rational levels of the discussion, such as shopping experiences, to esthetic and emotional experiences. At each step of the discussion, the moderator not only exposes increasingly subjective motives for consumers' brand choices but also expands scope of brand associations. The approach produces abundant semiotic data for new product development, brand positioning, and advertising.

For example, in developing safety features for a new model, an automotive manufacturer wanted to understand the meaning of safety and security for women drivers. Through laddering and free association, the moderator revealed that state-of-the-art technologies were not top of mind for consumers who had safety concerns that struck closer to their hearts and minds.

Example

INTERVIEWER: What is the most important feature you look for in a new vehicle?
R: Safety
INTERVIEWER: Have you noticed the state of the art safety features of the new Brand X?
R: Yes, but I am leaning toward Brand B.
INTERVIEWER: Why?
R: Brand B has a storage compartment under the front seat for my purse.
INTERVIEWER: Oh?
R: Yes. It's the best thing for staying safe.
INTERVIEWER: Really?
R. Last year I stopped for a red light and someone broke the front window and stole my purse. It was on the seat next to me.
INTERVIEWER: Tell me about it.
R: They got away with my purse.
INTERVIEWER: How did that feel?

R: I was terrified. Plus I had to fill out a police report, get the window repaired and deal with the insurance company.

INTERVIEWER: So when you think of security, you would say . . . .

R: Store your valuables in a secure place.

INTERVIEWER: Anything else?

R: Brand B has the storage space under the seat—they understand where I'm coming from. I can rely on them.

Although the manufacturer may think of vehicle security in terms of advanced automotive technologies, this driver's safety concerns relate to a personal trauma that she believes could have been avoided had she stored her purse rather than leaving it on the front seat. Furthermore, the woman feels a special bond with Brand B because she can rely on them.

The example points to the advantages of qualitative research for understanding consumers' deep-seated emotional motives for choosing on brand over another. Furthermore, by means of laddering and free association we found that the need for security translates into a need for a brand that consumers trust. Furthermore, this woman's seemingly random and very personal response to the safety question was not isolated but recurred in various forms with enough frequency to warrant further investigation, such as running the question by a much larger sample in a consumer survey.

Exercise 4.2 Moderating

Working in pairs, students practice laddering and free association techniques by means of a short interview exercise. Students can work with a topic suggested by the instructor or choose from the topics below. For the exercise to work, you must use indirect questioning. For example, raise the topic and wait for a reply, then probe the respondent until they lead you to the emotional motivations behind a behavior.

1. Find out the emotional basis for choosing one brand of pet food over another.
2. Identify social or emotional barriers to accepting a new office procedure.
3. The client wants to understand what motivates men to seek spa and beauty treatments.
4. A car dealership wants to understand how to sell to female customers.
5. You want to know why patients are reluctant to try a new pain relief medication.

Projective Techniques

Brands grow value in direct relation to (1) their relevance for consumers and (2) the depth and scope of the meanings that consumers associate with the brand name and logo, and (3) their resonance with consumers' deep-seated emotional motivations for making marketplace decisions. While direct questioning can elicit information about superficial attributes such as consumer demographics, lifestyle, and shopping behavior, projective techniques prompt consumers to reveal the deeper motivations for their lifestyle and marketplace choices. They are particularly useful for moving the in-depth interview to the discussion of feelings and unconscious ideation.

Projective techniques tap into the thoughts and emotions that hover beneath the surface of conscious thought by means of indirect methods such as free association. Rather than asking respondents head-on about their feelings, exercises disrupt the grip of the rational mind on consumers' thoughts, giving free reign to consumer creativity and emotion-laden ideation buried deep in the unconscious. Exercises such as free association and sentence completion resemble games. Since there is no "right" answer, projective exercises put the respondent at ease and inspire a flow of insights that elude direct questioning.

For example, a few years ago I was called in to help a large ad agency rescue a large qualitative study on the attitudes of 18- to 24-year-old men toward fashion brands. After conducting fifty in-depth interviews nationwide, the researcher determined that "young men just couldn't open up about fashion" because his questions were met with short, perfunctory replies. A cursory review of the discussion guide revealed that the direct interview style, not the young men, was the culprit. The questioning overlooked the difficulty young men encounter when asked to reveal their emotions and persona opinions, especially on topics related to personal fashion. When asked, "What do you feel about this tie?" or "Why do you like this brand?" they froze up like a deer in the headlights.

I redesigned the questionnaire for a new group of respondents using indirect questioning such as metaphor elicitation and storytelling. The new approach elicited rich information about the unmet needs of these respondents to gain confidence, belonging, and status from their fashion choices. When asked to choose their favorite outfit from a deck of men's fashion ads, then probing them about how they would they feel or others would perceive them in the outfit, or to describe an occasion when they would wear it, the new approach encouraged friendly discussion.

Rather than asking respondents to *describe* their feelings, indirect techniques *trigger* emotional responses, softened respondent's defenses and opened a window for the moderator to gently probe for more in-depth information.

Free Association

Projective exercises encourage respondents to generate free associations with a term in order to relax the grip of mental resistance and logic. Free association is a psychoanalytic technique developed by Freud ((1965 [1899]) to make sense of his patients' dreams. He observed that the mind disguises uncomfortable thoughts and forbidden feelings behind benign and apparently meaningless symbols. To explain a woman's recurring dream of being attacked by a snake, for instance, Freud might lead the patient along a chain of rhetorical associations from the idea of snakes to a buried sexual trauma. He revealed how she projected her negative emotions into the snake symbolism. He applied the same process to unravel the meaning of neurotic symptoms such as phobias and obsessions.

To practice projective techniques in consumer research, the moderator prompts the respondent to say the first thing that comes to mind in relation to stimulus such as a brand logo or the name of the product category. Let's say that the moderator asks, "What's the first word that comes to mind when you think of 'ride sharing'?" and the consumer responds, "convenience." Using laddering techniques, the moderator then prompts the respondent to think of an association for "convenience," and so on and so forth until they have nothing more to say. The exchange both expands the meaning of "ride share" and also sheds light on emotional drivers behind consumers' use of ride share services.

Sentence Completion
As the term suggests, sentence completion prompts respondents to simply fill in a missing word in a sentence provided by the interviewer. It is a very simple exercise that can be used to prepare respondents to participate in more complex exercises.

The Picture Sort
In a brand positioning study, the researcher is called upon to differentiate a set of competitors based upon the intangible benefits consumers associate with each brand. The exercise prompts respondents to select several pictures from a deck and match them with each brand based upon their emotional or esthetic resonance. True to the maxim that "a picture is worth a thousand words," the picture sort exercise stimulates the respondent's ability to free associate on the topic by expanding the range of their imaginations beyond the topic at hand. The researcher prepares a deck of pictures in advance to elicit from respondents a free flow of associations related to the emotional, social, or lifestyle attributes they associate with a given brand. I usually select two-dozen pictures from the Internet and have them printed on card stock. I include categories such as animals, landscapes, faces because they elicit comments about the mood state, relationship, and emotional drivers that respondents associate with the topic.

To begin, the interviewer asks the respondent to select four to five pictures from the deck that make them think of a specific brand. They continue the same process with each brand in the competitive set and then compare and contrast the "personalities" and other attributes of all the brands. The success of this exercise depends greatly upon the interviewer's ability to probe respondents to elaborate upon the reasons they selected each image. If they match a truck with a horse, for example, the interviewer probes the respondent to elaborate upon the connections between the two terms.

Storytelling

Storytelling prompts the respondent to complete a scenario prepared in advance by the interviewer. I use storytelling to amplify the personal and emotional attributes that consumers associate with brands. Since it requires more time and brand clarity than the other exercises, I usually place it toward the end of a series of projective exercises. The respondent now has a good idea of the qualitative distinctions between brands in a competitive set and can better imagine the brand as a character in a story.

I may ask the respondent to imagine all five brands in a group as individuals who have been shipwrecked and land on a deserted island in the Pacific. One by one I ask them to describe each brand as a character in the story. Then I ask them to imagine the roles each brand takes in order to survive and ultimately get off the island. Their stories provide detailed insights about things like brand reliability, originality, intelligence, and empathy.

Team Projects

The team projects enable the students to practice the rudiments of semiotics-based qualitative research. They pick a topic, decide and justify use of either focus groups or IDIs, define the respondent profile, design the questionnaire, and form a focus group from members of the team, and moderate a short discussion.

Alternative 1: Focus Groups

Using the sample Focus Group Guide in the appendix to this chapter, design a thirty-minute discussion guide that explores a topic related to the brand of your choice.

Appendix 1: Focus Group Interview Guide

Alternative 2: In-Depth Interview

Using the sample In-Depth Interview Guide in the appendix to this chapter, design a thirty-minute discussion guide that explores a topic related to the brand of your choice. Each member of the team will interview one person from the team or outside of the class who matches the study specifications.

Appendix 2: In-Depth Interview Guide

Case Examples

1. The project evaluates the importance of branding in the personal computer market. The interviewer presents respondents with an alternative between the lower-priced Dell and one of the more the expensive iconic brands such as the Samsung or Apple. Gauge the value consumers place on iconic branding in this category. Assume that all brands offer the same capabilities.
2. The client wants to gauge consumer preferences for either the lower-priced salads at McDonald's or the higher-priced salads with *exactly* the same ingredients at a new quick-serve chain called "Fresh."
3. Management wants to understand the social and emotional motivations behind the changing consumer preferences in on-line personal messaging. Specifically, why consumers have migrated from email and Facebook to newer media such as Instagram and WhatsApp.
4. The management of a surgical practice of highly reputable physicians wanted to understand why some patients decided to go elsewhere for their procedures after their initial visit to the office. Probe for things related to the facility, the offices, the staff, and the physician to identify any emotional barriers that discouraged a repeat visit.
5. City planners want feedback from residents regarding a developer's proposal to build a strip mall next to the high school.

Instructions

Working in teams, students will create the overall design of the study, including a clear statement of the research objectives, the consumer group targeted by the product, the recruitment screener, and the questionnaire guide. The guide should include laddering and at least one projective exercise. Each team selects a moderator to conduct the group. Other team members play the role of the consumers targeted by the study. Teams can also decide to conduct the research with members of another group.

Scope and Objectives

Purpose
Identify intangible benefits that motivate consumers to make brand choices in the category of your choosing.

Timing
Each student conducts a thirty-minute focus group or interview.

Data Set

Outline the demographic and qualitative specifications you would use to recruit respondents for this study.

Design

Design the questionnaire to follow a sequence from more superficial to more emotional questioning. Include laddering and at least one more projective task in your study.

Analysis and Report Production

Unlike quantitative research, which reports the results of statistical data in graphs and numerical charts, qualitative reporting summarizes key insights related to consumer motives, perceptions, and attitudes in plain language supported by visuals and consumers' exact words. The report includes:

- An Executive Report of key findings,
- A detailed Findings Summary organized along the lines of topics on the research guide.
- A list of Actionable Recommendations based on the findings.

The report is usually delivered in Power Point and follows the order of the topics listed in the discussion guide. Visuals from the projective tasks as well as grids that map the relationships among competitors on a binary grid support the verbal findings (Figure 4.4).

The Binary Analysis
Define the main cultural binaries that shape the meaning and value of brands in the product category. For example, if it's trucks, the categories might include Power, Styling, Handling, Comfort, Payload, and Price. Within the data set, consumers may be divided along the lines of their priorities, some putting their money on Power and Performance, and others selecting brands known for Handling and Styling. Consumer preferences usually align with the brand attributes they associate with one brand or another.

Brand Mapping
Referring to the binary grids used in Chapter 2, please create at least two double-axis grids based upon the key binaries you identified in the analysis. The example

in Figure 4.4 maps the competitive positionings of truck brands according to consumer preferences for some combination of the brand attributes of Power, Handling, Payload, and Comfort. Map the various brands you studied in the quadrant that best describes their positioning.

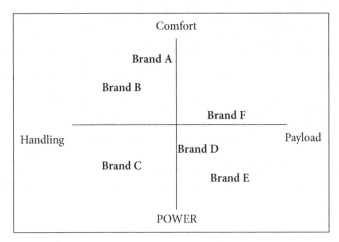

Figure 4.4. Brand mapping in the truck category

In the interest of budget concerns, clients may opt to trim the live presentations from the project due to budget constraints, the live presentation to the brand team is critical for implementing findings that otherwise may be buried on the client's desk. The live presentation enables the researcher to report details that cannot be captured in PowerPoint bullets, stimulate discussion within the team, and generate ideation for putting into action the project recommendations.

Concluding Remarks

The objective of qualitative research is to deliver depth of insights rather than calculate responses from a list of close-ended questions. By noting the drift of consumer attitudes in one direction or the other, the researcher generates deep insights motivations, values, and other intangible factors on consumer behavior. These kinds of insights usually elude quantitative surveys because they need to be teased out by means of specialized interview methodologies.

In my experience working in advertising research, clients may simply draw from these insights to create stories and themes for a specific ad campaign or for developing overall creative strategy. However, when working with brand managers to build long-term strategy for things like brand positioning, new product development, or new market development, the client will most likely distill qualitative insights into a survey questionnaire to gauge more precisely the generalizability of qualitative findings for the general population.

Appendices

Focus Group Guide

1.a. A BASIC PRE-GROUP RESCREEN **[Respondents complete prior to the interview]**			
VEHICLE PURCHASE STUDY			
Date	Location	Participant Name	Group # and Time

DEMOGRAPHIC SURVEY [Respondents complete prior to the group.]

Please answer the following questions in the spaces provided or check the most appropriate answer.

1. Age. _____

2. Gender. ☐ Male ☐ Female

3. Family Status. ☐ Married ☐ Single

4. Children. ☐ No ☐ Yes (How Many?)

5. How would you describe your job?
   ☐ Blue Collar
   ☐ Clerical
   ☐ Middle Management
   ☐ Education
   ☐ Professional
   ☐ IT
   ☐ Medical, other than physician
   ☐ Homemaker
   ☐ Other _____

6. Are you the primary decision maker in vehicle purchases? ☐ Yes ☐ No (Disqualify)

7. How many vehicles do you own? _____

8. What is the Brand and Year of your new vehicle? _____ (Prior to 2013, Disqualify)

9. When did you purchase your last vehicle? _____

10. Describe the primary use of the vehicle (check one, several, or all).
    ☐ Commute to Work
    ☐ Work or Business
    ☐ Family Activities
    ☐ Leisure
    ☐ All of the above

11. Any additional questions as per the objectives.

1.b. A BASIC FOCUS GROUP GUIDE			
VEHICLE PURCHASE STUDY			
Date	Location	Participant Name	Group # and Time

Facilitator's welcome, introduction, and instructions to respondents.

Welcome and thank you for taking part in this focus group. Your point of view is very important for this research and we appreciate that you took time out of your busy day to participate.

Please hand in the short survey you completed in the waiting room.

Introduction: This discussion is designed to assess your behaviors, thoughts, and feelings as they relate to your recent purchase of a vehicle.

Anonymity: The discussion will be taped for research purposes but the identities of individual participants will remain anonymous. When the research is completed, the discussion tapes will be destroyed. To protect the privacy of individual members, please refrain from discussing what is said in the group when you leave here.

Sometimes our research partners will observe the group through the two-way mirror at the end of the room.

Ground rules

- The most important rule is that only one person speaks at a time.
- There are no right or wrong answers.
- You do not have to speak in any particular order.
- You do not have to respond to all the questions, but do not hesitate to participate when you want.
- You do not have to agree with the views of other people in the group.
- Does anyone have any questions?
- OK, let's begin.

Warm up: First, I'd like everyone to introduce themselves with the brand name of their vehicles as we go around the table.

Introductory question

I'm going to give you a few minutes to think about the last time you bought a new vehicle. Thinking about the decision to buy, the brand choice, the sales process, and so on—what stands out the most and why?

(Wait 4 minutes.)

Would someone like to begin?

Does anyone wish to respond to that?

Etc. Involve the group in the discussion. Try to probe for one aspect of the purchase process at a time (i.e., the decision to buy, the brand choice, the sales process, etc.).

Guiding questions

- Purchase Decision
  - Why did you decide to buy a new car?
  - Who was involved?
  - Were you the primary decision-maker?
- Brand Choice
  - Loyalty?
  - Peer influence?
  - Advertising or other media?
  - A promotional sale?
  - Did you switch brands? Why?
  - Are you happy with your choice?
- Sales Process
  - How did you prepare your search?
    - On-line research (consumer reports, etc.)
    - Word-of-mouth—friends and family
    - Other
  - How many dealerships did you visit?
  - Describe good and not so good experiences.
  - How did you decide to purchase with one dealership?
  - Did someone accompany you to the dealership?
  - Describe the sales experience.
    - Introduction to the salesperson
    - The sales approach
    - Did you test drive the vehicle?
    - Did you negotiate price?
    - How did you feel in the process?
    - Did you make any compromises on what you originally wanted in a vehicle?
  - How could the experience have been improved?
    - Communication
    - Personality
    - Convenience
    - Comfort
    - Responsiveness (respect, pressure, timing, etc.)
  - Did the sales experience motivate you to switch brands?
- Post-Purchase Experience
  - Did you second-guess your decision?
  - Did you need to contact the dealership again after the purchase?
    - If so, describe the experience.
    - Evaluate the post-purchase service.
  - Would you recommend the dealership to a friend or family member?
    - Why/Why not?
- Summary
  - What are the main advantages of a good sales experience?

- What are the main barriers to a good sales experience?
- Assessment of the Client's New Service

Our client has developed an online purchase software to make the car sales process easier. It invites customers to check off their vehicle preferences from a list of options. The software would then calculate the total price as well as provide alternative vehicle options that would lower the price.

- Have you tried this process before?
- Pros and cons about this sales approach?
- Would you try it?
- What would you include in the new software to make it work for you?
- Any other comments?

Conclusion

- Thank you for participating. This has been a very successful discussion and your opinions will be a valuable asset to the study. I would like to remind you that your comments will remain anonymous. Please refrain from discussing the comments of other members of the group when you leave here.
- Please let the receptionist know if you would like to register any praise or complaints about today's discussion.
- Please pick up your incentive checks at the front desk.
- Good day/evening.

END AND GOODBYE
C DISCUSSION GUIDE

A Basic In-Depth Interview Guide

2.a. A BASIC PRE-INTERVIEW SURVEY [Respondents complete prior to the interview]				
Trucks: A Strategic Exploratory Study				
Objectives: The purpose of this study is to identify unmet needs in the truck market by understanding the consumer culture of truck owners, including their lifestyles, values, and brand perceptions.				
Date	Location	Participant Name	Truck Brand	IDI # and Time

DEMOGRAPHIC SURVEY [Respondents complete prior to the interview.]

Please answer the following questions in the spaces provided or check the most appropriate answer.

1. Age. _____

2. Gender. ☐ Male☐ Female

3. Family Status. ☐ Married ☐ Single

4. Children. ☐ No ☐ Yes (How Many?)

5. How would you describe your job?
   ☐ Blue Collar
   ☐ Clerical
   ☐ Middle Management
   ☐ Education
   ☐ Professional
   ☐ IT
   ☐ Medical, other than physician
   ☐ Homemaker
   ☐ Other _____

6. Are you the primary decision maker in vehicle purchases? ☐ Yes ☐ No (Disqualify)

7. How many vehicles do you own? _____

8. What is the Brand and Year of your new vehicle? _____ (Prior to 2013, Disqualify)

9. When did you purchase your last vehicle? _____

10. Describe the primary use of the vehicle (check one, several, or all).
    ☐ Commute to Work
    ☐ Work or Business
    ☐ Family Activities
    ☐ Leisure
    ☐ All of the above

11. Any additional questions as per the objectives.

2.b. A BASIC IN-DEPTH INTERVIEW GUIDE				
Trucks: A Strategic Exploratory Study				
Objectives: The purpose of this study is to identify unmet needs in the truck market by understanding the consumer culture of truck owners, including their lifestyles, values, and brand perceptions.				
Date	Location	Participant Name	Truck Brand	IDI # and Time

Facilitator's welcome, introduction, and instructions to participants

Welcome and thank you for taking part in this study. Your point of view is very important for this research and we appreciate your willingness to participate.

Before we get started, please hand in the short survey you completed in the waiting room.

Anonymity: The interview will be taped for research purposes, but the identities of individual participants will remain anonymous. When the research is completed, the interview tapes will be destroyed. Please refrain from discussing what is said in the group when you leave here.

Sometimes our research partners will observe the interviews through the two-way mirror at the end of the room.

Introduction: I'm a researcher. I do not represent any truck company. I was hired to learn more about the people who drive trucks. I'll be asking you about your vehicle preferences and what went into your purchase decision. We will also discuss what makes you "tick" (i.e., values, lifestyles, and attitudes). Your views are very important to us, and I hope you will enjoy the process. The interview will last about 90 minutes. Do you have any questions?

[Note: Do not reveal the identity of the client's brand until the very end, if at all.]

[Note: Questions marked with a box ☐ involve projective tasks and call for special stimuli.]

Warm up

- [Name] please tell me how your day is going so far? (If it's early morning, you may ask "Do you have plans for this evening?")
- How did you get to the facility?
- Have you ever participated in a consumer interview before? [Probe about the experience.]
- Refer briefly to their answers on the written survey to re household composition, marital status, children, job and job satisfaction? [Probe re their brand, number of cars they own, their role in purchase decision, etc.]

Self and Lifestyle Topics

Personality
- What makes you happy?
- How do you balance social and alone time?
- What do you look for in others?
- Anything you want to avoid in life?
- How do others perceive you?

Leisure

- Activities
- With others or alone?
- Define a "get away"—[travel or local?]
- Does your truck fit into leisure experiences? Probe for frequency and the role of the truck in making the experience memorable.

Culture

- Do you celebrate Thanksgiving?
  ☐ No [Ask what they do on that day and skip to the next section.]
  ☐ Yes.
- Who is with you? [Probe number of guests; family, friends or both?]
- Describe the meal and any special family recipes.
- Describe any unique family traditions at Thanksgiving.

Media Use

- How much time to you spend on social media?
- What are your favorite networks?
- Any household rules regarding mobile phone use, etc.?
- In the truck, how important are the smart features in your truck?
- How often do you use the voice-prompted text technology in the truck?
- What sources do you use to find information about products such as trucks?
- Did advertising play a role in your current truck choice?
- Other

Car and Driver

- Tell me about the vehicles you own. [Probe for brand choices and loyalty, who drives which vehicles, etc.]
- Tell me about the companies that make those trucks [Probe for issues about country of origin, American-made, image, and reputation, etc.]
- Have you always driven a truck [Probe for first truck, family traditions, local truck culture, etc.]?

Shopping and Purchase

- Describe the shopping process for your current truck. [Probe for the decision to purchase a truck; brand preferences; the ease or difficulty of process, etc.]
- Discuss research process. [Internet, advertising, consumer reports, WOM, and loyalty, sales promotions, etc.]
- Any advertising that jumped out?
- Describe the sales experience. [Probe—who was with them, salesperson's style, negotiating the price, etc.]

- Describe the purchase decision [Probe for salesperson's role, the price, did they switch brands from their original choice, etc.]
- Describe the post-purchase experience [Probe re buyer's regret, customer service, after-market accessories, etc.]

The Driving Experience

- What's it like to drive your [brand]? [They bring in a picture that describes how they feel in the truck. Probe.]
- Tell me how it feels. [Probe for occasions, moods, and behaviors such as speeding.]
- Do you ever just take the truck out on the open road and drive for pleasure? [Probe. Do they turn off the cell phone, where do they go, is anyone with them, etc.?]
- Probe for handling. [Compare to Car and SUV.]
- Was there something about the [brand] engineering that motivated your choice?
- [Probe for smart technology needs and likes in addition to media.]

The Brand Experience

- ☐ Using the image that respondents brought in as a stimulus, ask respondents why the image reminded them of their truck, then probe for their top of mind comments about feelings and experiences they associate with their truck brand.

Moderator: Tell me why you associate this image with your truck.

- Tell me about your truck [Probe for the driving experience, relationship to the truck, the features they prefer, after-market accessories, etc.]
- Relate the discussion to the respondent's brand.
- What do people think about you when they see you in your truck?
- Anything about your truck that you couldn't do without?
- Anything you'd change about your truck?

Brand Perceptions

- ☐ Brand Ranking Exercise [10 minutes]. [Moderator gives the respondent a stack of cards each marked with the brand logo of key competitors in the truck market (i.e., Ford, Dodge, Chevy, Toyota, GMC, etc.).]
  - Introduction: We are changing gears and will walk through some exercises to gauge your brand perceptions. Looking at this deck of cards, do you recognize these logos?
  - Please rank the brands from High (5) to Low (1) according to their attributes.
  - [Go through each attribute separately until they complete the exercise.] Price, Reliability, Quality, Power, Styling
  - [Probe for short explanations.]
  - Would you like to add any other brand attributes that make a difference to you?

Brand Rank (High = 5)	Value	Reliability	Power	Styling
5				
4				
3				
2				
1				

☐ Picture Sort

The picture sort is a projective exercise structured to elicit respondents' top of mind emotional perceptions of brands in the competitive set.

- Drawing from a set of images prepared in advance by the moderator, the respondent matches 4-5 images with each brand in the competitive set that communicate that brand's experience, personality, and other intangible attributes.

- Each card is marked with a number to facilitate the reporting. Make note of the brand associations elicited by the exercise.

BRAND	Picture Numbers	Free associations
Ford		
Dodge		
Chevy		
Toyota		
GM		

☐ The Brand Persona

The questioning in this exercise directs the respondent to imagine each brand as a person, with a specific personality, job title, and fashion style.

Moderator:

- If (x brand) walked into the room, describe them as a person. Include gender, dress, job field and title,

- Next, imagine what they say when you ask them what they want.

- How do you relate to them?

BRAND	Gender	Job and title	Dress	Relationship to you
Ford				
Dodge				
Chevy				
Toyota				
GM				
other				

Final Questions

If the project calls for assessing consumers' responses to a product upgrade or advertising campaign, the moderator reveals here the client's brand name and briefly presents the innovation or advertisement and gauges top of mind responses.

Conclusion

- Thank you for participating in this study. This has been a very successful discussion and your opinions will be a valuable asset to the study. I would like to remind you that your comments will remain anonymous and to refrain from discussing the research when you leave the facility.
- Please let the receptionist know if you would like to register any praise or complaints about today's discussion.
- Please pick up your incentive checks at the front desk.

Good day/evening

END AND GOODBYE
C DISCUSSION GUIDE

Reading 4
*Marketing Semiotics

Christian Pinson
INSEAD
Fontainebleau, France

Semiosis, i.e. the process by which things and events come to be recognized as signs, is of particular relevance to marketing scholars and practitioners. The term marketing encompasses those activities involved in identifying the needs and wants of target markets and delivering the desired satisfactions more effectively and efficiently than competitors. Whereas early definitions of marketing focused on the performance of business activities that direct the flow of goods and services from producer to consumer or user, modern definitions stress that marketing activities involve interaction between seller and buyer and not a one-way flow from producer to consumer. As a consequence, the majority of marketers now view marketing in terms of exchange relationships. These relationships entail physical, financial, psychological, and social meanings. The broad objective of the semiotics of marketing is to make explicit the conditions under which these meanings are produced and apprehended.

Although semioticians have been actively working in the field of marketing since the 1960s, it is only recently that semiotic concepts and approaches have received international attention and recognition (for an overview, see Larsen et al. 1991; Mick, 1986, 1997; Umiker-Sebeok, 1988; Pinson, 1988). Diffusion of semiotic research in marketing has been made difficult by cultural and linguistic barriers as well as by divergence of thought. Whereas Anglo-Saxon researchers base their conceptual framework on Charles Peirce's ideas, Continental scholars tend to refer to the sign theory in Ferdinand de Saussure and to its interpretation by Hjelmslev.

The Symbolic Nature of Consumption

Consumer researchers and critics of marketing have long recognized the symbolic nature of consumption and the importance of studying the meanings attached by

* The first part of this reading has been republished from the author's previous chapter "Marketing Semiotics" in Pinson C. (1998) *Concise Encyclopedia of Pragmatics* (pp. 538–44). Published by Elsevier Science.

consumers to the various linguistic and non-linguistic signs available to them in the marketplace. In a seminal article, Sidney Levy (1959) suggested that products are "symbols for sale." What he meant was that products are often purchased and consumed for their symbolic as well as their pragmatic value.

Products (and services) serve three symbolic purposes. First, products allow consumers to create meaning for themselves, to symbolize to themselves who they are (self-concept theory). The self-concept comprises all of an individual's thoughts and feelings about himself/herself. It is an articulated schema (knowledge structure) that functionally controls how self-referent information is processed and structurally organized in memory. Second, products are signs that are essential for creating an identity, a status in the eyes of significant others. The study of status symbols goes back to Veblen's 1899 book *The Theory of the Leisure Class* in which he strongly criticized the "conspicuous consumption" and "conspicuous waste" that he saw around him. Consumers acquire very early the "language" of consumption symbols (see for example Holbrook and Hirschman 1993; Richins 1994; Wiley 1994). They learn to make inferences about others based on their choices of consumption objects and prefer products with images more similar to their self-concept and "ideal self-concept" (how the individual would ideally like to see himself/herself or be seen by others). Finally, products may be instrumental to the symbolic extension of the self. Extension of the self through the display of possessions corresponds to a long research traditional in anthropology and sociology and some of these works (e.g. Appadurai 1986; Dittmar 1992; McCracken 1988) have eventually led to the emergence of a new stream of consumer research (called "postmodernist"), which has been the subject of considerable controversy involving methodological and philosophical issues (see Belk 1995; Brown and Turley 1997; Featherstone 1991; Gottdiener 1995; Hirschman and Holbrook 1992; Sherry 1995).

Products are not the only consumption objects that consumers can use to create meanings. Brands too can be bought for their symbolic value and the affectional bonds they allow to develop. This explains that they are an increasingly concern for marketing researchers (e.g. Cross and Smith 1995; Fournier and Yao 1997) and applied semioticians (e.g. Semprini 1992). Noting that consumers often imbue brands with human personality traits, some authors (e.g. Aaker 1997; Fournier 1998; Heilbrunn 1998) have developed an anthropomorphic representation of the brand as a person.

Products as Language

Products are often perceived and described as being part of a family, constellation or system of complementary or substitutable objects (e.g. Baudrillard 1968) and can be conceptualized as a text, a discourse (see Semprini 1995). This suggests that products are not only signs but also form sign systems and that they are analyzable in terms of paradigmatic and syntagmatic relations.

While paradigmatic relationships refer to both similarities and differences between the products under consideration, syntagmatic relationships correspond to a formal proximity, a co-presence, of these products in the same purchase or usage strings. A purchase/usage "string" or "chain" consists of all the products bought/used by the consumer in the course of fulfilling his/her consumption goal. A product paradigm is a class of products that can occupy the same place in the syntagmatic string or, in other terms, a set of products, each of which is compatible with or substitutable for the other in the same usage context (e.g. toque—hood—bonnet). These products belong to the same associative set by virtue of the function they share.

Syntagmatic product relations refer to the permissible ways in which products succeed each other or combine together in a usage string. These products are brought together by virtue of syntactic rules as in clothing codes (e.g. shirt—blouse—jacket) or culinary codes (appetizer—entree—dessert). These rules reflect cultural or aesthetic conventions. They may also correspond to functional constraints (other than "part–whole" or metonymic relations) which suggest certain ordering as in the following syntagm: facial cleanser—pre-shave lotion—shaver—after-shave lotion.

While the paradigmatic dimension of the language of products has been well researched and is ingrained in almost any market-structure and product-image and positioning studies, the topic of product syntax and syntagmatic relations has received comparatively little attention from scholars and marketing practitioners. For the most part, marketing researchers have looked at usage situations to get a feel for which products are perceived to be similar, hence substitutable (paradigmatic relationships), and have largely ignored how product combinations arise (syntagmatic relationships). The objectives of syntagmatic research in marketing have been described (Kehret-Ward, 1988) as involving the following five steps: (a) itemize the string of complementary products required by consumers to achieve a particular consumption goal; (b) identify temporal and/or spatial combinatorial categories for objects which are functionally related to that goal; (c) identify principles for establishing prominence among the combinatorial categories; and (d) describe any systematic differences in the combinatorial rules observed by different user groups.

Critics (e.g. Nöth 1988) have objected that students of consumption syntax do not have firm bases on which to decide what constitutes an "acceptable" combination of products, and that the product combinations studied so far are rudimentary (e.g. additive) operations involving cultural or aesthetic rules and conventions which simply restrict the possibility of combining certain products for reasons which might be more pragmatic than syntactic in nature.

Meaning and Structure in Advertising

Advertising constitutes one of the major fields of applied semiotic research (see Aoki 1988; Appiano 1991; Bachand 1988; Henny 1987; IREP 1976, 1983; Peninou 1972; Perez Tomero 1982; Semprini 1996). Following Barthes (1964), one can distinguish three types of messages in an illustrated advertisement: the linguistic message (brand name, text...), the un-coded iconic message in which the "photographic" image denotes the material object advertised and finally the coded iconic message. Eco (1968) introduces three additional elements: the verbal and visual tropes, or rhetorical figures; the loci, or topoi, of argumentation and the enthymemes, i.e. the incomplete or apparent syllogisms used to persuade emotionally rather than logically.

Metaphor and metonymy are two examples of tropes frequently used by advertisers. Geis (1982) argues that advertisers (like many other speakers) often employ the strategy of implying rather than asserting claims and that they should be held responsible for these invalid "conversational implicatures" (Grice) that derive from what they say. Grunig (1990) offers a well documented study of how advertisers "play with words" to seduce their readers. Durand (1970) identified virtually all of the rhetorical figures used in advertisements and suggested classifying them according to four rhetorical operations: addition/suppression/substitution/exchange, and four relationships between the variable elements: identity/similarity/difference/opposition.

In recent years, researchers have shown an increasing interest in studying the rhetorical structure of ads (e.g. Leigh 1994; McQuarrie and Mick 1996; Scott 1994a; Stern 1990; Tanaka 1994). One rhetorical figure which has been particularly studied is the metaphor (e.g. Bremer and Lee 1997, Forceville 1996; van den Bulte 1994).

Indexicality

The "signifier–signified" dichotomy introduced by de Saussure and Hjelmslev to distinguish between the material object or ostensible representation of the sign ("signifier") and the mental concept to which it refers ("signified") has been considered by many applied semioticians the key to advertising analysis. The importance of semiotic connotations has been clearly shown in the work of Roland Barthes on advertising images. Denotative signifieds are "first-order" signifying systems. They correspond to the literal meaning of the advertising sign, to what is "objectively" referred to in the advertising image. Connotative signifiers are introduced by the receiver of the advertising message. They correspond to "second-order" signifying systems—systems which build on already existing ones. While the denotative meaning of an advertising image is generally viewed as a non-coded, iconic message, its connotative meaning involves a coded iconic, or symbolic, message that requires interpretation by means of cultural conventions or codes. Barthes, like other critics of advertising (e.g. Dyer 1988; Goldman 1992; Wernick 1991; Williamson 1978), identifies connotation with the operation of "ideology" and production of "myth." He also suggests that denotation itself is not innocent or neutral and participates in the manipulation of the public by creating the illusion that "it is the first meaning."

Literary criticism (see Stern 1989, 1995) and hermeneutics (see Arnold and Fischer 1994; Thompson 1997) are two neighboring disciplines of semiotics which have been also increasingly used to interpret textual and visual persuasive messages. For example, Thompson and Haytko (1997) offer an interesting hermeneutic study of how consumers use fashion discourses to inscribe their consumption behavior in a complex ideological system of folk theories about the nature of self and society. Stern (1996a) shows how Jacques Derrida's concept of deconstruction can be applied to the reading of an exemplar text—the Joe Camel campaign. Peirce's division of signs between icon, index and symbol provides another way of looking at advertising signs. Iconic advertising signs (e.g. photographic pictures) are used to make the signifier–signified relationship one of resemblance to the "real" object or person.

Some advertising signs are used indexically to indicate a further meaning to the one immediately and obviously signified. The index sets up a relation of "natural" or existential contiguity. For example, the co-presence of a woman in front of the Eiffel Tower in the advertisement for Yves Saint Laurent's "Paris" perfume indexically suggests French "Parisienne." The relationship between signifier and signified is often not based on resemblance nor on a natural link. In the case of symbols, the signified is related to the signifier by convention or contract as where a crown is used as a trademark for a beer.

Structuralist semioticians offer still another research paradigm. The so-called School of Paris and Algirdas Greimas in particular (see Greimas and Courtès 1979) has inspired many applied studies of the "deep" as opposed to "surface" structures of advertising messages. A key principle of this research tradition is that the meaning of a sign can be assessed only in relation to its structural relationship with other signs. The procedure of commutation (i.e. artificially changing an element in the advertising message to observe whether the change modifies the meaning) provides one way of recognizing semiotic units. Differences between surface and deep messages correspond to different levels of meaning and (intensive and extensive) complexity. Greimas' model of the generative trajectory of discourse represents the production of meaning as a pathway which starts at the deep level with abstract relations (e.g. the semiotic square), ensuring the minimum conditions for signification, and progresses through semio-narrative and discursive structures to the complex patterns underlying the manifestation of advertising discourse, whether verbal, visual, or otherwise.

The elementary structure of signification involves recognition of the existence of two basic types of opposition: contradiction (privative relation in the Jakobsonian sense) and contrariety (qualitative relation). For example, "female" and "male" are in a qualitative or contrariety relation whereas "male"/"non-male" (or "female"/"non-female") correspond to a privative or contradiction relation. The relations "male"/"non-female" and "female"/"nonmale" correspond to complementarity relations and the operation which constitutes them is called implication. Greimas' celebrated semiotic square is a visual representation of these relations and elementary structure. The interest of the semiotic square for advertising researchers lies in its ability to model virtual and predictable relations. Potential semantic positions and processes can be entered onto the semiotic square to produce, ultimately, the specific items of advertising discourse.

Semio-narrative structures are viewed by Greimasians as the depository of fundamental signifying forms. They exist at the deep level and correspond to imaginary universals. These plots or stories are generated from a finite number of elements, disposed in a finite number of ways, and can be represented according to a model known as the "narrative schema." Derived from Propp's studies of folktales and myths, the schema describes the four major elements which comprise the basic structure of all narratives: contract competence—performance—sanction. The advertising message can therefore be studied as a "contract" proposed by its enunciator to the addressee. To fulfil the "contract," the enunciator needs to display the competences which will allow for the performance expected by the addressee to occur. Once the performance has been accomplished, the enunciator will receive a positive or negative sanction reflecting how closely his performance matches the addressee's expectations. The advertising message quite often establishes an intersubjective relationship which has as its effect the modification of the status of each of the subjects involved. The addressee, therefore, should not be viewed as a given but rather is constructed through the portrait of the "model reader" (Eco) presented in the message, to which the receiver is invited to conform. It is in this sense that the receiver is invited to become a co-enunciator, as in the Black & White advertising campaigns studied by Bertrand (1988): in this campaign, the addressee is identified as someone who is endowed with the ability to enjoy the use of irony in advertising.

The discursive structures correspond to the spatial, temporal, and personal representations which define the thematic and figurative universe of each advertising discourse. It is through the discursive structures that the virtualities offered by the semionarrative structures are selected and ordered by the enunciator to fulfil a particular narrative function. It is the task of the semiotician to identify the thematic and figurative roles held by the "actants" (actantial model) and to study the various forms of narrative programs as well as the values which recur within them. For example, Floch (1990) shows that car advertising campaigns can be classified and studied according to four major types of values which may be invested in the car-object: utilitarian, utopian, critical, and hedonic. These four values can be "projected" onto a semiotic square to identify which positional values are currently invested, semantically, by car producers in their advertising discourses and which ones are still available for future campaigns and product positioning or repositioning attempts.

Jakobson's model of the six functions of communication has received considerable attention from advertising researchers. It is seen as a useful and simple representation of the major tasks of any advertising campaign. It also enables advertisements to be classified on the basis of which functions are predominant. It will be recalled that the referential function focuses on the referent (the product or service advertised), whereas the expressive, or emotive, and conative functions are oriented toward building the enunciator and the addressee, respectively. The conative and referential functions are particularly important in marketing where producers and sellers are attempting to segment their potential markets by creating unique images for their products and intended product users. Advertisers have often been accused of neglecting these marketing objectives in their attempts to capture the audience's attention (phatic function) or to produce autotelic messages (poetic function), i.e. the message has no other function beside itself. The sixth function, the metalinguistic, corresponds to communication strategies where advertisers try to install a code of communication between themselves and target customers. This code may involve the use of music (as in the famous DIM pantyhose campaigns), color (e.g. Marlboro's distinctive red and white shapes), or any other element.

Building on Cornu (1990), Julien (1997) uses a Peircean semiotic framework to study the olfactory dimension contained in 300 advertisements for perfumes. She shows that consumers can consciously or unconsciously use the various iconic and non-iconic signs available in these ads (e.g. the brand name, the logo, the bottle...) to retrieve from their memory the olfactory sensations they may have developed in case of prior exposure to the perfume advertised. If they have not been physically exposed to it, the many signs contained in the ad (the colors, landscape, scene, characters... used) can alternatively trigger the evocation of olfactory sensations which can then be used as weak cues to infer the likely olfactory properties of the perfume advertised. In this case, the fragrance is not communicated through the retrieval of a sensory memory trace. Rather it is built through an interpretive process, which because of its subjectivity partly escapes the control of the advertiser. The olfactory concept built by the reader of the ad may be at variance with the olfactory reality of the perfume and the message (product positioning) intended by the advertiser.

While early semiotic approaches had relegated the receiver of the advertising message to a rather secondary or passive position, more recent approaches (e.g. Everaert-Desmedt 1984; Fouquier 1988; Jensen 1995), mainly inspired by theories of pragmatics (Austin, Searle, Ducrot) have assigned the receiver a crucial role in the reception of the message, apparently indicating a resurgence of interest in the subjective aspect of semiosis. Cook (1990) suggests that ads are a new discourse type that do not simply try to attract receivers' attention and persuade them to buy the product. They may also fulfill a societal need for "light-hearted code play" and display which is no longer satisfied—at least for some people—by the more traditional discourse types. Pragmatics takes into account factors which are external to the message and is founded on the idea of an intersubjective position on which the (advertising) discourse acts. In this framework, it is essential to define the enunciator and addressee as discursive entities which may be totally distinct from the real sender and receiver of the message. Signification is globally dependent on the context in which the communication act occurs. The "illocutionary force" (Austin) of a successful communication, which determines how it is going to be received, is determined by such factors as what precedes and follows it (the co-text), what it refers to (referential context), the physical and social surroundings in which the act takes place (situational context), the activities or intentions of other "speakers" participating in the communicative situation (actional context), the expectations, motivations, interests, the explicit and implicit images that the sender and the receiver have of themselves and of the communication (psychological context).

Other Semiotic Applications

Although advertising is by far the most visible application area, semiotic approaches have also been successfully applied to other elements of the marketing-mix, particularly to such varied domains as branding, the design of logos, packaging, products, stores, promotional objects, the media, and so forth. The interested reader is referred to Pinson (1988), Umiker-Sebeok (1988), Floch (1990), Dano (1996), Semprini (1996), and Nöth (1997) for a presentation of some of these studies. They testify that, over the past twenty years, semiotics has taken on a significant role in marketing research.

Semprini's (1992) work on brand identity is particularly worth mentioning. Using a Greimassian approach, Semprini explains how the identity of a brand is gradually built through three stages or levels, referred to as axiological, narrative, and discursive. Semprini also shows how Floch's (1990) four axiologies of consumption: utilitarian, utopian, critical, and hedonic can be used to produce a 'semiotic mapping' of such well known brands as Benetton, Swatch, Perrier, Lee, Virgin, Gatorade... Semprini's framework can be used by marketers to better understand the discourse, functions, and underlying core values of various brands competing in the same market. These values and functions have to be studied in the broader theoretical context of how social discourses are produced and diffused (Veron 1987). A recent study by Chandon and Dano (1997) suggests how a semiotic analysis can be fruitfully combined with the types of statistical analyses traditionally used in market research. In the first stage of this study, a structural semiotic analysis of consumers' discourses about the packaging of two products (rice and shampoos) resulted in a five-class partition of consumers. Then a confirmatory cluster analysis of consumer questionnaire data was carried out to empirically validate the semiotic partition.

Future work is expected to give us a better understanding of the principles governing the production and reception of an expanded range of discourse, in particular of discourses that are mediated through shapes, materials, colors, and other plastic elements ("plastic discourse"). In this context, Floch's work is worth reporting. Floch (1995) draws on C. Levi-Strauss's ([1963] 1974) concept of "bricolage" to offer a broad-ranging, innovative framework for understanding the process of building and managing the visual identity of a product, a brand, a corporation. His analysis of the logos of Apple vs. IBM is particularly interesting: Floch shows that the logo of Apple can be "deducted" from the logo of IBM by a process of plastic inversion or opposition. The fact that this opposition can also be found when comparing the corporate strategies and discourses of these two companies—Apple clearly wanting to position itself against IBM in the mind of the target customers, lends credence to Floch's main philosophical position: a visual identity does not simply correspond to a combination of signs, it is a narrative and dialectical process where one needs to creatively combine tradition and innovation.

Postscript: Why and How I Came to Semiotics

My initial training in management and in sociology/psychology did not give me the opportunity to study semiotics. It was only later, after completing my Ph.D. in Marketing (Northwestern University) and returning to France, that I understood all the possibilities semiotics could offer to academic and applied researchers in marketing.

At that time (1970s–'80s), semiotic studies were already frequently run by the leading French and European market research and advertising/design agencies. These studies were usually drawing their inspiration from cultural anthropology (C. Lévi-Strauss, V. Propp) and language (R. Jakobson, E. Benveniste, R. Barthes, U. Eco) theories. C. Peirce's theories, which are so ubiquitous in Anglo-Saxon semiotic circles, were generally ignored or even disregarded. This reaction can be explained by cultural and linguistic factors but also by the fact that the conceptual framework proposed by Peirce, although intellectually attractive, was perceived by most applied researchers to be abstruse and too difficult to implement.

By and large, French and European semioticians have favored the theoretical developments of A. J. Greimas, who had set himself the project of developing a structuralist approach to semiotics that would be independent of connotation, a notion in his eyes charged with too much subjectivity. This project was to give birth to the so-called Paris School of Semiotics. For a curious mind, it was difficult not to take a close interest in this development. That's what I did.

As a member of the scientific committee of IREP (Institute of Research and Advertising Studies), which played a leading role in promoting semiotics, I had the opportunity to meet and interact with many leading applied semioticians and more particularly with Jean-Marie Floch, an ardent propagator of the structural semiotics advocated by A. J. Greimas. Until his untimely death in 2001, we exchanged a lot and he strongly contributed to my incursions, investments, and experiences in semiotics.

I quickly understood that structural semiotics, and in particular the" semiotic square," would allow me to throw a new look at the problem of how to best define a concept. I had previously tried to tackle this issue, particularly in the book *Metatheory and Consumer Research* (co-authored in 1972 with J. Zaltman and R. Angelmar), by heavily relying on the Philosophy of Science literature (M. Bunge, R. Carnap, H. Feigl, C. G. Hempel, E. Nagel, K. R. Popper...). I later carefully examined the psychological works of E. Rosch and her followers on cognitive categories and felt it necessary to go back to Aristotle's "logical square" (or square of Apuleius) as well as to the more contemporary, "logical hexagon" (R. Blanché, A. Sesmat) which extends Aristotle's square of opposition to six logical statements. As I remember it, I did not get the answer I was looking for, i.e. a comprehensive way to represent the logical and semantic relations between a given concept/term and the concepts/terms with which it is bound. This is how I was drawn into Greimassian semiotics, which did not, of course, prevent me from being attentive to other disciplines.

Starting from the fundamental Saussurian idea that "meaning occurs only in and through differences," structural semiotics gave itself as a project to go beyond the existing relationship between the expression plane (the signifier) and the content plane (the signified). It posits that a term/concept makes sense only in relation to another term/concept. The goal is to move from simply capturing the differences that produce the meaning of a message to establishing a true "topography of meaning" based on the relationships that underlie the conceptual universe under consideration, for example the terms good/bad. The semiotic square represents a "contrariety" relation of semantic nature (e.g. good vs. bad or not good vs. not bad), a relation of "contradiction" which corresponds to a negation of logical order (e.g. bad vs. not bad or good vs. not good) and finally a relation of "assertion," which corresponds to either a positive implication (not bad → good) or a negative implication (not good → bad).

We thus obtain four inter-defined positions that can be invested to "make sense of things." For example, the opposition "good" vs. "bad" can lead to concepts such as euphoria ("I'm fine") vs. dysphoria ('I'm bad') or client satisfaction ('it was good') vs. dissatisfaction ('it was bad'). Similarly, one can use the square "sexual confusion" vs. "sexual distinction" to describe the targets of the brand Calvin Klein as portrayed in the launch campaigns of the following four perfumes: Obsession ('no sexual distinction'), Eternity, ("sexual distinction"), CK One ("sexual confusion"), Escape ("no sexual confusion"). One may also remember that in 1997 Calvin Klein launched his new "CK Be" perfume using the slogan " be good, be bad, just be," that is to say, the combination (the meta-term) "good + bad."

Compared to other "tools," the semiotic square is simple to construct and easy to communicate. It encourages creativity. It is particularly useful for studying past positioning strategies as well as for identifying "meaning territories" that have not yet been exploited. As I have seen in my own teaching and consulting interventions, the opportunity to identify positions not yet invested is indeed a real advantage when it comes to search for new concepts of products, packaging, advertising, or innovative ways of segmenting the market.

The semiotic square represents what is happening at the deepest level of the so-called "generative trajectory of signification." It is at that level that fundamental choices must be made. For example, the company may decide to position itself on the pole of the square "discontinuity" by opposition to the pole "continuity," in other terms to opt for a strategy of disruption by breaking up with its past or with competitors' offers. In a different context, the company may use the opposition "utilitarian vs. emotional values" or the "natural vs. cultural" opposition to position its products or services. Floch's studies on the opposition between the IBM vs. Apple logos, the typology of Metro travelers, and the design of a hypermarket are brilliant demonstrations of the power of structural semiotic analysis as an aid for managerial decision-making.

At each context, its semiotic square! This choice made, it is necessary to choose a narrative function or plot, i.e. a "mise en intrigue" (semio-narrative structures) then to decide how the plot will be staged, i.e. a "mise en scène" (discursive structures) and finally which signs, i.e. the "surface manifestations" (textual structures) will be used to convey the intended meanings. These signs and accompanying stories must be easily accessible, intelligible, and must carry the values desired by consumers in each targeted market segment. This can represent real challenges in terms of creativity. Take for example the semiotic square "formal vs. casual." While it would be relatively easy for a designer to imagine a range of clothing or furniture that fits into one or the other of these two registers, investing with new product lines the "not casual" or "not formal" poles would clearly require much more creativity.

Over the last twenty years, the major challenge of post-Gremassian semiotic research was to develop a new paradigm that would take greater account of perceptions, passions, emotions, and consumption axiologies. This implies accepting a more multidisciplinary approach. These developments which are carried by researchers such as J. Fontanille or C. Zilberberg, to name but two, remain for the moment at a level of abstraction and theory that makes them difficult to access by practitioners and beginner semioticians.

Author Profile: Christian Pinson

Christian Pinson is Emeritus Professor of Marketing at INSEAD. He holds graduate degrees in law, management, sociology and a PhD in Marketing from Northwestern University. He co-founded and headed The French Marketing Association and was editor-in-chief of *Recherche et Applications en Marketing*, the leading francophone marketing journal. He is currently editorial advisor for the French publisher Dunod. He is co-author of *Metatheory and Consumer Research* (Dryden Press), co-editor of *Marketing Research: Applications and Problems* (Wiley) and guest editor of "Semiotics and Marketing Communication Research", *The International Journal of Research in Marketing*, Nos 3 & 4, 1988. Pinson has published on consumer information processing, marketing theory, marketing research and semiotics in marketing. He was an active promoter of applied semiotics since the early 1980s.

5

Semiotic Ethnography

"Semiotic ethnography accounts for the complex and dynamic character of meaning production and the tentative nature of any particular interpretation of consumer behavior." Laura Oswald, *Creating Value*

Introduction

Consumer ethnography is essentially a semiotic enterprise inasmuch as the ethnographer is tasked with making sense of a situation or behavior through interviews and observations (Geertz 1972a & b). Unlike in-depth interviews and focus groups, which take place in the rarefied atmosphere of the recruitment facility, ethnography embeds consumer speech in the complex semantic context of consumers' lived environments. Beginning with a broad agenda and a semi-structured interview protocol, ethnographic methods enable development of a rich, multi-dimensional data set that sheds light on relationships between what consumers say and what they do, including the decisions they make about the disposition of goods in the home, the organization of their living spaces, their social interactions and their brand choices. The semiotic analysis of this data set decodes the patterns or codes that structure meaning production across multiple consumer encounters and also identifies tensions between the various dimensions of the study.

This chapter puts into play the skills and semiotic principles learned in the four previous chapters as they relate to research design, management, execution, and write-up of ethnographic consumer research for marketing. I wrote the reading for this chapter, a case study related to a prolonged ethnography of community gardening on the West Side of Chicago.

A cursory review of the literature throughout the twentieth century suggests that semiotics evolved from the implication of structural linguistics and the social sciences beginning with the early work of contemporaries Ferdinand de Saussure (2011 [1916]) and Emile Durkheim (1995 [1912]), rather than structural linguistics alone. This trend prevailed in the work of the Moscow Linguistic Circle in the early 1900s (for example Jakobson 1990 [1956] and Volosinov 1986 [1929]); the Bakhtin Circle (Bakhtin (1993 [1934–1935]; 1981) and the Prague Linguistic Circle in the 1930's (Toman) , and the post-war structuralist movement in Paris (i.e. Pierre de Bourdieu 1984 [1976]). The specific application of semiotics to the

Laura R. Oswald, *Semiotic Ethnography* In: *Doing Semiotics: A Research Guide for Marketers at the Edge of Culture.*
Edited by: Laura R. Oswald, Oxford University Press (2020). © Laura R. Oswald, Reading 5.
DOI: 10.1093/oso/9780198822028.003.0005

practice of ethnography was fostered by Claude Levi-Strauss (1974 [1963]), who influenced American anthropologists such as Clifford Geertz (1973a &b), Marshall Sahlins (1976). (For more detail see Oswald 2015, ch. 6.)

After introducing the basics of consumer ethnography, I will illustrate the specifically *semiotic* nature of semiotic ethnography in discussion, exercises, and class activities. The learnings on ethnographic research build throughout the chapter, beginning with an exercise to develop awareness of the environmental factors that shape consumers' retail experiences and closing with a team ethnographic study of consumer behavior in multicultural households.

Between Semiotics and Anthropology

Marketers commission ethnography to discover deeper, more nuanced consumer insights to maintain competitive edge, identify new opportunities for growth, and create impactful, relevant advertising. Researchers also use ethnographic methods for more general purposes, such as exploring what motivates consumer acceptance of new technologies or to simply collect stories for social media content.

A Multi-Coded Environment

The ethnographic environment is a multi-coded sign system that consists of words, visuals, public space, and consumer narratives. Inasmuch as commercial ethnography derives inspiration from anthropology, it emphasizes the importance of on-site observations to enrich consumer insights beyond the scope of the structured interview. Broad and deep in scope, semiotics-based ethnography relies to a great extent upon the researcher's ability to make sense of the visual, social, and environmental cues that comprise the ethnographic setting. By tracking recurring patterns of meaning throughout a data set, the ethnographer teases out the broad cultural codes that structure the meaning of goods, rituals, and social spaces in a given market.

The semiotician decodes the ethnographic encounter by employing the basic tools of semiotics-based research that we applied in the four previous chapters to advertising, brand positioning, design, and consumer narratives. They begin with the formal analysis of individual artifacts, environments, or consumer statements, then classify findings into cultural categories, and organize the cultural categories into a binary system or paradigm that represents the broad cultural dimensions of the market. By anchoring the interpretation of culture in the theory of codes rather than the researcher's subjective lens, semiotic ethnography supports insights with concrete evidence based on a structural analysis of these patterns in the data.

Inasmuch as commercial ethnography derives inspiration from anthropology, it emphasizes the importance of on-site observations to enrich consumer insights beyond the scope of the structured interview. Ethnographers observe how shared cultural codes shape consumer behavior and how consumers in turn modify the codes in day to day life. Broad and deep in scope, semiotics-based ethnography relies to a great extent upon the researcher's ability to make sense of the visual, social, and environmental cues that comprise the ethnographic setting. By tracking recurring patterns of meaning throughout a data set, the ethnographer teases out the broad cultural codes that structure the meaning of goods, rituals, and social spaces in a given market.

The semiotician decodes the ethnographic encounter by employing the basic semiotic tools we applied in the four previous chapters to advertising, brand positioning, design, and consumer narratives. They begin with the formal analysis of individual artifacts, environments, or consumer statements, then classify findings into cultural categories, and organize the cultural categories into a binary system or paradigm that represents the broad cultural dimensions of the market. By anchoring the interpretation of culture in the theory of codes rather than the researcher's subjective lens, semiotic ethnography supports insights with concrete evidence based on a structural analysis of these patterns in the data.

By interviewing consumers in their lived environments, ethnographers can observe how well consumer statements hold up in the light of their behaviors. A typical example was an interview with a housewife who took pride in "only serving the family all-natural fresh foods." Since we interviewed her at home, we took a peek into her refrigerator and noticed fast food sandwiches leftover from last evening's meal, and a generous stock of frozen meals from Walmart. Such tensions between consumer behavior and speech often betray emotional tensions about one's fitness as a "good mom," or their denial about some other aspect of their lives that they block from memory. For this reason, consumers may be required to keep a journal of a given behavior for two weeks prior to the interview as a memory aid.

Cracking the Code on Chronic Pain

In an ethnographic study of chronic pain patients (see Oswald 2012, ch. 6), patients reported that they suffered more from a loss of control over their lives than from the physical symptoms themselves. Loss of control was evident in the chaotic disposition of possessions in the home.

For example, medicine traditionally belongs to the sacred realm of consumption inasmuch as it can only be obtained through medical professionals and distributed through legally licensed pharmacies. In the home, the medicine cabinet preserves the sanctity of medications by setting them aside from the "profane" spaces in the home where consumption is free from regulation and control. However, depending on the duration of the illness from 3 months to multiple years, chronic pain patients gradually moved their pain medications from the privacy of medicine cabinets in the bathroom to living spaces such as kitchen cabinets and eventually to public spaces such as coffee tables in the living room. The breakdown of clear boundaries between sacred and profane areas of consumption was symptomatic of their lack of control.

Lack of control was also manifested in hoarding behaviors that reflect a disruption in patients' ability to manage their possessions. The hoarding grew more prevalent the longer patients lived with chronic pain, impinging on family life and personal safety. In the first few interviews, we noticed that informants would set aside a closet or spare bedroom where they stored old furnishings, clothing, and even newspapers, but we did not immediately interpret these behaviors as evidence of pathological hoarding. It was only after the recurrence of hoarding behavior across half a dozen interviews that we recognized how chronic pain broke down the cognitive mechanisms that preserved order, hygiene, and balance in human life. We confirmed and refined these initial observations in the remaining interviews.

In the course of twenty-four ethnographic interviews with chronic pain patients we also confirmed that the longer one lived with chronic pain, the likelier the hoarding would take over the patient's life. In patients in advanced stages of the disease, hoarded goods encroached on all the living spaces and surfaces in the home. In several homes the hoarded goods blocked the front entrance to the home and made it difficult to find uncluttered seating to conduct the interview. At this stage of the pathology, kitchen counters, beds, and even bathroom fixtures were covered with discarded goods. Order had collapsed into chaos, reflecting once again patients' complaints that the loss of control was paramount in their experience of chronic pain.

A Note on the Back Room

This example brings to mind a methodological issue that warrants discussion. Clients usually want to observe the interviews, either live or through a remote video-cast, because they are used to observing interviews and focus groups at a facility from the back room through the two-way mirror. The presence of client-observers in the room runs the risk of disturbing the informant, particularly when discussing medical conditions. Furthermore, even if the client observes the interview off-site through a video interface, observations early on in a study may foster confusion, since the client cannot see where the interview is going. Unlike focus groups, which provide immediate answers to specific questions, the most important insights from ethnographic research emerge over multiple interviews as recurring patterns come to the surface. In a large-scale ethnographic study, I usually notice traces of a pattern in the first half-dozen interviews or so and the pattern grows clearer in the course of subsequent interviews. The pattern also shows up across multiple semiotic systems in the data, as we noticed earlier in the disposition of medications in the home discussed earlier, in informants' perform-ance of projective tasks, and in their own statements. If the client insists upon viewing interviews "live," it is a much more reassuring and successful experience if they come in after we have developed some initial insights that can guide their observations.

Exercise 5.1 Assessing Semiotic Dimensions of an Environment

This exercise is designed to build awareness of the semiotic dimensions of the lived environment from the floor plan and traffic flow to architectural dimensions and furnishings. Working individually, students develop a floor plan of their living environment. If there are multiple levels of the home, please focus on the main floor and describe simply the rooms on the upper floors.

The Floor Plan

1. Referring to the sample floor plan in Figure 5.1, name and number each room.

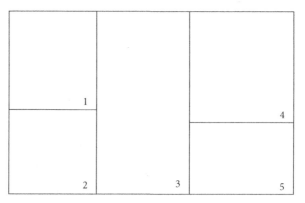

Figure 5.1. A sample floor plan

The Semiotic Analysis

- Referring to Table 5.1 in the Appendices, list the semiotic dimensions of each room, including their functions, decor, the people who use them, and the flow of people through the space.

Discussion

Based on the semiotic dimensions of this household, what can you infer about the resident(s)' lifestyle?

Degree of Formality
In a formal environment, the functions and social uses of each space are more discrete than in a casual household. For example, the boundaries separating public and private as well as sacred and profane spaces are more strictly observed.

The formal style of the layout is usually reiterated in other semiotic systems in the home, including decor and artwork, as well as the use of storage space to separate architectural elements of the space from the stuff of daily life (from food and dishes to linens and clothing).

Does the home include both formal rooms and casual spaces where the rules are relaxed? Is there a space with multiple functions, such as working, entertaining and even sleeping? A space where anyone can enter and stuff is left out in the open rather than stored away?

Social Organization
The placement of furnishings and technologies in the home also suggests the social style of the residents. Describe the organization of furnishings in the living areas of the home and explain how they either encourage conversation or entertainment or while other areas invite quiet solo activities such as reading or working at the computer.

Reporting

Summarize your findings in no more than five Power Point slides. It is up to the discretion of the instructor to schedule live presentations of the report by students. The report will include:

1. The floor plan with numbered spaces with their functions.
2. A key with the semiotic dimensions of each space.

3. A summary that explores the lifestyle implications of the semiotic analysis for the consumers who dwell there.

Exercise 5.2 The Disposition of Possessions in the Home

In this exercise, students take a closer look at the environment they analyzed in Exercise 5.1, paying close attention to the disposition of goods in the home other than furnishings, from the food in the refrigerator to clothing, books, and supplies.

Instructions

- Start by making a new list of the rooms in your floor plan and describe in general the kinds of products you would find in each space.
- Take a few snapshots or a short video to bring to life your observations in the report.

Inventory

Take an inventory of the placement of goods in the home. Table 5.2 (Appendices) represents a sample inventory guide.

Congruity

In addition to listing goods that are located in rooms that are congruous with the cultural category, such as foodstuffs in the kitchen, students should keep track of possessions that end up in incongruous locations, such as food in the living room. Describe how they got there, because this detail may reveal something important about the consumers' lifestyle. Perhaps you find a computer in the bedroom or medications in the kitchen or you have a yoga mat in the living room. State whether these incongruous placements are more or less permanent or temporary, and how often the movement of these goods takes place.

Analysis

Describing the disposition of goods in the home is the initial step in the semiotic analysis. At this stage students discuss how the disposition of goods in the home reflect the meanings consumers associate with the things themselves or the rooms in which they are located.

- Does the disposition of goods in the home reflect something about the consumer's personality, lifestyle, or character? Discuss for example the organization of goods in cabinets, refrigerator, and other locations.

- Is there a place for everything and for everything a place? How often does the consumer move goods from their "proper" place to other rooms in the home?
- Are the incongruous goods placed there temporarily or permanently? For instance, does the bedroom always double for an office, or does the consumer place the computer there occasionally to avoid the noise in the living room?
- Does the disposition and displacement of goods in the home suggest something about the meanings the consumer assigns to certain goods or spaces in the home? Explain and support your thoughts with evidence from the analysis.
- Do you notice anything else about the disposition of goods in the home?

Reporting

Organize your findings in about five PowerPoint slides and add the slides to the report you created for Exercises 5.1 and 5.2, making sure to include visuals that will support your findings. It is up the discretion of the instructor to schedule live presentations in front of the class.

The Research on Semiotic Ethnography

The underlying objective of ethnographic practice is to make sense of the marketplace. This principle is based upon the assumption that goods, rituals, and social spaces make meanings, and that these meanings are shared by groups of consumers. Although French sociologist Émile Durkheim (1997 [1893]) claimed that shared beliefs and behaviors were the basis of social organization, it was Claude Lévi-Strauss (1974 [1963]) who explained that a system of cultural codes is responsible for the collective nature of social life. Inspired by the work of Ferdinand de Saussure (2011 [1916]), Levi-Strauss drew parallels between structural linguistics and anthropology most notably with regard to the theory of codes. In *Structural Anthropology*, Levi-Strauss moved the focus of ethnography from the description of isolated events to an exploration of the underlying patterns in consumer behavior that define the cultural system.

As discussed throughout this book, the theory of codes accounts for the very possibility of communication and social organization in the marketplace. Code theory also forms the scientific basis of semiotics-based research because it roots the interpretation of cultural meanings in the recurring patterns and networks of signs and symbols across given data set.

Symbolic Consumption

It was the pioneering work of Mary Douglas and Baron Isherwood (1996 [1979]), an anthropologist and an economist, respectively, that bridged structural anthropology, economics, and consumer behavior, showing a direct relationship between value creation and the meanings consumers invest in their possessions. They emphasized that consumer behavior is not only motivated by rational choice or finances but also the social benefits they derive from using goods for self-display, sharing, and communicating with others. These interpersonal experiences, rather than quantitative measures such as supply and demand, shape to a great extent how consumers assign value to goods.

For example, people place added value on luxury goods because they are scarce and out of reach. They may use luxury goods to boost their social status or mark rank in a hierarchy. In any case, the perception of luxury value cannot be pinned down to an economic formula because it relies to a great extent upon the cultural codes that define value in a given market. What constitutes luxury differs from one culture to the next. While ostentatious display, rare gems, and expensive clothing may represent luxury in an emerging market such as China, in the United States, consumers place higher value on technologies, housing, and services such as a personal concierge or a private jet.

Douglas and Isherwood acknowledge a debt to Lévi-Strauss, who discovered the fundamentally semiotic character of culture. He revolutionized current theories about kinship affiliation, for example, by showing that the importance granted to fathers, mothers, or uncles in a given society is not determined by biology, but by long-standing social codes that define the meaning and value of some relationships over others in the family group.

Structural Anthropology

Lévi-Strauss not only discovered the symbolic dimension of cultural phenomena but also looked to structural linguistics to develop a scientific approach to the study of cultural meanings. In *Structural Anthropology* (1967), Lévi-Strauss credits Saussure (1901), the founder of structural linguistics, with establishing the scientific foundations of linguistics and laying the groundwork for a general semiotics of non-linguistic sign systems.

First of all, Saussure changed the focus of linguistic studies from the analysis of specific statements or texts to the abstract system of codes that linked phonetic signs to meanings. He also segmented speech into its constituent units, including sounds (phonemes), words (signs), and sentences (discourses). In this way Saussure insisted upon the dependence of meaning production on cultural norms and linguistic codes, rather than any natural or historical affiliation.

By teasing out objective, structural elements of sign systems from their implementation in specific statements, Saussure also freed linguistic science from the interpretive authority of the linguist. Lévi-Strauss was particularly interested in the idea that the codes structuring language speak for themselves, therefore reducing the influence of researcher bias on research findings. He states, "We might say then, that insofar as language is concerned, we need not fear the influence of the observer on the observed phenomenon, because the observer cannot modify the phenomenon merely by becoming conscious of it," (1967: 57). His theory of structural anthropology sought to achieve the scientific status of Saussure's theory for the study of culture.

Linguistics and Semiotics

The debates about parallels between linguistics and anthropology that Lévi-Strauss summarized in 1967 all stumbled on the incompatibility between sounds or "phonemes," the material stuff of language, and cultural phenomena such as artifacts, interpersonal relationships, and rituals. This insight deserves a brief explanation.

A key element of structural linguistics is the notion that the relationship of signs to meaning is arbitrary rather than motivated by natural affinity. Saussure further insisted that the meaning communicated by a sign does not refer to the thing it references in the real world, but to the concept of the thing. He illustrates this concept in the famous illustration in Figure 5.2.

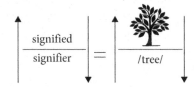

Figure 5.2. The conceptual structure of the sign

The linguistic sign is a dialectical structure that associates a phonetic signifier and a concept. There is no natural affinity between the sounds/tree/and the concept of a tree—the association is entirely governed by linguistic codes. For example, the French use the signifier /l'arbre/ for a tree, and speakers in other languages use their own culture-specific signifiers for tree.

Since the relation of sounds to meaning is arbitrary, the sounds themselves can be recombined with other sounds to create an infinite number of meanings. The abstract nature of the phonetic signifier contributes to the flexibility and fluidity of language. For example, the phonemes /t//r//ee/ are not owned by the concept "tree." Speakers can recombine them with other phonemes indefinitely to communicate something new, for example adding an /s/ in front and a /t/ at the end and gives us "street."

To illustrate this point, Roman Jakobson gives an example where communication hinged on the binary contrast of two vowels, /i/ and /e/. Suppose a customer in a cafe is unhappy with their tea and tells the waiter, "This tea is b/i/tter." Due to the noise level at the cafe, the waiter hears the word, "b/e/tter," and serves another round of the tea. In other words, the waiter filled in his version of the sound uttered by the customer in order to make sense of the event, even though it was incorrect.

In contrast with linguistics, no such claims can be made of anthropological artifacts. They may have a dual function as "things in the world" and also signifiers for abstract meanings, but they will never have the conceptual aspect of phonetic signs. Although a luxury watch may represent status, savoir faire, and success, a watch is still a watch and cannot be recombined with other things indefinitely to produce new meanings.

The Meaning of Things

It is a credit to Lévi-Strauss that he prevailed in his quest for a science of anthropological inquiry by looking past the differences between linguistics and non-verbal sign systems and emphasized similarities between their underlying discursive functions. In effect, Lévi-Strauss, along with contemporaries in areas such as Christian Metz in cinema semiotics (including [1971] 1991; [1977] 1981), Roland Barthes in literary criticism (including [1964] 1977; [1964] 2000), Douglas and Isherwood in consumer behavior ([1979] 1996), and Pierre Bourdieu in sociology (1984) [1976], are responsible for forging a science of semiotics by highlighting underlying discursive functions that language shares with other forms of communication, including code theory, the binary organization of meaning, and the ability to transcend the materiality of the signifier to commu-nicate abstract concepts.

Exercise 5.3 Show and Tell—My Favorite Thing

In this exercise, students learn to organize their thoughts about the meanings that they invest in sacred possessions—the priceless objects or rituals that consumers preserve and set aside from everyday commodities. Sacred possessions have value for consumers because of the meanings they attach to them.

Directions

Students identify a sacred possession or ritual and prepare a five-minute show-and-tell presentation that explains how they came to endow it with meaning and value.

Discussion

In addition to summarizing how the possession or ritual acquired sacred status, please answer the following questions.

- In what way is the possession a non-verbal sign? Is there anything about the object that suggests the meaning it has for you, or are the meanings entirely subjective and personal?
- Do other people know about the sacred possession and recognize its meaning?
- Do you benefit from thinking about sacred possession in your daily life or is it something you remember from time to time?

Reporting

Organize your discussion in a PowerPoint slide and add it to the report you created for Exercises 5.1 and 5.2.

Culture as a Semiotic System

As I reiterate throughout my writing, the semiotic analysis may begin with a textual analysis of semiotic elements in a single unit of meaning, such as an artifact, an image, or a dwelling. However, as noted in the chronic pain ethnography, it is only with reference to multiple examples of a given phenomenon such as hoarding that a pattern of meaning emerges that reveals the code structuring a given behavior, i.e., hoarding is a signifier for the lack of control experienced by chronic pain patients.

In some cases, a study may extend to multiple international markets in order to compare and contrast behaviors that represent how different cultures perform a given task, such as serving a meal. The comparative analysis defines and refines understanding of the codes structuring one's own culture, which we take for granted in daily life. For instance, to understand France's distinctive culinary culture, the semiotician might compare it to China's culinary traditions. We begin by identifying a set of key cultural categories at play in food service, including Consumer Behavior, Time, Preparation, Presentation, and Social.

Without examining in rich detail the dining rituals of French and Chinese meal service, I contrast some basic elements of these two cultural systems in order to highlight for the reader how to observe and analyze cultural difference and the ways consumers or cultural change might even modify the cultural codes.

FOOD SERVICE CULTURE

Cultural Categories	French /	Chinese
Consumer Behavior	Formal /	Informal
Time	Seqential /	Synonymous
Preparation	Discrete Food Groups /	Blended Food Groups
Presentation	Artful /	Casual
Social	Individual /	Shared

Figure 5.3. A Paradigmatic Analysis of Cultural Difference

In general, French meal service calls for a linear sequence of service that begins with hors d'oeuvres and leads predictably to the cheese and dessert. Each dish represents a discrete food group—meat, vegetables, or dairy—served individually to each diner. The presentation highlights the visual appeal of each dish. In contrast, Chinese diners, expect to be served all courses of a meal at the same time from a large rotating tray that encourages sharing among the diners. Even on formal occasions, the food presentation mixes up cultural categories such as main dish, side, and soup. The dishes themselves may mix up vegetables and meats or fish, with or without noodles, on a single plate.

By mapping these contrasts on a binary table, the semiotician identifies the paradigmatic system—the set of binary pairs—that define each culture. The France/China comparison generates a paradigmatic set of binaries, including formal/informal, sequential/non-sequential, distinct/blended food categories, artful/casual presentation, and individualized/shared service. Figure 5.3 maps the cultural paradigm on a binary grid.

Cultural Analysis

The comparison casts in high relief the distinctive features of one's own culture that we take for granted. Americans may assume, for instance, that "everybody" would prefer a gift of a dozen roses to just one. Isn't the dozen more valuable? In fact French consumers do not agree. My research with affluent French consumers in Paris (Oswald 2015, Ch. 6) found that the French value "la discretion" and restraint in their self-presentation and they would gift an attractively wrapped single rose rather than an ostentatious large bouquet. The example sheds light on America's love affair with excess and show.

Exercise 5.4 The Binary Analysis of the Customer Experience

The exercise calls for a comparative analysis of consumer culture at each end of the informal dining service spectrum: fast food and small sole proprietor restaurants. Working in teams, students conduct prolonged visits in two restaurants and take stock of the semiotic dimensions of consumer culture at a service setting, including architectural elements and consumer behavior. By comparing and contrasting the semiotic elements of each site, teams analyze the broad binary dimensions of informal dining service culture.

Directions

Teams choose one restaurant from each dining category and note the locations. They assign research roles to each member of the team. Plan to spend at least one hour in each location.

Teams produce a research guide before visiting the sites to structure the on-site visits. Please see Table 5.3 (Appendices) for a sample guide. The guide lists the semiotic dimensions of dining service, including: design and architectural features, staffing, service processes such as ordering and delivering food, restaurant messaging and merchandising, the payment process, and consumer behaviors and dining rituals.

Store Visits

Conducting research in commercial sites raises the issue of access, since management may have concerns about disturbing diners or violating corporate privacy. If management expresses these kinds of concerns, it is better to find alternative restaurants and employ a participant-observer methodology that would enable researchers to conduct their work while blending in with the other diners in the restaurant.

In order to take photographs of the site as inconspicuously as possible, I limit photography to a few well-chosen details in each store and snap the photos toward the end of the visit. The team photographer can also pretend to take photos of other team members while focusing on the restaurant design. Photos that include customers or staff must conceal the individual's facial identity. It is also important to limit any ad hoc conversations with service staff and other customers to a few minutes.

The teams visit each site and assess the semiotic dimensions listed on the guide. Teams note their observations on the guide sheet and complete one sheet for each site visit.

Methods

Teams will sketch floor plans of each restaurant they visit, observe customers and staff at all stages of the service experience, and engage staff and customers in ad hoc conversations about their experiences. They will take photos of design elements in each store, beginning outside, making sure to protect the privacy of people in the space by avoiding shots that reveal the identities of individuals.

The Floor Plan

Sketch simple floor plans of each restaurant you visit. The floor plan should show how architectural elements structure the movements of consumers and staff at the restaurant. After tracing the spatial elements, discuss in more detail the effects of spatial organization on consumer behavior. Using the guide in Table 5.4 (Appendices), note how firm is the boundary between the areas of food production and consumption? Is the transaction counter a barrier or a window onto the service space? How frequently do customers use any digital ordering kiosks? Note the mood in the waiting area and what customers do to pass the time.

Consumer Behavior

Observe how consumers enter and exit the restaurant, the pace of the service, the wait for seating in the sole proprietor restaurant or the waiting line for ordering food in the fast food restaurant. What do consumers do while waiting? Are diners alone, in couples, with children or families? Describe the pace of service, formality of the service and dining behaviors of customers, etc. Note the amount of time diners spend in each restaurant.

Individual team members engage diners and staff in brief, casual chats to gauge their restaurant choice, loyalty, and menu preferences. To conceal the purpose of the chats, keep them brief and do not take notes until you find your own seat.

Analysis

Perform a binary analysis of the data from the two restaurants, using the analysis of French and Chinese dining (Figure 5.3) as a model. Identify six to eight prominent design elements and behaviors that represent, in broad brushstrokes, key differentiators between the culture of fast food dining and sole proprietor dining. Referring to Table 5.5 (Appendices), teams create a grid that maps the cultural binaries you identified by means of this comparative analysis.

In addition to the summary of key binaries on the grid, summarize any details that you discovered about design and consumer behavior in the informal dining space that you believe may be relevant for understanding this market.

Reporting

Organize the team findings in a brief PowerPoint report and support your analysis with the floor plan for each restaurant, the binary grid, photographs from the sites, and any relevant verbatims from consumers and staff.

Key Learning from Exercises 5.1, 5.2, and 5.3

In the first two exercises students learned to pay attention to the semiotic dimensions of the lived environment and what they communicate about the people who live there. They also became aware of the mobility of goods from places where they are congruous with the location to places where they are incongruous, and to analyze what this means about the meanings consumers assign to goods and spaces in the home.

In Exercise 5.3, students learned to assess the symbolic function of goods by discussing the meanings they assign to a sacred possession or ritual behavior. Exercise 5.4 assimilated learnings from the first three exercises order to understand the integration of all elements of the service environment and how they differentiate one type of informal food category. They began with a detailed analysis of customers, service staff, and environmental elements in the fast food and sole proprietor service categories. They then compared and contrasted their findings from each site in order to clarify the binary codes that structure each service category.

Deconstructing the Cultural Binaries

Critics of semiotics often complain that the binary analysis rigidly oversimplifies the complexity of meaning production, consumer identity, and culture. This complaint is not backed up by the facts. The binary analysis is not an end in itself, but a tool for sorting out the elementary cultural codes that enable consumers to communicate in the first place. These codes form the condition of possibility of social life and economic exchange because we generally agree on what they mean. In the analysis of dining service culture, for example, we identified a group of codes that differentiate service categories from one another in the informal food industry. These kinds of distinctions are very practical and are responsible for the ways marketers assign value and consumers assess value in a given market. Furthermore, by structuring service styles in binary terms, semiotics also provides a methodology for deconstructing the prevailing codes and creating something new and different.

Beyond the Binary Structure of Culture

As the cases below illustrate, rather than killing creativity, the binary analysis leads to creativity because it actually clarifies cultural norms so that we can change them.

McCafé: A New Cultural Space for Fast Food

In order to grow market share in the profitable café coffee market, McDonald's, the fast food giant, had to develop a strategy for incorporating a new line of espresso drinks into the regular fast food menu. The initiative demanded that management blend very distinct marketing cultures—American fast food and European coffee traditions—in a single brand.

For most of us, fast food means cheap, standard fare and restaurants devoid of class, comfort, or glamour. In contrast, we associate branded espresso cafés with specialty fare whose prices suggest luxury. Rather than simply add the new product line to the current fast food menu, McDonald's decided to create a peripheral environment in the restaurants to provide context for the new products. The space incorporated cultural equities from the branded café world.

In place of bright primary colors, plastic tables and florescent lighting, cafés are decorated in sophisticated earth tones, natural materials, and mood lighting. Figure 5.4 illustrates how McDonald's bent the codes to create a new brand.

Fast Food / Branded Café	McCafé in McD's
Cheap / Expensive	Good value
Standard / Specialty	Specialty drinks, average beans
Primary Colors / Earth tones	Earth tones
Plastic / Natural materials	Natural and plastic
Florescent lighting / Accent lighting	Accent lighting

Figure 5.4. Code blending for innovation

Repositioning Luxury for Chinese Consumers

In exploratory research with affluent Chinese consumers in Shanghai, researchers from Marketing Semiotics identified a cultural barrier that threatened the long-term growth of the European luxury market in China. Out of twenty interviews, most respondents did not relate emotionally to brands or relate to the idea of a brand personality or identity. They did not recognize emotional cues in advertising, did not differentiate brands from one another, and were not loyal to any given brand. Inasmuch as long-term growth depends upon brand distinctions and sustainable brand loyalty, we predicted an eventual slowdown of the market as the luxury sector matured and Chinese consumers looked to brands that reflected something of their own national identity.

To shed light on the matter, we conducted a semiotic analysis of print advertising for luxury brands such as Louis Vuitton, Gucci, Chanel, and Dior. All of the ads reflected the priority given to individual identity in the West by casting individual models against a neutral backdrop, isolated from their social and natural contexts. This interpretation of human existence is deeply engrained in the metaphysical tradition in European philosophy. In contrast, Chinese philosophy conceives of the self as a detail in the expansive order of Nature and the Cosmos. The classical tradition in Chinese landscape painting, which lasted roughly from the twelfth to the twentieth centuries, represents humans as tiny figures in vast mountainous landscapes. In the modern era, communist ideology extended this perspective in Socialist art that subordinates the individual to the will of the group, taken up by sweeping social forces.

Furthermore, the newly rich Chinese consumers we interviewed valued Confucian ideals of material austerity, family, and restraint, and placed more importance on lifestyle brands than on ostentatious display. While they consumed luxury brands to mark their social status and success, they invested a large percentage of their income in savings, investments, and property.

The Semiotic Square

In order to mitigate consumer resistance to Western brands, European manufacturers would have to translate luxury into semiotic strategies that would connect with Chinese consumers. A semiotic approach to the problem begins with a binary analysis of the underlying cultural tensions at play in this market, such as West/East, Individualistic/Part of the Whole, and Appearance/Lifestyle. We then deconstruct these binaries using a methodology developed by Algirdas Greimas (1984 [1966]) called the semiotic square.

The semiotic square is a kind of matrix for exposing semantic tensions within discourse. These tensions are formed by the dual effects of the binary structure of cultural categories themselves (i.e. ego/harmony) and the superimposition of multiple cultural categories in any given instance of discourse (i.e. personal identity/lifestyle/fashion). By overlapping several cultural binaries on a multi-dimensional double-axis grid, the semiotic square breaks down the rigid binary analysis into secondary types of associations including contrariness, and implication (Figure 5.5). The analysis both differentiates between rigid, insurmountable differences between two cultural systems and areas of semantic overlap that draw meanings from both systems to form a new cultural space.

Though these new cultural spaces form sites of cultural creativity and innovation, they fall short of forming a synthesis of the binary terms into a single meaning. As Greimas insists, the overlap of multiple relationships and cultural categories in active meaning production constantly shifts and reframes the semantic context of discourse. This dynamic suspends indefinitely the possibility of a synthesis of binary oppositions into a final interpretation or meaning. It is as if the semiotic square exposes a kind of border space where these tensions continue to play in daily life.

A Note on Method

The radical implications of Greimas' theory for post-structural semiotics and consumer behavior are often oversimplified in the marketing literature. For example, Jean-Marie Floch (2001 [1990]) narrows the semiotic square to the structural analysis of cultural data in order to articulate the meanings and values consumers associate with various aspects of a research project. The structural analysis yields sharp insights for solving strategic marketing problems such as brand positioning, advertising, and service site design. It makes sense that Floch avoids the more nuanced aspects of structural semantics in his case studies, where the emphasis is on problem solving. However Floch's interpretation of the semiotic square obscures the more nuanced implications of Greimas' theory for understanding the resistant areas of consumer behavior and culture which defy assimilation, synthesis, or a final solution.

Contraries

A contrary relationship is a more flexible approach to cultural difference because it plays within the tensions between binaries, rather than synthesize them into a common identity. In emerging markets and multicultural American markets, ethnic consumers may not ever completely assimilate to a new culture, but participate in both local and global cultures at various occasions throughout the day (see Oswald 1999). In Figure 5.5, for instance, due in part to their traditions in Taoist philosophy, the Chinese view themselves as part of a larger whole, from community to the cosmos. In the West, we pride ourselves in our individuality and independence. Although these two philosophical traditions may strongly contrast with each other, we identified a point of contact between /Individual/ and /Part of Whole/ in the notion of "Context." As a point of contact, the notion of Context does not exactly merge Eastern and Western philosophies, but creates a cultural space for adapting Western brands to the priorities of Chinese consumers.

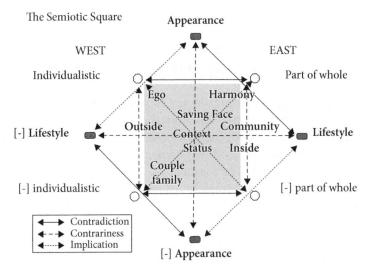

Figure 5.5. Deconstructing the luxury market

Louis Vuitton

Louis Vuitton, the most popular luxury brand in China, leveraged the logic of contrariness to reposition brands in China without losing the brand's European essence. Management found a point of contact between Western Individualism and Eastern Part of Whole values that centers on Context. Rather than adopt wholeheartedly the Chinese point of view, the LV brand leveraged tensions between the two cultures, showing models and iconic celebrities—Individuals—in social and spatial contexts. They aligned branding and marketing strategy with the values Chinese consumers place on family, social responsibility, and purpose.

For example, LV's "Life is a Journey" campaign represents Western celebrities from politics and entertainment in the context of their lived experiences. For instance, one ad represents Sophia and Frances Ford Coppola working on a script in Buenos Aires, with the tagline, "For every story there's a beautiful journey." More recent Journey campaigns "translate" the message and visuals for the China market in advertising that featured ethereal representations of Chinese landscapes, Eastern music, and nameless people.[1]

Implications

Next, relations of implication structure more intimate relations between cultural terms, such as cause-effect or part/whole. For example, with its emphasis on the Individual, Appearance, and status, Western luxury brands would seem to contrast with the Chinese emphasis on inner harmony and being a Part of the Whole.

---

[1]   https://www.youtube.com/watch?v=XckKFdAOeaM

However, Chinese social life is deeply influenced by the practice of "saving face" looking good in the social group to avoid shame and humiliation. Although saving face does not actually equate with Ego, it serves a self-centered need of Chinese consumers to manage their outside identities in order to maintain balance and social harmony.

On the subject of marketing luxury to China, it is interesting to note that the consumers we interviewed had little awareness of the luxury traditions that evolved during China's rich imperial past. Since the nineteenth century, invasions, European imperialism, and modern Communism not only destroyed ancient traditions but allowed Western merchants to pave the way for a new modern luxury culture in pre-war China influenced by the West.

Hermès—*Shang Xia*

This much said, Chinese consumers are beginning to turn to locally produced luxury goods that speak to their evolving values and tastes as modern consumers. To meet this demand, Hermès did not stop with blending contrary cultural terms in advertising, but developed a new Chinese luxury brand, *Shang Xia*,[2] that implicates contemporary Chinese values for home, tradition, and harmony in French luxury values for rarity, elegance, and discretion.

Shang Xia not only aligned communications and marketing strategies to Chinese traditions, but developed a product line that includes both traditional luxury goods such as fashion, leather goods, jewelry, and also a full line of furnishings, interior design, and other goods for the home. The design and branding elements evoke rich luxury traditions from China's imperial past, as well as the historical implication of French and Chinese luxury cultures going back over a century.

Extended Team Project: An Ethnography of a Multicultural Household

The chapter ends with an outline (Appendices) of an extended team project that walks students through a multicultural ethnography. The project is designed as the semester-long final project for graduate students in the social sciences, marketing, and other research disciplines. The instructor may choose to adapt the scope of the project for use in undergraduate courses.

A detailed outline of the project is presented in the Appendix.

The project serves as an effective tool for student evaluation because it puts students through a rigorous application of semiotic principles and methods summarized in Chapters 4 and 5 on the design, execution, and write-up of

---

[2] http://www.shang-xia.com/EN/space.html

findings for semiotics-based consumer research. More importantly, the study offers students an opportunity to gain and integrate valuable insights about the ways immigrants use goods symbolically to navigate the marketplace, define identities, and contribute to the current multicultural society.

For more insights about conducting and writing up an ethnographic investigation with consumers in a multicultural household, please read my paper on multicultural consumer behavior in a Midwestern Haitian household (Oswald 1999).

Appendices

Table 5.1 Semiotic dimensions of the lived environment (see Exercise 5.1).

Name and function	i.e. living area, kitchen, den, etc. What is is used for?
Dimensions	Approximate square feet.
Furnishings, appliances,	Mark the placement of windows, furnishings, appliances, and technologies, when/how they are used (work, entertainment, dining, etc.).
Décor	Color scheme (uniform throughout?), window treatments, artwork, rugs or carpet, etc.
Public/private	Who goes there?
Sacred/profane	Is the space "sacred," i.e. set off from the rest of the house for personal use, quiet time, and a single purpose, i.e. sleeping or working? Is it "profane," i.e. is it used for multiple purposes, such as a guest room used as an office space, etc.?
Traffic flow	Mark hallways, doorways, entrance/exit to home.Trace a typical pathway from one end of the floor plan to another.
Storage	Mark closets, cabinets, and other storage places and what's stored there.
Other	

Table 5.2 Sample inventory of goods (see Exercise 5.2).

Location	Goods	Congruity
1. Kitchen Cabinets, countertops and other surfaces, refrigerator and freezer		
2. Living room Surfaces, cabinets, other.		
etc.		

Table 5.3 Sample research guide (see Exercise 5.3).

Floor plan	Include entrance, windows, traffic flow, placement of counters, kiosks, tables, and other elements. Observe how customers move through the services spaces.
Dimensions	Approximate square feet.
Design	Note design elements, color scheme, lighting, mood, merchandising and other messaging.
Service processes	Include customer seating, food ordering and delivery, payment, and clean up, and other processes.
Staff	Note the customer relationship, service pace, mood, etc.
Menu	Describe the scope and specialties. Note menu design and location.
Furnishings	Design, esthetics, comfort, convenience.
Timing	How long does the dining experience last, from entrance to exit? Do people linger, order additional food, etc.?
Atmospherics	Describe the mood, sociality, customer relationship, formality, etc.
Other	

Table 5.4 Dining behavior guide (see Exercise 5.4).

Logistics and population	Note location and time of day. Note consumer demographics; gauge the number of customers from beginning to end of the visit.
Sociality	Are customers alone? With other people and who?
Food service	Note the time customers take to review the menu and order. How many people take food out? Dine fast and leave? Linger?
Service relationship	Is the restaurant a "third living space"? Personal or impersonal? Friendly or matter of fact?
Dining behavior	Note the etiquette for each place: finger food or cutlery? Slow or fast eating? Napkins or not? Etc.
Consumer inquiry	Why did they choose restaurant? Are they loyal? Do they choose the same meal or mix it up with each visit? What drives their choice of restaurant for this occasion?
Other	

Table 5.5 Binary analysis grid for Exercise 5.4

Cultural categories	Fast food/	Sole proprietor
	/	
	/	
	/	
	/	
	/	

Directions for an Extended Ethnographic Study

An Exploration of Food Consumption in a Multicultural Household

The final project puts into play chapter learnings by walking students through the various stages of an ethnographic inquiry. The ethnography explores the various rituals, goods, and behaviors that ethnic consumers associate with food consumption. The exercise highlights the effects of cultures in contact in the multicultural home, as consumers make decisions about food shopping, preparation, and service.

Since first-generation multicultural consumers have one foot in their home cultures and the other in their current host culture, the research will expose binary distinctions between each cultural system and explore how consumers negotiate these differences at different occasions during the day. For example, do they mix ethnic food products with mainstream food products at a single meal, or do they use them separately? Do they shop at both the supermarket and the local ethnic grocery? Are there traditional foods that they always eat? Any mainstream food rituals or meals that they or their families have adopted?

Before beginning the project, please read and review carefully all the directions and obtain a signed Consent Form from all informants that you interview.

Research Design

Working in teams, students will conduct a multi-stage ethnographic study with ethnic consumers who identify with a clear subsegment based on ethnicity, lifestyle choices, or other subgroup identification. Each team member will complete a single ethnography at a multicultural household of their choice. They will coordinate with the team to review, analyze, and synthesize findings from all the interviews for the final report.

One member of the team conducts secondary research about the ethnic population under investigation to gain background on the customs and traditions of the home culture, and which ones they maintain in the host culture, such as holidays and favorite foods. Find out basic demographic data about their participation in the new culture.

The project includes five stages:

- A brief review of the secondary data on your research population;
- A 90-minute in-depth interview in consumers' homes;
- A 30-minute visit with them to the market or markets, as needed;
- Up to a 60-minute visit at a social gathering with the respondent and family or friends;
- A 30-minute follow-up visit at the respondent's home;
- Write up field notes;
- Coordinate findings from all team members.
- Collaborate on a final report in PowerPoint.

Recruitment

Each informant must sign a brief consent form that grants permission to the researcher to conduct the research. The form includes the name of the researcher and the informant, the date, a summary of the research and how it will be used, a statement about the confidentiality of the research, and the researcher's signature.

If possible, the informants should be first-generation consumers in the host country. Though each team member is responsible for one interview, all the team members should select a respondent belonging to the same general ethnic group in order to infer generalizations about the consumer behavior of a given population.

Team members must rely upon their network of contacts to recruit informants for the study. You may promise a simple gift or other favor as an incentive, but the best way to persuade respondents is to explain your purpose and express your enthusiasm for finding out more about them and their culture.

Research and Guides

To maintain consistency of the interviews across all team members, teams develop guides in advance to structure the time they spend with the informant, including a long interview guide, a store visit outline, and key points for the event observations. Each team member will plan his or her own follow-up interview.

The Long Interview Guide

The interview guide will include at least five key sections, including:

- Introduction and explanation of the purpose and structure of the interview.
- Demographic information—age, background, ethnicity, time in the host country, language(s), education, family status.
- Relationship to the home country. Do they identify more with home or with the new, host culture? Is their extended family here or there? Ask about the ethnic identifications of other family members.
- Home Tour. Midway into the interview, ask the informant to walk you through the home, noting details about their home and possessions, making note of souvenirs, photos, and artifacts that reflect their cultural priorities. Ask about who uses the dining room and when.
- Explore the kitchen, including the foods in the cabinets and the freezer and refrigerator. Continue the discussion of multicultural behaviors in the kitchen.
- Return to the seated interview.
- Follow up on your observations in the kitchens, as well as the meals they prepare for the family and for entertaining. Find out if they serve some foods for their mainstream friends and others for holidays and children's friends. Do they usually eat in the kitchen or the dining room?
- Close the interview, thank the informant, and say goodbye.

The Store Visit Plan

Teams create a brief outline of key topics for the walk around at the stores, Teams should develop a short guide to plan the store visits. The visit should note the store environment, but the main focus will be on the informant's product choices and how they contribute to the informant's multicultural behaviors with food. Discuss the different kinds of products they purchase at the supermarket and those they purchase at the ethnic market. Note the differences in branding and packaging at both markets and relate them to the informant's cultural traditions.

The Social Gathering and Follow-up Meeting

For the social gathering, a formal guide is not required. It suffices to prepare a plan for observing the ways consumers use food to represent cultural identity. Please note the cultural setting, food preparation, and the informant's social behavior. Do your observations complement or add something new to your learnings so far?

The final follow-up meeting provides closure to the interview process and enables the interviewer to ask any lingering questions that may have come up since the last interview. It should last no more than thirty minutes.

Fieldwork

Each team member is responsible for conducting all phases of their interview. I recommend working together with another team member, each one helping out the other when it's their turn. While one person is conducting the interview, the other can take notes, manage the audio or video technology, and review the interview with their partner. The two-person team may be less important for the walk through of the store and the other events.

The fieldwork includes:

- Conduct a 90-minute in-depth interview at the informant's home;

- Video or audiotape the interview;

- Take notes and photographs at all sites and include key verbatim comments ("verbatims" in the industry) by informants;

- Organize notes from the long interview in the sections provided on the field guide;

- Pay particular attention to findings about cultural attitudes, rituals, and buying behaviors that characterize the ethnic culture, and the ways consumers integrate mainstream culture into these aspects of their food consumption.

Field Notes Write-up

Each researcher writes up a summary of their findings, including key quotes and photos from the fieldwork. The team should agree to write up findings using a single format or Write-Up Form in order to facilitate coordination of findings from all the interviews at the report production stage. The Write-Up Form should parallel the main sections of the Guide. Each section of the Write-Up Form should be marked with consistent headings in order to easily integrate the information from all the interviews in the report. Include any additional topics that may have emerged during the fieldwork.

Include key quotes and photos to share with the team. If you used video to record the interview, choose a few clips that could be used in the report.

The Team Report

The team meets to coordinate findings from all the interviews and develop a strategy for producing a final PowerPoint report.

At the report meeting, choose a team scribe or scribes to take notes. Each researcher in turn distributes to the team their completed Write-Up form and presents their findings to the group. Once all the data is in, the team compares and contrasts findings. To help sort out the key insights from all the interviews, the scribe writes a list of relevant findings and themes from the data on a white board and the team whittles down the list to a few key insights.

To ensure that the report does not just list the key findings from each interview, develop a strategy for synthesizing the data into a clear story about your collective experiences and observations in the field. List specific households, events, observations, and consumer statements to support your claims.

Analysis and Presentation

Make use of the various analytical tools that you learned in both Chapters 4 and 5, in particular the binary analysis of cultures in contact. Create a binary table first, showing a series of binaries associated with the research, then plot the binaries on a double-axis grid that illustrates how the two cultures intersect in each quadrant.

Marketing Implications

Think of an example where your findings could be used to develop a new food brand or service targeted to both ethnic and mainstream consumers. Make use of the learnings related to "blending cultures" to create a multicultural brand that would translate an ethnic food for mainstream consumption.

Reading 5

A Semiotic Ethnography of Community Gardening in Chicago's Inner City

Methods and Case Analysis

Laura R. Oswald
Marketing Semiotics, Chicago

The research summarized here illustrates how findings from a semiotic ethnography mitigated a cultural divide between the Garfield Park Conservatory, a public institution, and the local community it meant to serve on the West Side of Chicago. Research findings have important implications for public policy, cultural production in the inner city, and urban gardening.

In 1999 the Conservatory Alliance of civic leaders commissioned this study to gain insights into the programming interests of local residents, identify any barriers to acceptance, and recommend strategies for targeting this population through marketing campaigns. I donated much of my time and scheduled field-work to fit into my business calendar. I usually visited the West Side in the company of a videographer or a volunteer from the Alliance. The research unfolded in two stages, including research with community leaders to gain an overview of the local market and an ethnographic exploration of local consumers at home and in public spaces.

Background

At the turn of the twentieth century, the Conservatory represented the high-cultural ambitions of Chicago's new rich who built their mansions along tree-lined streets leading west from downtown (see Reed 1996, 1999). By the 1990s, the West Side had devolved into an underserved inner-city community and the Conservatory risked demolition. Before World War II, the Conservatory boasted one of the largest horticultural centers in the world, housing a range of rare plants such as orchids, palm trees, and cacti. They used to host lavish seasonal flower shows for a far-reaching population of visitors.

The neighborhood's socioeconomic stability was challenged after World War II when hundreds of thousands of blacks migrated north to Chicago from the rural

South in search of jobs, housing, and education. By the 1960s, the neighborhood experienced rapid decline as businesses and the white moneyed classes fled to the suburbs, leaving massive unemployment, street crime, and abandoned buildings in their wake. At the time of the study, the Conservatory's West Side location claimed the highest rates of unemployment and violent crime in the city of Chicago. Abandoned buildings and empty lots were the enduring legacies of the 1968 race riots that followed upon Dr. King's assassination. Visitors from downtown and local residents alike were deterred by the reputed dangers of walking these streets and the Conservatory itself was threatened with demolition in the face of diminishing attendance, rising maintenance costs, and lack of community support.

Study Objectives

In addition to improving programming that appealed to the local residents, the Alliance needed to convince funding agencies of the Conservatory's positive impact on the welfare of the local African American population across the West Side, including Garfield Park, West Humboldt Park, Austin, and Lawndale. The Alliance claimed that horticulture was a proven means of improving personal well-being and that the greenhouse experience could counteract negative forces in the neighborhood. They also anticipated that the Conservatory would ultimately stand as a catalyst for uniting the community around a shared experience and cultural identity. We would discover the fallacy of these assumptions in due time.

Early stage interviews made clear that developing the right program, brochure, or publicity campaign would not by itself succeed in attracting local residents to the Conservatory. Nor would we reach this population through traditional marketing channels such as direct mail or mass media. Due to the fragile commercial and social infrastructure of the community, it was not immediately clear how to identify informants or plan a research agenda. Recruiting grew from a list of school groups that had recently visited the Conservatory. Through informal networking, I developed a generous database of teachers, community leaders, and eventually local residents.

We were challenged to deliver on the original marketing objectives because of the inaccessibility of many residents. Many local residents were transient or had fallen away from the social networks that bind communities together due to unemployment, drug addiction, and lack of institutional support. Even if residents wanted to visit the Conservatory, fear of gang activity and cuts in public transportation stood in their way. Still other residents were isolated in senior residences or halfway houses.

We recommended that the Alliance work with local agencies and charities to fund private transportation to and from the Conservatory and senior residences, churches, and halfway houses. We also suggested that they leverage informal social networks within the community to market Conservatory programs according to the accessibility of each population segment. We also encouraged the Alliance to work with community leaders to support advocacy initiatives aimed at improving the neighborhood infrastructure, including public transit and public safety. An investment in the community was also an investment in the Conservatory.

Early stage findings also suggested that residents would probably not adopt the Conservatory as a catalyst for social cohesion due to the cultural barriers dividing these two worlds. The Conservatory is the rarefied product of white European culture and had low appeal for the local community, which consisted primarily of working-class African Americans who, for the most part had migrated to Chicago from the agricultural South in the 1950s and 1960s.

An Exploratory Ethnography of Community Gardening

In the course of multiple informal conversations with residents at aldermanic meetings, churches, and community centers, I learned about a thriving tradition of community gardening that already claimed the hearts and minds of local residents. I pursued this line of investigation in an extended ethnography of community gardening. I employed semi-structured methodologies that include emergent design, social networking, and prolonged engagement in the community.

Emergent Design

The research design, direction, and even recruiting emerged in response to day-to-day findings. An example of "emergent design" (Belk, Wallendorf, and Sherry 1989), the fieldwork proceeded apace without a structured guide, recruitment specifications, or fixed variables for interpreting findings. Ethnographic methods, including prolonged, informal contact with the community, social networking, and participant observation enabled me to insinuate myself into the local culture and recruit informants.

Social Networking

Recruitment evolved from informal social networking. For example, a local teacher told me about two retired grandmothers who spent their spare time clearing and developing empty lots into lush gardens. Since I did not have their address or phone number, I just showed up at the garden and asked around until

I found them. I continued in this manner until I had a list of gardens in Austin, Lawndale, and Garfield Park.

Prolonged Engagement

I visited the gardeners on multiple occasions over a six-month period and even helped out in the garden on occasion. By way of an incentive for their time, I donated gift certificates from a nursery supply store. I also spoke with heads at community centers, gardening organizations, and educational programs that were involved in the neighborhood, including the Open Lands Project, Bethel New Life Center, Primo Women's Center, The Field Museum Center for Cultural Understanding, and the Urban Horticulture and Environment Program at the University of Illinois Extension. From these contacts, I learned of other gardens across the West Side.

I knew when I had recruited a sufficient sample of informants when I began to observe a common set of characteristics among gardeners who were spread across multiple neighborhoods. They are working-class homeowners with a stake in the community; they became social activists when City Hall neglected demands for cleanup and public safety; and they leveraged the symbolic importance of gardening and green space for cultural identity and social organization in the African American community. The following summaries focus on five gardeners: Earle and Lorrean, retired activists in Lawndale, Betty and Mary, retired grandmothers in Garfield Park, and Doretha, the neighborhood matriarch, also in Lawndale.

The Gardeners*

Earle and Lorrean and The Slum Busters Project

Earle and Lorrean became activists when they retired in the late 1960s and took stock of the deterioration of the neighborhood. Garbage and abandoned cars were piling up in empty lots, abandoned buildings were home to drug dealers, and businesses dumped construction materials in the alleys.

> We say the slums is in the people. The neighborhood was nice, but the people come and they didn't care.... you can work on your car and leave car parts out on the streets. Somebody might be growing grass, maybe one person out of the whole block, and [the people] didn't care about what they did, they'd run all over it ... like they didn't see the paper and the bottles and garbage.... Then we used to go to meetings and talk to the alderman. And they still didn't seem to get the picture.—Earle.

Figure R5.1. A Slum Buster garden. Photo by Gerald Earles

Earle is a retired auto mechanic whose family migrated to Chicago from New Orleans in the 1940s. Lorrean is a retired clerk for a utility company. Her family migrated to Chicago from Mississippi in the 1940s because she said her father didn't want his daughters to grow up in the Jim Crow South (see Lehman 1992). Earle and Lorrean own two three-flat buildings in Lawndale. In 1993, President Clinton awarded them a Thousand Points of Light Award for cleaning up a total of fifty city blocks on the West Side, through personal initiative and community activism. They even created a community garden for rehabilitating inmates on the Cook County Jail campus.

They took things into their own hands. Beginning with a shovel and a garbage bag, they began cleaning empty lots in Lawndale. They then planted grass, flowers, vegetables, and trees in lots all over Lawndale (Figure R5.1). Earle and Lorrean view their work as a calling. Earle emphasizes the deeply spiritual rewards associated with gardening, both as a source of beauty and of personal empowerment.[1]

---

[1] The author thanks the informants for providing access to their lives and enabling publication of these insights.

> Some people are chosen to be a minister or a physician. We were chosen to be Slum Busters because of what we saw that needed to be taken care of. We tried to get the neighbors involved. People want something for their time. A lot of them want to get paid. Some think we're getting paid. The main thing was to make the area look nice. People say "Do you get paid for this?" and I say yeah, I get paid when I see the grass and flowers growing and looking good. Instead of a check, we get grass and flowers and vegetables growing.—Earle.

As they extended their efforts to other blocks, they organized volunteers into a group they named "Slum Busters" and demanded help from City Hall to clear empty lots of abandoned cars and construction debris, tear down abandoned buildings, and maintain sidewalks. They hold fundraisers to purchase materials for the fences, plants, and other materials.

To "make people see," they use photography and video to garner media attention and "make people see" in presentations to public officials. They invite the press to cover Slum Buster events such as the "Say No to Slums March," to which they invite the mayor, the alderman, state representatives, congressmen, and the police superintendent. By taking control of media narrative, they empower the community and expose its positive side. One of their media events even caused an alderman to lose an election.

Earle was inspired by Martin Luther King Jr., who was organizing on the West Side in 1968. Earle recalls sitting on the beach one morning back then and hearing an announcement inviting people to come to a meeting of Operation Breadbasket.

> I decided to go, and saw people who wanted to make a difference, including the Reverend Jessie Jackson. I learned how to deal with doing things, how to call up the mayor and speak to him, and go see the superintendent of police.

The garden next to Earle and Lorrean's home is traversed by an elevated train running east and west from downtown, forming a dramatic contrast between the lush vegetation of the garden below that includes collard greens, peppers, squash, and flowers, and the periodic roar of the train overhead. The couple invites school groups to the garden for the fall and spring clean-up. They also started a 4-H club and donated part of one garden to 4-H members, not only to teach children horticulture but also to keep them busy after school. He and Lorrean are informal grandparents to the children in the community because their own parents are apathetic and dump garbage in the street, no matter how often they clean up.

Doretha and the Prairie Street Block Club

Doretha's parents had been farmers in Louisiana before moving to Mississippi in the 1940s for better jobs. As a teenager in the 1950s, Doretha migrated north to the

West Side of Chicago and stayed with relatives until she married. She and her husband sent their three children to Catholic school. She worked for almost thirty years as a nurse's assistant at a local hospital. Her husband died twenty years prior to our interview and her children grew up and moved to the suburbs. Rather than follow her children, Doretha preferred to stay in Chicago, her home for over fifty years, and wants to maintain the equity in her two-flat building.

Doretha works in the garden most days with other members of the block club and involves neighborhood children in cultivating and planting. These days Doretha is known as "Mom" to many of her neighbors, even adult men. She holds sway with gang members on the street. Doretha, a deacon at a Baptist Church, gently asks them to move on with an encouraging, "God bless."

> They respect us because I don't talk down at them. [She says,] "I love you. I know you're gonna work; you need to get a job. You can't get a job if you're gonna get out here and do this sellin' for someone else. Not here, the kids gotta get out and play." So we work together; so they go somewhere else. Every once in a while you hear them out there trying to do something, but not often.... They're just kids just like my kids.... Anywhere from 13 to in their 20s.... If I see somebody—a strange face come out there and I know they're not supposed to be there,... I'll call them and say, "Come over here sweetheart," and we'll sit down and have a talk. [They say,] "Yes mam, yes my Momma, I understand." [She says,] "That's okay, I love you." And they're on their way.—Doretha

When she retired, Doretha and her neighbors revived the Prairie Street Block Club to counteract the decline of the neighborhood, the rise of gangs, and drug traffic. Doretha explains that in the 1970s people were moving out of the neighborhood because they could not obtain jobs, security, and basic services. Residents abandoned buildings when they could no longer pay taxes, and even the Catholic Church down the street was demolished for lack of funding. Sunday services are now held in the school gymnasium.

Findings from the Prairie Street block club provide insights into the role of informal social practices in the movement of consumer culture on the West Side. These practices are grounded in African American culture and include broad, informal kinship networks, an economy of borrowing and reciprocal exchange, social activism, and the articulation of sacred space through signage, fencing, and plantings. These practices recur in various configurations in all of the gardens under analysis.

The block club pressured the City of Chicago to tear down an abandoned building on the street and leased the lot from the city. They marshaled the help of greening organizations such as Open Lands to prepare the ground and donate plants for a garden. The result was Crystal's Peace Garden, a lush oasis of flowers and vegetables. Crystal's Peace Garden is filled with a variety of roses, perennials, and annual flowers visible from the street, as well as an abundance of vegetables, including collard greens, peppers, squash, onions, corn, beans, and okra that they distribute to neighbors (Figure R5.2). They harvest collard greens as late as November and preserve produce year-round in the freezer in plastic bags.

Figure R5.2. Crystal's Peace Garden. Photo by the author

Doretha's block is an oasis of well-maintained two- and three-flat buildings and groomed yards in this distressed neighborhood. The gardeners' impact on the neighborhood occurs within the "multitude of rituals, situations, gestures and experiences" of daily life (Maffesoli [1988] 1996), rather than at the level of political activism.

As we saw over and over again, the effects of these gardening efforts on social organization, cultural reproduction, and even food supplies far exceeds their esthetic function. Fencing, naming the gardens, and homemade signs form inter-pretive frames around the gardens and set them aside from the street as green space. The signs outline the block's rules of civic behavior, including a ban on drinking, drug dealing, loud noises, speeding, or weapons. Informants throughout the study stated that in the inner city, "green space is sacred space," not only for residents but also gangs and dealers who leave the gardens alone.

The academic literature supports the view that green space can have positive impact on the psychological well-being of inner-city residents (see Coley, Kuo, and Sullivan 1997; Taylor, Kuo, and Sullivan 1998; Kweon, Sullivan, and

Wiley 1998; Taylor, Kuo, and Sullivan 2001, 2002; Kuo 2001; Kuo, and Sullivan 2001). "Green space" is a place of calm and beauty, and many of the gardens call attention to young victims of street violence in one of the most crime-ridden neighborhoods in Chicago, such as the Peace Garden, Rachel's Garden, or the Reconciliation Garden. During our visit with Doretha, one of her fellow gardeners began to weep because it was the anniversary of the death of her son, found shot to death nine years before.

The interpretive frames that set green space apart from the street—including fencing, naming, signage, and codes of civic comportment—contribute to the symbolic dimensions of gardening that both reproduce the community's southern agricultural heritage and also define the community's collective cultural identity in urban centers in the North. "Everyone had [community] gardens in the South....they shared the harvest among themselves" (Doretha). Some block clubs even plant cotton and tobacco to commemorate the southern black experience on plantations and sharecropping farms. Local gardens and gardening thus transcend their practical functions and stand as icons for the community's collective identity and solidarity, a function that public institutions would be hard-pressed to supply.

The Informal Social Order

The first two gardening stories illustrate how underserved communities resort to informal social strategies to compensate for their lack of power and material resources (Laguerre 1994). Through individual activism, volunteering, and reciprocal exchange, they meet social, safety, and material needs where formal agencies fall short (see Stack 1974: 39–40; Wellman 1990: 195; Drake and Clayton 1993 [1945]). Community elders patrol the neighborhood at night, they hold fundraisers, help residents with paperwork, and even grow fresh produce to compensate for the lack of local supermarkets.

Their services are not simply charity, however, but represent moments in a complex reciprocal economy (Stack 1974: 40) that obliges the receiver of benefits to return the favor at some point in time, even if not in the same way. It is a subtle but powerful form of give-and-take that supports social networks in communities such as these, which on the surface seem to lack meaning and coherence (see Wellman 1990). In the informal society, customs and informal social bonds are stronger and more resilient than formal contracts or even family ties. In this system of favors and debts, community leaders are not reciprocated in kind, but in the form of social support that empowers them to obtain even more benefits from the formal sector (agencies, institutions, government) and so on in an ongoing social dynamic.

Ethel and Betty and the Maypole Street Block Club

Ethel and Betty are retired grandmothers who formed the Maypole Street Block Club just west of the Garfield Park Conservatory after they retired. They have lived in the neighborhood most of their adult lives and have been working in three gardens on their street for over fifteen years.

Betty's family migrated to Chicago from Mississippi in the 1940s via St. Louis, where she still attends large family reunions. She lives in a single-family home with her husband and the oldest of her four children and two grandchildren. She and her neighbor of forty years, Ethel, had always grown flowers in their back yards, but only after they retired did they begin cleaning up the block. Both had worked for over twenty-five years at the same jobs, Ethel with the utility company, Betty at a hospital. Their children and grandchildren moved to the suburbs as adults.

Ethel grew up on her father's farm in Alabama, where she and her siblings each had small gardens and competed among themselves to produce the best produce and flowers. She and her husband moved to the West Side of Chicago via Detroit, where he worked in a factory after the war. She said when they bought their two-flat building in Garfield Park in the 1950s, the streets were lined with trees and the Park was still the center of community activities such as boating, swimming, and lounging on the grass—a stark contrast with the current situation. By the 1990s, the local high school could not even hold gym in the Park because of the threat of gangs.

Ethel and Betty developed abandoned lots with help from City Hall and local greening organizations that cleared the land and provided plants and shrubs. Unlike Earle, Lorrean, and Doretha, Ethel and Betty grow only flowers in the street gardens, but cultivate vegetables in their back yards. Like the other gardeners, the women are motivated to some extent by maintaining the equity in their homes. In addition to beautifying the block, gardens such as these are informal sites for spreading news and networking, both within the block and with other blocks. The women compete in annual gardening contests with other block clubs, share resources with other gardeners, and pass along information of relevance to the community as a whole. They built a gazebo where the neighbors hold parties and meetings.

Like other gardeners, Ethel and Betty involve the local schools in their work, teaching children how to plant bulbs, pull weeds, and sow seeds. Gardening thus empowers the gardener to move out of the realm of personal satisfaction and into the realm of social commitment and transformation.

Like Earle and Lorrean, Betty took advantage of these kinds of networks to claim benefits from the formal sector. During the Clinton Administration, Empowerment Zone grants were established for inner-city residents to pay for improvements to the exteriors of their homes. In order to benefit from the grant, residents had to submit application forms with details about their property. Betty went door to door in a twelve-block radius from her home to distribute information, help people fill out the forms, and mail them to the government.

Gardening as Cultural Reproduction

Ethel and Betty reiterate that though the gardens beautify the neighborhood, it is not so much the end product as the gardening process itself that has value for residents. This point was underscored when a rich white man from the suburbs— an outsider—hired professionals to create a garden across the street from Betty and Ethel's garden. In an interview, this benefactor from the suburbs reported that he hired a team of landscapers and contractors rather than engage local residents in the project. They planted mature trees and shrubs, installed an expensive fountain, lighting, and a brick fence, and finished the whole job in several months—"because I wanted it to be ready by summer," he said.

Although the new garden dwarfed the women's garden in terms of material and architectural advantages, and though the white man named the garden after Betty, observations at the site over the months following the installation confirmed that the residents by and large neglected it. The rejection of the new garden was dramatically illustrated during a block party Betty and Ethel organized to celebrate completion of the fancy garden, since, they had the audacity to hold the party not in the rich man's garden but *in their own garden across the street!* I videotaped the party and interviewed the neighbors. Over fifty people attended the luncheon, which included barbecue, and homemade ice cream and cake. No one so much as looked across the street toward the white man's contribution, though they were too respectful to criticize it when directly questioned. When interviewed at the party, the white man was undeterred, saying he was staking out other sites on the West Side to build new gardens— but only in areas "where people really want to take care of them." Contrary to his expectations, the community did not occupy or maintain the garden because it did not engage their struggles for personal emancipation, social engagement, and social reproduction through community activism.

Summary

Bridging Local and Institutional Garden Cultures

This last example returns us full circle to the social service ambitions of the Conservatory Alliance to rehabilitate local residents, increase their engagement in Conservatory programs, and serve as a beacon for community unity and solidarity. Findings from the ethnography make clear that the meaning of community gardening for the local population already serves these purposes. The benefits of community gardening draw directly from the informal ties, actions, and cultural identity themes that gardening puts into play. Neither formal programming, nor gifts, nor cultural symbols borrowed from the Conservatory can substitute for the sense of empowerment, civic responsibility, social cohesion, and cultural distinction that the residents derive from creating and maintaining green space on the blocks where they reside. Stated in more theoretical terms, community gardening has a powerful impact on inner-city neighborhoods because it puts into play the collective actions of meaning production and cultural reproduction. As I show in the following section, Conservatory horticulture and community gardening form two incompatible semiotic systems and these distinctions pose substantial hurdles to achieving the Conservatory's goals.

How Do Gardens Mean?

If we agree with Clifford Geertz (1973a, 5) that "the concept of culture...is essentially a semiotic one," then the tensions formed by cultures in contact create a kind of *semiotic dissonance* that eludes dialectical synthesis and forms lines of resistance between groups. In the case of the Garfield Park Conservatory, semiotic dissonance centered on contrasting interpretations of the meaning of gardens, public space, culture, and social organization by the parties involved. I mapped these contrasts along binary oppositions such as European American/African American and urban/rural, elite/popular culture (Figure R5.3).

Community Gardens   **Conservatory**
African American   Eurpoean American
Informal Culture   **X** Formal Culture
Rural   Urban
Popular Culture   Elite Culture
Reciprocal Economy   Cash Economy
Contingent Eco-System   Self-Contained
Open Discourse   Closed Discourse

Figure R5.3. Cultural dissonance: How do gardens mean?

The Conservatory gardens are derived from an urban, European elite cultural tradition, are maintained by professional horticulturists, and exist within an artificial, controlled, and self-contained eco-system. The walls and glass ceilings shield the visitor from the real "profane" world of the inner city. Conservatory greenhouses are sustained by a capitalist cash economy through memberships, fees, and endowments, and represent a closed system of social discourse. Signage in the Conservatory reflects back on the plants rather than referencing the social reality of the visitor. Communication is one way, from the work of experts outward to the visitor, who is admonished at every turn not to cross the lines separating them from the plants. In other words, the social discourse of the Conservatory references a closed system of horticultural science that transcends the realities of history and urban society. This context is reiterated in the architecture, the plantings, the brochures, and signage.

On the other hand, the West Side community gardens are derived from a rural African American popular culture tradition, are maintained by volunteers, and exist in an outdoor eco-system contingent on such factors as weather and available help. Community gardens are sustained by a reciprocal exchange economy and represent an open system of discourse. The semiotic world of the community gardens opens onto the fields of history, community, and social activism. From the names of the gardens, to the use of signage, to the choice and distribution of plants, to the very existence of the gardens themselves, community gardens on the West Side are sites for the production of community solidarity and the reproduction of urban African American culture.

Managerial Implications

Michael Porter (1995, 59) finds that "Most products and services have been designed for white consumers and businesses. As a result, product configurations, retail concepts, entertainment, and personal and business services have not been adapted to the needs of inner-city customers." For the Garfield Park Conservatory to develop a successful business model for reaching the local market, they would need to take into account for cultural factors that form barriers to acceptance by the local population.

The challenge for the Conservatory Alliance was to develop a culture-focused strategy for satisfying community needs and building long-term relationships with community stakeholders. Although they had initially planned to reconfigure current programs to meet the interests of the local population, findings from the ethnography suggested the need for a fresh approach that aligned with the community's indigenous gardening culture. The Conservatory took steps to send horticulturalists out to the neighborhood to help gardeners improve planting and yields and even made changes to the physical operations of the Conservatory campus itself, which occupies 184 acres of parkland. Just south of the Conservatory, they constructed a Demonstration garden the size of a city lot, where residents who do not have gardens can learn about growing methods for urban gardens, organic planting, and the plants that best grow there. At the north end of the building, the Alliance holds a weekly Farmers Market that features produce from local organic farmers.

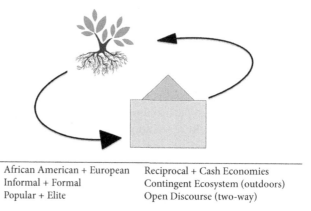

African American + European	Reciprocal + Cash Economies
Informal + Formal	Contingent Ecosystem (outdoors)
Popular + Elite	Open Discourse (two-way)

Figure R5.4. Community gardening at the Conservatory

These kinds of initiatives mitigated the firm cultural contrasts between the Conservatory and the local community that at one time seemed insurmountable. By reaching out to local growers in their own gardens, extending the Conservatory's footprint beyond the walls of the institution to the Demonstration Garden, and marketing the organic produce of urban farmers, the Conservatory created a space for cultural inclusion, dialogue, even market exchange that neither appropriates nor assimilates the local culture (Figure R5.4).

Theoretical Implications

These observations of cultures in contact challenge the assumptions of public policy agencies regarding the role of public institutions in the inner city. The reader may recall that the Conservatory Alliance originally assumed that the local community "needed" them, not only for sharing horticultural expertise but also for enabling social organization and rehabilitation and personal well-being. Findings from the ethnography disproved these assumptions by exploring the positive effects of the community's informal gardening culture on social organization and community improvement.

Furthermore, recommendations led to creation of a hybrid cultural space where the active flow and exchange of cultural influence, goods, and knowledge between the institution and the local community could play out. This strategy fostered cultural and social exchange but left each cultural system—the Conservatory and the local gardening culture—intact. According to the latest visitor data, local residents still prefer community gardening to the Conservatory's greenhouse exhibits, and the Conservatory's traditional programming still draws thousands of visitors from beyond the community every year.

Furthermore, the study illustrated that cultures in contact do not as a matter of principle end with the assimilation of one culture into the other. For example, our "flow" model resists *synthesizing* cultural binaries into a third meaning, the space of assimilation and acculturation. On the West Side, we observed an active process of flow and exchange *across* cultural binaries rather than synthesis or assimilation. The Conservatory's cultural strategy enabled this flow when they carved out a "border space" for meeting, exchanging goods and information, and gaining understanding of the other's cultural priorities. This border space became a pivotal site for the movement of people, knowledge, and cultural influence back and forth across the boundaries of cultural difference.

Author Profile: Laura R. Oswald

I am trained in theoretical semiotics and poetics and came to consumer research and marketing communications rather late in my career. I work across intersections between theory and consulting to industry: theory feeds the practice of marketing semiotics and the practice feeds theory. As principal of the Marketing Semiotics Company in Chicago, Illinois, I have worked with a variety of blue chip organizations and non-profits on projects ranging from brand equity management, strategic planning and new product development to design strategy and new business acquisition strategy. I also publish in peer-reviewed articles on poetics, cinema semiotics, consumer behavior and marketing communications and have held academic positions at Northwestern University, the ESSEC Business School in Paris, Nanyang Technological University in Singapore, and the University of Illinois Urbana-Champaign.

Bibliography

Aaker, David A. (1991). *Managing Brand Equity: Capitalizing on the Value of a Brand Name*. New York: Free Press.

Aaker, Jennifer (1997). "Dimensions of Brand Personality." *Journal of Marketing Research* 34: 347–56.

Altman, Lynn (2006). *Brand It Yourself: The Fast, Focused Way to Marketplace Magic*. New York: Portfolio.

Aoki, S. (1988). "Semiotics of Significance in Advertising Text." *Studia Semiotica: Journal of the Japanese Association for Semiotic Studies* 8: 249–64.

Appadurai, Arjun, ed. (1986). *The Social Life of Things: Commodities in Cultural Perspective*. New York: Cambridge University Press.

Appiano, A. (1991). *Pubblicità Communicazione Immagine*. Bologna: Zanichelli.

Aristotle ([347–322 BC] 1984). *The Rhetoric and Poetics of Aristotle*. Translated by W. Rhys Roberts and Ingram Bywater. New York: Random House.

Arnold, Stephen, and Eileen Fischer (1994). "Hermeneutics and Consumer Research." *Journal of Consumer Research* 21 (June): 55–70.

Arnould, Eric J., and Craig J. Thompson (2005). "Consumer Culture Theory (CCT): Twenty Years of Research." *Journal of Consumer Research* 31(4): 868–82.

Askegaard, Søren, Dorthe Brogård Kristensen & Sofia Ulver ((2017). "Consumers' Collective Action in Market System Dynamics: A Case of Beer." *Marketing Theory*. 17, 1, pp. 51–70.

Bachand, D. (1988). "Marketing Icons: A Survey of Advertising Semiotics." *Semiotic Inquiry* 3: 277–95.

Bakhtin, Mikhail M. (1981 [1934–1935]). "Discourse in the Novel," in *The Dialogic Imagination*, translated and edited by Michael Holquist and Caryl Emerson. Austin: University of Texas Press, pp. 259–422.

Bakhtin, Mikhail M. (1993). Rabelais and His World, translated by Hélène Iswolsky. Bloomington: Indiana University Press.

Barthes, Roland (1977 [1964]). "Rhetoric of the Image." In *Image, Music, Text*. Translated by Stephen Heath, 32–51. New York: Hill and Wang.

Barthes, Roland (2000 [1964]). *Elements of Semiology*. Translated by Annette Lavers and Colin Smith. New York: Hill and Wang.

Baudrillard, Jean (1968). *Le Système des Objets*. Paris: Gallimard.

Baudrillard, Jean (1983). *Simulations*. New York: Semiotext(e).

Beasley, Ron, and Marcel Danesi (2002). *Persuasive Signs: The Semiotics of Advertising*. The Hague: Mouton de Gruyter.

Belk, Russell (1988). "Possessions and the Extended Self." *Journal of Consumer Research* 15(2): 139–68.

Belk, Russell (1995). "Studies in the New Consumer Behaviour." In *Acknowledging Consumption: A Review of New Studies*, edited by D. Miller, 58–95. London: Routledge.

Belk, Russell, Melanie Wallendorf, and John F. Sherry, Jr. (1989). "The Sacred and the Profane in Consumer Behavior: Theodicy on the Odyssey." *Journal of Consumer Research* 16(1) (June): 1–38.

Belk, Russel & Rana Sobh (2019). "No Assemblage Required: On Pursuing, Original Consumer Culture Theory," Marketing Theory, 19(4), 489–507.

Benveniste, Émile (1967). "La Forme et le sens dans le langage." In Actes du XIIIème Congrès de la philosophie de la langue française, 29–40. Neuchatel: La Baconnière.

Benveniste, Émile (1971 [1966]). "Man and Language." In Problems in General Linguistics, translated by Mary Elizabeth Meek, 195–248. Coral Gables, FL: Miami University Press.

Bertrand, D. (1988). "The Creation of Complicity: A Semiotic Analysis of Advertising Campaign for Black & White Whisky." International Journal of Research in Marketing 4: 273–89.

Bonwell, Charles C., and James A. Eison (1991). Active Learning: Creating Excitement in the Classroom. Washington, DC: ASHE-ERIC Higher Education Reports.

Bourdieu, Pierre de (1984) [1976]. Distinction: A Social Critique of the Judgment of Taste. Translated by Richard Nice. Cambridge, MA: Harvard University Press.

Bourdieu, Pierre de (2010). Distinction: A Social Critique of the Judgement of Taste. Abingdon: Routledge.

Bremer, C., and M. Lee (1997). "Metaphors in Marketing: Review and Implications for Marketers." Advances in Consumer Research 24: 419–24.

Brown, S., and D. Turley, eds. (1997). Consumer Research: Postcards from the Edge. London: Routledge.

Brown, Tim (2009). Change by Design: How Design Thinking Transforms Organizations and Inspires Innovation. New York: Harper Business.

Brunel, Frederic F., and Michelle Nelson (2000). "Gender Responses to 'Help-Self' and 'Help-Others' Charity Ad Appeals: An Analysis of the Mediating Role of World-Views and Values." Journal of Advertising 24(3): 15–28.

Ceschin, Fabrizio, Carlo Vezzoli, and Salvatore Zingale, eds. (2014). "An Aesthetic for Sustainable Interactions in Product-Service Systems?" In Product-Service System Design for Sustainability, 200–17 Sheffield: Greenleaf Publishing.

Chandon, J. L., and F. Dano (1997). "Analyses typologiques confirmatoires: Évaluation d'une partition hypothétique issue d'une étude sémiotique." Recherche et Applications en Marketing 12(2): 1–22.

Clatworthy, Simon (2012). "Interaction Design: Services as a Series of Interactions." In This Is Service Design Thinking: Basics, Tools, Cases, edited by Marc Stickdorn and Jakob Schneider, 80–7. Hoboken, N.J.: Wiley.

Coley, R. L., F. E. Kuo, and W. C. Sullivan (1997). "Where Does Community Grow? The Social Context Created by Nature in Urban Public Housing." Environment and Behavior 29(4): 468–94.

Cook, Vivian (1990). Why Can't Anybody Spell? New York: Touchstone.

Cornu, G. (1990). Sémiologie de l'image dans la publicité. Paris: Les Editions d'Organisation.

Croce, Nia (2018). "Emory Jones Talks 'Bet on Yourself' Puma™ Collab and Why Nike™ Should Have Hired Virgil Abloh First." FB: Fashion Business, September 26. https://footwearnews.com/2018/influencers/athletic-outdoor/emory-jones-Puma™-bet-on-yourself-collection-1202684699/.

Cross, R., and J. Smith (1995). Customer Bonding. Lincolnwood, IL: NTC Business Books.

Danesi, Marcel (2008). Why It Sells: Decoding the Meanings of Brand Names, Logos, Ads, and Other Marketing and Advertising Ploys. Lanham, MD: Rowman & Littlefield.

Dano, F. (1996). "Packaging: Une approche sémiotique." Recherche et Applications en Marketing 11(1): 23–36.

Darley, W. K., and R. E. Smith (1995). "Gender Differences in Information Processing Strategies: An Empirical Test of the Selectivity Model in Advertising Response." *Journal of Advertising* 24(1): 41–56.

Derrida, Jacques (1976). *Of Grammatology*. Translated by Gayatri Chakravorty Spivak. Baltimore and London: Johns Hopkins University Press.

Derrida, Jacques (1983 [1972]). *Dissemination*. Translated by Barbara Johnson. Chicago: University of Chicago Press.

Design Council (2005). "A Study of the Design Process." *Design Council* (Vol. 44).

Dittmar, H. (1992). *The Social Psychology of Social Possessions: To Have Is To Be*. London: Harvester Wheatsheaf.

Douglas, Mary, and Baron Isherwood (1996 [1979]). *The World of Goods: Toward an Anthropology of Consumption*. 2nd ed. New York: Routledge.

Drake, St Clair, and Horace Clayton ([1945] 1993). *Black Metropolis*. Chicago: University of Chicago Press.

Durand, J. (1970). "Rhétorique et image publicitaire." *Communications* 15: 70–96. Translation: (1988). "Rhetorical Figures in the Advertising Image." In *Marketing and Semiotics*, edited by J. Umiker-Sebeok, 295–318. Berlin: Mouton de Gruyter.

Durkheim, Émile (1995 [1912]). *The Elementary Forms of Religious Life*. Translated by Karen E. Fields. New York: The Free Press.

Durkheim, Émile (1997 [1893]). *The Division of Labor in Society*. Translated by George Simpson. New York: The Free Press.

Dyer, G. (1988). *Advertising as Communication*. London: Routledge.

Eco, Umberto (1968). *La struttura assente*. Milan: Bompiani.

Eco, Umberto (1979). *A Theory of Semiotics*. Bloomington: Indiana University Press.

Elliott, Stewart (2013). "Apple Passes Coca-Cola as Most Valuable Brand." *New York Times*, online, September 29. https://www.nytimes.com/2013/09/30/business/media/apple-passes-coca-cola-as-most-valuable-brand.html.

Everaert-Desmedt, N. (1984). *La Communication publicitaire: Etude sémio-pragmatique*. Louvain-la-Neuve: Labay.

Featherstone, M. (1991). *Consumer Culture and Postmodernism*. London: SAGE.

Floch, Jean-Marie (2001 [1990]). *Semiotics, Marketing and Communication: Beneath the Signs, the Strategies*. Translated by Robin Orr Bodkin. New York: Palgrave MacMillan.

Floch, Jean-Marie (1990). *Sémiotique, marketing et communication*. Paris: P.U.F.

Floch, Jean-Marie (1995). *Identités visuelles* Paris: P.U.F.

Forceville, C. (1996). *Pictorial Metaphor in Advertising*. London: Routledge.

Fouquier, E. (1988). "Figures of Reception: Concepts and Rules for a Semiotic Analysis of Mass Media Reception." *International Journal of Research in Marketing* 4(3): 331–48.

Fournier, S. (1998). "Consumers and their Brands: Developing Relationship Theory in Consumer Research." *Journal of Consumer Research* 24(4): 343–73.

Fournier, S., and J. L. Yao (1997). "Reviving Brand Loyalty: A Reconceptualization within the Framework of Consumer-Based Relationships." *International Journal of Research in Marketing* 14(5): 451–72.

Frankel, Alex (2004). *Word Craft: The Art of Turning Little Words into Big Business*. New York: Three Rivers Press.

Freud, Sigmund (1955 [1909]). "Analysis of a Phobia in a Five-Year-Old Boy," in "Two Case Histories," trans. James Strachey, from *The Standard Edition of the Complete Psychological Works of Sigmund Freud*. London: The Hogarth Press: Vol. 10: 1–149.

Freud, Sigmund (1965 [1899]). *The Interpretation of Dreams*, trans. James Strachey (ed.). New York: Avon.

Gay, Paul du, Stuart Hall, Linda Janes, Anders Madsen, Hugh Mackay, and Keith Negus (2013). *Doing Cultural Studies: The Story of the Sony Walkman*. 2nd ed. London: SAGE.

Geertz, Clifford (1973a). "Thick Description: Toward and Interpretive Theory of Culture." In *The Interpretation of Cultures*, 3–30. New York: Basic Books.

Geertz, Clifford (1973b). "Notes on a Balinese Cockfight." In *The Interpretation of Cultures*, by Clifford Geertz, 435–53. New York: Basic Books.

Geis, M. L. (1982). *The Language of Television Advertising*. New York: Academic Press.

Genette, Gérard (1972). "Métonymie chez Proust." In *Figures III*, by Gérard Genette, 41–63. Paris: Editions du Seuil.

Goldman, R. (1992). *Reading Ads Socially*. London: Routledge.

Gottdiener, M. (1995). *Postmodern Semiotics: Material Culture and the Forms of Postmodern Life*. Cambridge, MA: Blackwell.

Grayson, Kent and Radan Martinec (2004). "Consumer Perceptions of Iconicity and Indexicality and Their Influence on Assessments of Authentic Market Offerings." *Journal of Consumer Research* 31(2): 296–313.

Greenberg, Zack O'Malley (2019). "Kanye's Second Coming: Inside The Billion-Dollar Yeezy Empire." *Forbes*, The Daily Cover, July 9, 2019, 08:00 A.M. https://www.forbes.com/sites/zackomalleygreenburg/2019/07/09/kanyes-second-coming-inside-the-billion-dollaryeezy-empire/#398e57b65ec3.

Greimas, A. J., and J. Courtès (1979). *Sémiotique: Dictionnaire raisonné de la théorie du langage*. Paris: Hachette. Translation: Larry Christ, Daniel Patte, James Lee, Edward McMahon II, Gary Phillips, & Michael Rengstorf (1982) *Semiotics and Language: An Analytical Dictionary*. Bloomington: Indiana University Press.

Greimas, Algirdas (1984 [1966]). *Structural Semantics: An Attempt at a Method*. Translated by Daniele McDowell, Ronald Schleifer, and Alan Velie. Omaha: University of Nebraska Press.

Grunig, B. N. (1990). *Les Mots de la publicité*. Paris: Les Presses du CNRS.

Gunasti, K., and B. Devezer (2016). "How Competitor Brand Names Affect Within-Brand Choices." *Marketing Letters* 27(4): 715–27.

Gurvitch, Georges (1955). "Le Concept de structure sociale." *Cahiers Internationaux de Sociologie*, New Series, 19 (July–August): 3–44.

Hall, Edward T. (1966). *The Hidden Dimension*. New York: Anchor Books.

Hall, Stuart (1980). "Encoding/Decoding." In *Culture, Media, Language*, edited by Stuart Hall, D. Hobson, A. Lowe, and P. Willis, 128–38. London: Unwin Hyman.

Heilbrunn, B. (1998). "My Brand the Hero: A Semiotic Analysis of the Consumer-Brand Relationship." In *European Perspectives in Consumer Behavior*, edited by M. Lambkin et al. 102–15 London: Prentice Hall.

Henny, L., ed. (1987). *Semiotics of Advertisements*. Aachen: Raderverlag.

Herzfeld, Michael (1983). "Signs in the Field: Prospects and Issues for Semiotic Ethnography." *Semiotica* 46: 99–106.

Hirschman, E., and M. Holbrook (1992). *Postmodern Consumer Research: The Study of Consumption as a Text*. London: Routledge.

Hodge, Robert, and Gunther Kress (1988). *Social Semiotics*. Ithaca, NY: Cornell University Press.

Holbrook, Morris B., and Elizabeth C. Hirschman (1993). *The Semiotics of Consumption: Interpreting Symbolic Consumer Behavior in Popular Culture and Works of Art*. New York: Mouton de Gruyter.

Howarth, Sophie, and Jennifer Mundy (2015). "Marcel Duchamp: Fountain." London: The Tate Gallery, June 15, 2019. https://www.tate.org.uk/art/artworks/duchamp-fountain-t07573.

Interbrand Group (2018). Best Global Brands 2018: Rankings. New York. https://www.interbrand.com/best-brands/best-global-brands/2018/ranking/.

IREP (1976). *Les Apports de la sémiotique au marketing et à la publicité*. Paris: IREP.

IREP (1983). *Sémiotique II*. Paris: IREP.

Jakobson, Roman (1990). In *On Language: Roman Jakobson*, edited by Linda Waugh and Monique Monville-Burston, Cambridge, MA: Harvard University Press.

Jakobson, Roman (ibid). "Two Aspects of Language and Two Types of Aphasic Disturbances," 115–33.

Jensen, K. B. (1995). *The Social Semiotics of Mass Communication*. London: SAGE.

Julien, M. (1997). *L'Image publicitaire des parfums*. Paris: L'Harmattan.

Kehret-Ward, T. (1988). "Combining Products in Use." In *Marketing and Semiotics*, edited by J. Umiker-Sebeok, 219–58. Berlin: Mouton de Gruyter.

Klein, Naomi (2000). *No Logo: Taking Aim at the Brand Bullies*. Toronto: Alfred A. Knopf.

Krueger, Richard A., and Mary Anne Casey (2014). *Focus Groups: A Practical Guide for Applied Research*. 5th ed. Thousand Oaks, CA: SAGE.

Kuo, F. E. (2001). "Coping with Poverty: Impacts of Environment and Attention in the Inner City." *Environment & Behavior* 33(1): 5–34.

Kuo, F. E. and W. C. Sullivan (2001). "Aggression and Violence in the Inner City." *Environment and Behavior* 33(4): 543–71.

Kweon, B. S., W. C. Sullivan, and A. Wiley (1998). "Green Common Spaces and the Social Integration of Inner-City Older Adults." *Environment and Behavior* 30: 832–58.

Laclau, Ernesto (2007). "L'Articulation du sens et les limites de la métaphore." *Archives de Philosophie* 70(4): 599–624.

Laguerre, Michel S. (1994). *The Informal City*. New York: St. Martin's Press.

Lakoff, George (1992). "The Contemporary Theory of Metaphor." In *Metaphor and Thought*, 2nd ed., edited by Andrew Ortony, 202–51. Cambridge: Cambridge University Press.

Larsen, Hanne Hartvig, David Glen Mick, and Christian Alsted, eds. (1991). *Marketing and Semiotics: Selected Papers from the Copenhagen Symposium*. Copenhagen: Handelshøjskolens Forlag.

Lawes, Rachel (2002). "Demystifying Semiotics: Some Key Questions Answered." *International Journal of Market Research* 44(3): 251–64.

Lawes, R. (2020). *Using Semiotics in Marketing: How to Achieve Consumer Insight for Brand Growth and Profits*. London: Kogan Page.

Lehman, Nicholas (1992). *The Promised Land: The Great Black Migration and How It Changed America*. New York: Vintage Books.

Leigh, J. H. (1994). "The Use of Figures of Speech in Print Ad Headlines." *Journal of Advertising* 23: 17–34.

Lévi-Strauss, Claude (1974 [1963]). *Structural Anthropology*. Translated Claire Jacobson and Brooke Schoepf. New York: Doubleday Anchor.

Levitt, Theodore (1960). "Marketing Myopia." *Harvard Business Review* 37 (July–August) 24–47.

Levy, Sidney J. (1959). "Symbols for Sale." *Harvard Business Review* 37 (July–August): 117–24.

Levy, Sidney J. (1981). "Interpreting Consumer Mythology: A Structural Approach to Consumer Behavior." *Journal of Marketing* 45(3) (Summer): 49–61.

Maffesoli, Michel (1996 [1988]). *The Time of the Tribes: The Decline of Individualism in Mass Society*. Translated by Don Smith. Thousand Oaks, CA: SAGE.

Martin, K. (2017). *Famous Brand Names and Their Origins*. New York: Pen & Sword.

Massanari, Adrienne L. (2010). "Designing for Imaginary Friends: Information Architecture, Personas and the Politics of User-Centered Design." *New Media & Society* 12(3): 401–16. https://doi.org/10.1177/1461444809346722.

McCracken, Grant (1986). "Culture and Consumption: A Theoretical Account of the Structure and Movement of the Cultural Meaning of Consumer Goods." *Journal of Consumer Research* 13 (June): 71–84.

McCracken, Grant (1988). *Culture and Consumption.* Bloomington: Indiana University Press.

McCracken, Grant (1990). *Culture and Consumption: New Approaches to the Symbolic Character of Consumer Goods and Activities.* Bloomington: Indiana University Press.

McQuarrie, Edward, and David Glen Mick (1992). "On Resonance: A Critical Pluralistic Inquiry into Advertising Rhetoric." *Journal of Consumer Research* 19 (September): 180–97.

McQuarrie, Edward, and David Glen Mick (1996). "Figures of Rhetoric in Advertising Language." *Journal of Consumer Research* 22: 424–38.

Merriam, Sharon B. (2015). *Qualitative Research: A Guide to Design and Implementation.* 4th ed. Hoboken, NJ: John Wiley.

Merton, Robert K. (1964). *Social Theory and Social Structure.* 9th ed. Glencoe, IL: Free Press/Collier-Macmillan.

Metz, Christian (1981 [1977]). *The Imaginary Signifier.* Translated by Ben Brewster, Annwyl Williams, and Celia Britton. Bloomington: Indiana University Press.

Metz, Christian (1991 [1971]). *Film Language.* Translated by Michael Taylor. Chicago: University of Chicago Press.

Mick, David Glen (1986). "Consumer Research and Semiotics: Exploring the Morphology of Signs Symbols, and Significance." *Journal of Consumer Research* 18 (September): 196–13.

Mick, David Glen (1997). "Semiotics in Marketing and Consumer Research." In *Consumer Research: Postcards from the Edge,* edited by S. Brown and D. Turley, 249–62. London: Routledge.

Mick, David Glen, and Claus Buhl (1992). "A Meaning Based Model of Advertising Experiences." *Journal of Consumer Research* 19 (December): 317–38.

Morris, Charles W. (1971 [1946]). "Signs, Language and Behavior." In *Writings on the General Theory of Signs,* by Charles Morris, 73–97. The Hague: Mouton.

Muniz, Albert M., Jr., and Thomas C. O'Guinn (2001). "Brand Community." *Journal of Consumer Research* 27, no. 4 (March): 412–32.

Nessler, Dan (2016). "How to Apply a Design Thinking, HCD, UX or Any Creative Process from Scratch." *Digital Experience Design.* https://medium.com/digital-experience-design/how-to-apply-a-design-thinking-hcd-ux-or-any-creative-process-from-scratch-b8786efbf812

Neumeier, Marty (2006). *The Brand Gap.* Berkeley, CA: New Riders.

Norman, Don A., and Verganti, R. (2014). "Incremental and Radical Innovation: Design Research vs. Technology and Meaning Change." *Design Issues* 30(1).

Nöth, W. (1988). "The Language of Commodities." *International Journal of Research in Marketing* 4: 173–86.

Nöth, W. ed. (1997). *Semiotics of the Media.* Berlin: Mouton de Gruyter.

Nuessel, Frank (2010). "A Note on Names for Energy Drink Brands and Products." *Names* 58: 102–10.

O'Connell, Liam (2019). "Revenue from Footwear Segment of Nike, Adidas and Puma from 2010 to 2018 (in billion U.S. dollars)." *Statista.* https://static1.statista.com/statistics/278834/revenue-nike-adidas-puma-footwear-segment/, Mar 21, 2019.

Oswald, Laura R. (1987). "Toward a Semiotics of Performance: Staging the Double in Jean Genet." *Poetics Today* 8(2): 261–83.

Oswald, Laura R. (1989). *Jean Genet and the Semiotics of Performance*. Bloomington: Indiana University Press.

Oswald, Laura R. (1999). "Culture Swapping: The Ethnogenesis of Middle-Class Haitian-Americans." *Journal of Consumer Research* 25(4): 303–18.

Oswald, Laura R. (2010). "Marketing Hedonics: Toward a Psychoanalysis of Advertising Response." *Journal of Marketing Communication*, 16(3), 107–31. June, 107–31.

Oswald, Laura R. (2011). "What Do Chinese Consumers Want? A Semiotic Approach to Building Brand Literacy in Developing Markets," in *Cultural Marketing Management*, ed. Lisa Penaloza, Nil Ozcaglar and Luca Visconti. New York: Routledge 2011.

Oswald, Laura R. (2012). *Marketing Semiotics: Signs, Strategies, and Brand Value*. New York: Oxford University Press.

Oswald, Laura R. (2015). *Creating Value: The Theory and Practice of Marketing Semiotics Research*. New York: Oxford University Press.

Peirce, Charles Sanders (1988 [1955]). "Logic as Semiotic." In *The Philosophical Writings of Charles Sanders Peirce*, edited by Justus Buchler, 98–19. New York: Dover Press.

Peninou, G. (1972). *Intelligence de la publicité: Étude sémiotique*. Paris: Robert Laffont.

Perez Tomero, J. M. (1982). *La Semiotica de la publicidad*. Barcelona: Mitre.

Pinson, Christian, ed. (1988). "Semiotics and Marketing Communication Research." *International Journal of Research in Marketing* 4, nos. 3 and 4 (double issue).

Pinson, Christian, ed. (1998). "Marketing Semiotics." In *Concise Encyclopedia of Pragmatics*, edited by Jacob L. Mey, 538–44. London: Pergamon Press.

Porter, Michael E. (1995). "The Competitive Advantage of the Inner City." *Harvard Business Review* 73, no. 3 (May–June) 55–71.

Reder, Hillary. (2015). "Serial & Singular: Andy Warhol's Campbell's Soup Cans." *Inside/Out: A MoMA/MoMA PS1 Blog*. New York: Museum of Modern Art, posted April 29. https://www.moma.org/explore/inside_out/2015/04/29/serial-singular-andy-warhols-campbells-soup-cans/.

Reed, Christopher Robert (1996). "West Garfield Park." In *Chicago, City of Neighborhoods*, edited by Dominique A. Pacyga and Ellen Skerrett, 98–101. Chicago: Loyola UP.

Reed, Christopher Robert (1999). "Beyond Chicago's Black Metropolis: A History of the West Side's First Century, 1837–1940." *Journal of the Illinois State Historical Society*, Summer Issue.

Reynolds, T. J., and J. Gutman (1988). "Laddering Theory, Method, Analysis, and Interpretation." *Journal of Advertising Research* 28(1): 11–31.

Richards, I. A. (1929). *Practical Criticism*. New York: Harcourt Brace.

Richins, M. L. (1994). "Valuing Things: The Private and Public Meanings of Possessions." *Journal of Consumer Research* 21: 504–21.

Ries, Al, and Jack Trout (2000 [1981]). *Positioning: The Battle for Your Mind*. New York: McGraw-Hill.

Ritson, Mark, and Richard Elliot (1999). "The Social Uses of Advertising: An Ethnographic Study of Adolescent Advertising Audiences." *Journal of Consumer Research* 26(3): 260–77.

Roy, Marina (2000). *Sign after the X*. Vancouver: Advance Artspeak.

Sahlins, Marshall (1976). *Culture and Practical Reason*. Chicago: University of Chicago Press.

Sanders, M. S., and E. J. McCormick (1987). *Human Factors in Engineering and Design*. 6th ed. New York: McGraw-Hill.

Saussure, Ferdinand de (2011 [1916]). *Course in General Linguistics*. Edited by Perry Meisel and Haun Saussy. Translated by Wade Baskin. New York: Columbia University Press.

Schroeder, Jonathan E. (2002). *Visual Consumption*. New York: Routledge.

Scott, Linda (1994a). "Images in Advertising: The Need for a Theory of Visual Rhetoric." *Journal of Consumer Research* 21(2): 252–73.

Scott, Linda (1994b). "The Bridge from Text to Mind." *Journal of Consumer Research* 21(3): 461–80.

Sebeok, Thomas A. (1972). *Perspectives in Zoosemiotics*. Paris: Mouton.

Semprini, A. (1992). *Le Marketing de la marque: Approche sémiotique*. Paris: Editions Liaisons.

Semprini, A. (1995). *L 'Objet comme procès et comme action*. Paris: L'Harmattan.

Semprini, A. (1996). *Analyser la communication*. Paris: L'Harmattan.

Sherry, John F., Jr. (1987a). "Advertising as a Cultural System." In *Marketing and Semiotics: New Directions in the Study of Signs for Sale*, edited by Jean Umiker-Sebeok, 441–59. Berlin: Mouton de Gruyter.

Sherry, John F., Jr. and Eduardo G. Camargo (1987b). "'May Your Life Be Marvelous': English Language Labelling and the Semiotics of Japanese Promotion." *Journal of Consumer Research* 14 (September): 174–88.

Sherry, John F., Jr. (ed.) (1990). "A Sociocultural Analysis of a Midwestern Fleamarket." *Journal of Consumer Research* 17(1) (June): 13–30.

Sherry, John F., Jr. (1991). "Postmodern Alternatives: The Interpretive Turn in Consumer Research." In *Handbook of Consumer Behavior*, edited by Thomas S. Robertson and Harold H. Kassarjian, 548–91. Englewood Cliffs, NJ: Prentice-Hall.

Skinner, B. F. (1938). *The Behavior of organisms: An experimental analysis*. New York: Appleton-Century.

Souza, Clarisse Sieckenius de (2005). *The Semiotic Engineering of Human-Computer Interaction*. Acting with Technology Series. Cambridge, MA: MIT Press.

Spiegel, David L., Timothy J. Coffey, and Gregory Livingston (2004). *The Great Tween Buying Machine*. Chicago: Dearborn Trade Publishing.

Stack, Carol (1974). *All Our Kin*. New York: Basic Books.

Stanford Encyclopedia of Philosophy (2013)."Tropes." https://plato.stanford.edu/entries/tropes/#HisBac.

Statista website (2018). "Revenue from Footwear Segment of NIKE™, Adidas™, and Puma™ from 2010 to 2017 (in Billion US Dollars)." https://www.statista.com/statistics/278834/revenue-NIKE™-Adidas™-Puma™-footwear-segment/ (Visited August 27, 2018).

Stern, Barbara B. (1988). "How Does an Ad Mean? Language in Services Advertising." *Journal of Advertising* 17(2): 3–14.

Stern, Barbara B. (1989). "Literary Criticism and Consumer Research: Overview and Illustrative Analysis." *Journal of Consumer Research* 16: 322–34.

Stern, Barbara B. (1990). "Pleasure and Persuasion in Advertising: Rhetorical Irony as a Humor Technique." *Current Issues and Research in Advertising* 12: 25–42.

Stern, Barbara B. (1995). "Consumer Myths: Frye's Taxonomy and the Structural Analysis of Consumption Text." *Journal of Consumer Research* 22: 165–85.

Stern, Barbara B. (1996a). "Deconstructive Strategy and Consumer Research: Concepts and Illustrative Exemplar." *Journal of Consumer Research* 23: 136–47.

Stern, Barbara B. (1996b). "Textual Analysis in Advertising Research: Construction and Deconstruction of Meanings." *Journal of Advertising* 25(3): 61–73.

Tanaka, K. (1994). *Advertising Language: A Pragmatic Approach to Advertisements in Britain and Japan*. London: Routledge.

Taylor, A., F. E. Kuo, and W. C. Sullivan (2001). "Coping with ADD: The Surprising Connection to Green Play Settings." *Environment and Behavior* 33(1): 54–77.

Taylor, A., F. E. Kuo, and W. C. Sullivan (2002). "Views of Nature and Self-Discipline: Evidence from Inner-City Children." *Journal of Environmental Psychology*, Special Issue: Environment and Children, 22: 49–63.

Taylor, A., A. Wiley, F. E. Kuo, and W. C. Sullivan (1998). "Growing Up in the Inner City: Green Spaces as Places to Grow." *Environment and Behavior* 30(1): 3–27.

Taylor, Kate (2018). "Kanye West and Adidas™ Just Made a Major Play to One-Up Supreme." *Business Insider*, September 21, 8:56 AM. https://www.businessinsider.com/kanye-west-and-Adidas™-follow-supremes-front-page-ad-strategy-2018-9.

Thompson, Craig J. (1997). "Interpreting Consumers: A Hermeneutical Framework for Deriving Marketing Insights from the Texts of Consumers' Consumption Stories." *Journal of Marketing Research* 34: 438–55.

Thompson, Craig J., and Diana L. Haytko (1997). "Speaking of Fashion: Consumer's Uses of Fashion Discourses and the Appropriation of Countervailing Cultural Meanings." *Journal of Consumer Research* 24 (June): 15–42.

Toman, J. (1995). The Magic of a Common Language: Jakobson, Mathesius, Trubetzkoy, and the Prague Linguistic Circle. Cambridge, MA: MIT Press.

Umiker-Sebeok, Jean, ed. (1988). *Marketing and Semiotics: New Directions in the Study of Signs for Sale*. Berlin: Mouton de Gruyter.

Van den Bulte, Christophe (1994). "Metaphor at Work." In *Research Traditions in Marketing*, edited by G. Laurent et al., 405–25. Boston: Kluwer.

Veblen, T. (1899). New York: Macmillan.

Veron, E. (1987). La Semiosis sociale. Vincennes, France: Presses Universitaires de Vincennes.

Volosinov, Valentin N. (1986 [1929]). Marxism and the Philosophy of Language, translated by Ladislav Matejka and I. R. Titunik. Cambridge, MA: Harvard University Press.

Watercutter, Angela (2017). "Pepsi's Kendall Jenner Ad Was So Awful It Did the Impossible: It United the Internet." Wired. April 5, 3:12 PM. https://www.wired.com/2017/04/pepsi-ad-internet-response/.

Watkins, A. (2014). *Hello, My Name is Awesome: How to Create Brand Names That Stick*. Oakland, CA: Berrett-Koehler Publishers.

Wellman, Barry (1990). "The Place of Kinfolk in Personal Community Networks." *Marriage and Family Review* 15(1–2): 195–229.

Wernick, A. (1991). *Promotional Culture: Advertising, Ideology and Symbolic Expression*. New York: SAGE.

Wheeler, Alina (2003). *Designing Brand Identity*. New York: John Wiley.

Wiley, N. (1994). *The Semiotic Self*. Chicago: University of Chicago Press.

Williamson, Judith (1998 [1978]). *Decoding Advertisements: Ideology and Meaning in Advertising*. New York: Marion Boyers.

Wolfe, O. (1989). "Sociosemiology and Cross-Cultural Branding Strategies." *Marketing Signs* 3: 3–10.

Wolsko, Christopher, Hector Ariceaga, and Jesse Seiden (2016). "Red, White, and Blue Enough to Be Green: Effects of Moral Framing on Climate Change Attitudes and Conservation Behaviors." *Journal of Experimental Social Psychology* 65: 7–19. https://doi.org/10.1016/j.jesp.2016.02.005.

Zamara, G. (6/06/2018). "Why Metaphors Make Powerful Brand Names." *Brand Experience*, June 6. *https://www.bxpmagazine.com/article/why-metaphors-make-powerful-brand-names*

Lexicon of Key Words

Binary Analysis: The binary analysis accounts for the dialectical structure of cultural categories into a term and its opposite.

Brand: The associations that consumers make between the brand's proprietary symbols and a set of intangible benefits, such as status, fun, or pleasure.

Brand Audit: A research methodology that clarifies the brand's long-standing positioning by tracing the recurrence of signs and meanings across a set of the brand's historical campaigns.

Brand Equity: The value that exceeds a brand's functional attributes and derives from the brand's intangible benefits.

Brand Value Pyramid: An analytical tool that illustrates the coherence of various dimensions of the brand system, from the brand's functional attributes and value proposition to its cultural positioning and proprietary semiotic equities, including the brand name and logo.

Code Theory: A fundamental principle of structural semiotics, code theory accounts for the shared, normative aspects of verbal and nonverbal sign systems that structure meaning production within a given cultural context.

Cognitive Theory: An approach to meaning production that accounts for the intersection of semiotic associations and mental operations that account for our ability to read associations by similarity and contiguity in rhetoric and language.

Consumer Semiotics: The application of semiotic principles such as code theory and binary analysis to the study of consumer behavior, speech, and social organization.

Deconstruction: A postmodern critique of metaphysics that exposes the ideal closure of subject and object in phenomenology to the effects of ambiguity, cultural difference, and nonsense.

Design: A semiotic practice that shapes consumers' sensory and experiential interactions with objects, events, spaces, and processes in the marketplace.

Discourse Analysis: The articulation of a sign system, such as the elements of a brand system, into its syntagmatic (linear) and paradigmatic (recurring) elements.

Ethnography: A qualitative research methodology that interviews and observes consumers in their lived environments.

Focus Group: A qualitative research methodology that interviews groups of respondents, typically around a table in a commercial research facility.

In-Depth Interview: A long qualitative interview, usually held at a research facility, that probes beneath the surface of the respondent's rational statements to understand the psychological motivations for their behaviors.

Laddering: An interview moderating technique for moving the tone of the respondent narrative from the realm of rational choice to the deeper realm of consumer motives.

Marketing Mix: The marketing elements that form the ensemble of tactics used by the firm to communicate the brand value and positioning to consumers in product design, advertising, point of purchase display, and customer service.

Metaphorical Associations: Associations between a poetic signifier and signified on the basis of similarity, i.e., "Her boss barked at the group." [boss - dog].

Metonymical Associations: Associations between a poetic signifier and signified on the basis of contiguity, i.e., The White House responded immediately." [White House = the people in the administration of government in the U.S.A.]

Mood Board: A creative ideation tool that advertisers use to organize brand associations in words and visuals in a collage.

Paradigmatic Axis: The system set of signs and symbols that can be substituted for a given element of the brand's core message. For example, refreshment equals 'a break,' 'fun,' or 'socializing' in Coke's brand system.

Perception of Quality: Consumers brand perceptions of the brand's value on the marketplace, shaped by things like company reputation, product reliability, customer service, and communication strategy.

Phenomenology: A branch of philosophy that orients consciousness to an ideal of pure subjectivity based on the dialectical closure between sense perception and thought.

Projective Exercise: Interview techniques such as free association, image sorting, or storytelling, that probe consumers' emotional associations with a brand or other topic.

Rhetoric: In Aristotle, a compendium of figures of speech in terms of the specific ways they manipulate the literal meaning of a word to communicate a secondary, poetic meaning, i.e. metaphor and simile. Metaphors substitute the literal term with the figurative term, i.e. "the boss barked (yelled)." Similes align the literal and figurative terms in the statement, i.e. i.e. "the boss barked like a dog."

Semiotics: A discipline that draws from a hybrid of communication science and anthropology to identify the underlying code system responsible for meaning production in verbal and nonverbal communication.

Semiotic Analysis: The articulation of a text or a set of data into the codes and cultural categories that underlie the meaning of discourse.

Symbolic Consumption: A theory drawn from cognitive psychology that accounts for the symbolic function of goods and consumer rituals in cultural perspective.

Syntagmatic Analysis: The linear alignment of signs and symbols in a single text or statement, such as 'Coke is Refreshment.' [See also Paradigmatic Analysis.]

Index

Note: Page entries in bold type refer to illustrations.

Made in the USA
Las Vegas, NV
23 February 2022

44398831R10142